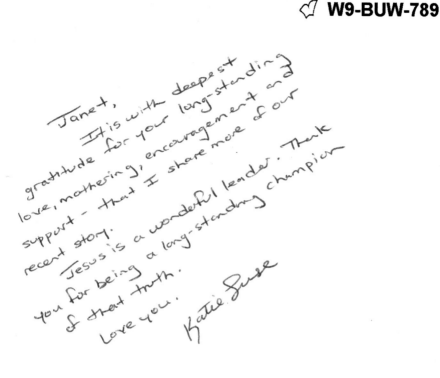

Janet,
It is with deepest
gratitude for your long-standing
love, mothering, encouragement and
support — that I share more of our
recent story.
Jesus is a wonderful leader. Thank
you for being a long-standing champion
of that truth.
Love you.
Katie Suse

Hello World,
I have a story to tell you.
It is called Ruby Joy.

Dedicated to all those who suffer
…and are brave to mine the suffering for joy.

Gratitude

Thank you to the following people for helping make
this book a reality...

Mitch, unwavering commitment.
Becki, strong mentorship.
Amanda, generous editing.
Sue, anointed expertise.
Victoria, Jenny, Julie and others, persistent belief.
Friends and donors, heartfelt support.

To the One who sat with me
and watched every word form,
I devote this work.

Contents

introduction:

**a word
is never just
a word.
a life
is never just
a life.**

Mine:
- That which belongs to me
- A pit or tunnel from which minerals are taken
- A bomb placed in the ground or in water, explodes upon touch —
- A rich source of something

Ruby:
- A deep red stone
- A jewel

Joy:
- A feeling of great happiness
- A source or cause of great happiness
- Something or someone that gives joy to someone
- Success in doing, finding, or obtaining something

A
womb –
the God-breathed tunnel from which

a
tiny jewel of life –
bombed
by cruel disease
exploded
into earth's atmosphere –

a
child,
a life...
the essence of Joy! Alive
Truly, completely.
Alive.

This is her story.

Prologue

There are times in life, holy moments, when we are entrusted with something much more valuable than we ever dared to expect. These times of underserved grace are like beauty interrupting the mundane, like waves of holiness invading the profane. Awe floods our hearts at the life that has found us. Like mining for gems, there is a discovery of the goodness of God, and the beauty of who He is.

While attending college in Philadelphia, I had a holy moment that impacted the trajectory of my life. I had been spending more time with another student I met on campus. She had light in her eyes, a strong celebratory streak, and an uncanny ability to find beauty in any setting. Her free spirit and abandon to life were foreign to me, but I couldn't deny the vitality and energy she brought to every room she entered. Her name is Katie.

One fall night, Katie and I were sitting in the car. We were parked in North Philadelphia talking and sharing our hearts, as hours passed like minutes, when our conversation took an abrupt turn. Unannounced, she suddenly leaned to the dashboard and turned her attention to something above the windshield. My eyes followed hers out the car window and upward, but there wasn't anything I noticed except the usual Philly row homes, streetlights, and skyscraper shadows. Ever so slowly, it dawned on me that she was not looking at any of the things I had observed.

"Look at the stars!" she exclaimed. "Aren't they beautiful?!" Her gaze had been arrested by something higher than the familiar city scene: the star-filled sky had her vivacious heart in rapt attention.

The realization of that moment pierced me and sent my heart reeling. Katie's purity and passion for life both rebuked and embraced me in the same movement. I dared to look again. With refined vision, I could now see that there is a sky full of beauty tucked behind the city lights, for those who have eyes to see it.

A few short years later, Katie and I were married and within a year we were pregnant. A season of unexpected trial and hardship ensued. We found ourselves dropped into a terrifying, dark pit. One which we could not escape. The intensity of the experience seemed to only refine Katie's eye for beauty and zeal for life. Her persistent upward gaze was a resonant match for our little girl, who carried a wealth of beauty with her, for those who have eyes to see it.

Some things only form in darkness, among them gems. Katie was pregnant with a girl, my girl. I am privileged to be that girl's dad and to share her story with you.

Mitch Luse

Part I

Choosing to Believe

Chapter 1

I wake up in the middle of the night and hear, "Ruby."

Ruby. I think to myself. *That is the most adorable name!*

The next day I approach my husband, Mitch. "What do you think about the name Ruby?"

His smile broadens, like it does, and he responds with an affirmative. "Yes."

"What do you think of Ruby Joy?" He dares to extend a conversation that has landed us in conflict a thousand times. How two opposite personalities are ever to decide on a single name for their child is beyond me.

I pause and then realize...I like it!

"Yes!" I reply.

We look at each other in mild shock.

"Ruby Joy?" he asks again.

"Yes!"

An 8-month conflict resolved at last. Just in time.

Her name will be...Ruby Joy.

~

Our car pulls up to the river and we sit still for a moment. I feel pending doom and don't know how to escape it. Mitch gets out first and then comes around to open my door. I exit the car and take a deep breath in the fresh air. I need this: space to breathe.

We walk down the path to the river, a familiar road in an unfamiliar time. I envy the walks we have had here without worry. People greet us along the trail with a congratulatory smile at our pregnancy. I stare to the ground. They have no idea what we are facing tonight. I suppose we have no idea what they are facing either.

Mitch and I walk for some time, mostly quiet. The peace that has ruled in our hearts still rules, but we are at a loss on how to proceed. A small bench calls our attention and we take a seat. Dialogue emerges. We are scared. What if the baby is deformed? What if she doesn't live?

Scattered conversation weaves through profound moments of silence. I fall into one of the moments, working to put the events of the day in order.

~

This morning we went for a late-term ultrasound. I am 39 weeks pregnant. We are expecting our first child, a baby girl, any day now. The midwife ordered the ultrasound this morning to check on the baby, who apparently has demonstrated slower growth the last two weeks. We were not concerned. We're both small. Everything has been normal. Normal. Healthy. *Normal.*

The technician began the ultrasound. I watched her face and, within seconds, I knew something was not right. Instead of the celebratory, "Here's her foot! Here's her ear!" she was silent, her face darkening with concern. I waited for her to say something. Nothing. Silence.

She began to shuffle nervously. She pulled out our records and started thumbing through previous reports. Still quiet. Her eyes went back to the screen and I watched her fight not to find what she knew she had found. I wanted to scream at her, demanding to know what she knew about my baby. Instead, I became gripped with fear and sat in front of her—just as silent.

At last, she spoke up. "I see some concerns with your baby. Serious concerns." Her eyes floated downward. I caught them and forced them back up. She continued. "I am looking at your 18-week ultrasound and everything reads normal." I brace myself. "However, I am seeing serious concerns today that need to be addressed immediately."

"Immediately?" I have no idea what she is talking about but am frustrated that she is not being direct with me.

The technician continues. "You need to go see your midwife this afternoon. I am going to send her this report and allow her to share it with you. I am so sorry."

"Sorry for what?"

No answer.

⌒

I let out a heavy sigh. Mitch hears me. He breaks our park bench silence. "What are you thinking about?"

"The technician," I respond flatly.

Silence falls again.

I continue recollecting.

⌒

Mitch and I are escorted upstairs. Our midwife looks very sad. She asks how much the technician shared with us. We relay that she told us nothing except that there were serious concerns. She seems surprised, now aware that the weight of the report is on her.

"Well," she said, "as you know there are concerns with your baby. This is not a conversation that I ever desire to have with parents."

We wait.

She continues. "Before I start, though, I want to tell you that ultrasounds are not always accurate. A lot of these things are guesses, and they could be wrong."

We wait.

"This baby is going to need to be born in the next 24 hours. When the baby is born, there will be an evaluation that supersedes all of this and may or may not reflect the ultrasound's findings."

We wait again.

The midwife lets out a heavy sigh and at last begins reading us the technician's report. Her voice is muffled and we press in to hear her. It's a long list of medical problems. I don't understand most of it. "Left ventricle of the heart…webbed stomach…incomplete development, etc." Other parts I do understand but wish I didn't. Like the report that the baby's head is six times the size of her body. My imagination screams.

The prognosis finally ends. Mitch and I sit still. The baby they are talking about is with us, in me. They are telling us she is severely deformed with incomplete development of major organs.

At last I speak. "What are we supposed to do?"

"Like I said in the beginning, there is a chance that this is wrong, at least in part, and that's what we can hope for. That said, it is not safe for the baby to remain in utero, as she may need medical intervention to keep her alive."

"Medical?"

"I am very sorry, but our practice cannot support you through this. We can refer you to a hospital, and I can give you the name of a doctor we recommend."

There goes our home birth. There goes our natural birth. There goes any thought we had of what this birth would be like. I wish our natural birthing classes prepared us for this.

"Do we have any other options?"

"I'm afraid not. But I am willing to come with you to the hospital to make sure you get settled. I would recommend you go right away. Do you want me to call them for you right now?"

"Now?! You want our baby to be born right now?"

The midwife gives me a nod.

I put on the breaks., "I know this is very serious, but I cannot go to the hospital right now to have this baby." I pause and then continue, "This is all happening too fast. Can we wait until tomorrow?" *If I'm honest, I hope that this whole thing will prove to be a mistake by tomorrow.*

"Tomorrow morning at the latest," she responds.

"I would prefer that." I let out a sigh.

"You understand there is risk in waiting?"

"Yes."

"Okay. Call me when you leave for the hospital. I will meet you there. Please do not delay. Tomorrow morning, first thing."

~

Tomorrow. That's the next day I'll see. That's the next time the sun rises. That's in a few hours. I shake myself out of the account of the day and turn my attention to Mitch, who is still sitting next to me on a park bench.

"What are you thinking?" I interrupt his silent gaze.

"I'm thinking about hope," he answers me directly.

Hope.

The thought of hope uncorks our silence and we find traction in our conversation for the first time this evening. Neither of us repeats the reports of the day. We were both there, no need to repeat it. Instead, we talk about hope.

As we talk, we realize that the enemy of this day is fear. It's not disease, deformity or disaster. It's fear. Fear lures us away from hope; hope crushes fear. When we talk through the filter of hope, we feel okay. When we stop, we feel endangered.

Therefore, we choose hope.

Together, we choose hope.

To hope for the best –
It is a *choice*.

Hope, our anchor of choice.

We pray.
We cry.
We wait.
We lay our hopes bare before God.

The sun sets. It's time to retreat. I ask Mitch for a moment alone before we leave the waterside. I need to hear from God. He graciously walks a few strides away, and I am left on the bench alone.

I sit and think. I wish I could hold onto this night forever rather than ever face tomorrow. I've never needed this much courage for anything, yet I am found lacking, trembling. I ask God if there is any way around this—over it, under it—anything instead of through it. I want out of this.

But I know I cannot escape. Somehow I know I must face it. Time does not relent in the face of tragedy. Tomorrow will come. I will either face it courageously or be tormented in it by timidity. *Make a choice.*

I look up into the darkening sky and ask God for courage. Then, I hear His voice. "I will uphold you with my victorious right hand." I hear it clearly, like a church bell resounding across the billows of the night clouds. It's a word from heaven—a word for me. I grab hold of this promise and tuck it deep into my heart. Deeper than deep, it is planted to become the roots of the tree from which I am held.

The page turns; the morning dawns. I was in mild labor through-out the night. I stayed awake hoping that the baby would just come, hoping that we would never need to reach the hospital chaos that demands our presence today. But the labor never picked up. I am still pregnant, and it is time to go.

I pack our things for a hospital birth, leaving our dreams of a home birth behind. I put together a small diaper bag of things for the baby. I look at it pitifully; the contents are scarce. I've never been a mom before; I have no idea what I'm doing. I throw the bag toward the front door. *It is what it is.* We pack an even smaller bag of things for ourselves. We will all be home in a day or two.

On the highway, we drive toward the hospital. It's the start of another hot, traffic-filled summer day. City fumes fill the air. The people inside the cars wear blank stares, revealing their monotonous routines. I wish I could trade my crisis commute this morning for any one of their mundane rides. We arrive at the hospital parking garage. Mitch parks the car in the lower level. I sit still.

"I don't want to get out." I stare at the windowpane from inside the car.

"You don't have to." Mitch's patience bounces off the windowpane back at me.

Time passes. I'm still staring at the windowpane, unmoved. My phone rings. The midwife wants to know where we are. I open my car door reluctantly and step out while telling her, "We are here." The moment I step out of the car, something inside of me shifts. I realize that avoiding this day is prolonging it, and, rather suddenly, I just want to be through it. Reluctancy meets anxiety, and the latter takes the lead. I grab Mitch's hand and make a beeline for the hospital entrance.

Inside the hospital, we check in. The receptionist looks tired; it must be the end of her night shift. She directs us to a room in Labor and Delivery. I put on a gown. Hooked up to monitors, I am attached to a world of being controlled by strangers.

The doctor is called in.

A short deliberation transpires.

It's time to have the baby.

~

I am escorted into an operating room. Sweat and chills reveal my troubled internal state. I sit down on the operating table and feel unpleasantly spotlighted. The anesthesiologist tells me to bend over so that he can administer the anesthetic into my spine. I lean forward and feel myself leaning into suffering.

I close my eyes and see vivid pictures of Jesus suffering; He is alive under my eyelids. He is suffering alongside me in this moment. He is on the cross; I am on the operating table. We are sharing in this together. In the encounter, it dawns on me that the fellowship of suffering is a real place. I just arrived.

Eyes still closed, I feel a depth of communion with God that is beyond what I have experienced before, even for a girl who has walked closely with God most of her life. This is new. There is a peace, comfort, and strength in God, and I experience it in the midst of my waking nightmare. It is quiet; it happens in solitude. It is real.

It's as if Jesus has come to me and is saying, "I am here. I entered into the worst pain and created there a safe place for those who suffer: the place of My Presence. My Presence will cover you, even on your darkest day. This is the fellowship of suffering. Katie, I am with you."

As this word washes over me, I know that He is not causing my pain but is making an invitation in it. To know God in pain is to know Him more deeply than I've known Him before. A friend who is willing to suffer with you is a true friend. I want to be more than a beneficiary of God; I want to be His friend.

I bow my head even lower; if Jesus is there, I want to go in. Upon this decision, peace settles over my heart, and I feel my love for God overtake my fear.

Needle goes in.

C-section begins.

I feel the cut more than I should. I scream. I vomit. Anesthetic is turned up. The room fills with specialists, gowned, afraid, panicked. I can feel the doctor removing the baby. It feels like I'm being robbed from the inside out. I cry. Agony arrests my heart and expels into weeping. No one seems to notice, the attention is no longer on me. Welcome to motherhood.

I cannot feel if the baby is in or out. The room is squirming. I glance at Mitch to try to get his attention; a neonatologist is relaying information to him. Mitch faints. Medics turn toward him. "Get him some water!" They catch Mitch from hitting the ground and begin spoon-feeding him water. A stranger in a blue gown bursts through the crowd of medics and I see that she is carrying the baby. For less than a second, the baby is held over my sick face.

"Ruby Joy," I whisper to myself. I cannot feel that she is mine. This bothers me. Has there been a mistake?

The stranger runs out of the room with my baby.

She's gone.

～

A few hours later, a nurse puts me into a wheelchair and brings me down to the Neonatal Intensive Care Unit (NICU) to meet Ruby. When I get to the double doors of the NICU, I realize there is a photographer at my heels. She is following me. I don't care much to find out who she is; I am on a mission to get to my baby.

When I arrive at Ruby's room, I see Mitch first. He looks like a different man to me. Something about him has changed. His eyes are shiny with love; his demeanor is plastered with adoration. I see a new identity on him, and it's bright.

I hear whispers as I enter the room. "Your husband…this dad… this man." Apparently, Mitch has shown up for Ruby in a way the world around him cannot help but commemorate out loud.

Mitch takes me by the hand and introduces me to Ruby. I peer over the ledge where she is lying and tenderly touch her. "Thank you, God." I whisper in gratitude.

She's alive.

I take a moment to stare at her. Memorize her, I must.

Ruby is tiny. Her legs are pulled up against her chest and she is lying curled up in a small tight ball. Her head is large. Her limbs are skinny. She has tiny eyelids that are tightly shut between a wide forehead and small chin. Her feet are flat, revealing webbed toes. Her fingers are long, and there is a sixth finger on one of her hands. Her ears are placed low on her head. Her hair is scarce. Wires and tubes protrude from her small frame.

This is our daughter, Ruby Joy.

I love her.

I glance up at Mitch and see pride radiating from his face. I don't know what has taken place between him and Ruby in the last few hours, but it is clear to me that they have established a bond. I marvel at its visibility. This new spark, new light, new strength—this new thing I see all over him—is *fatherhood*.

He was made for this.

I smile at Mitch, and the photographer I saw at my heels comes around the corner and inches toward us.

"Can I take a few pictures?" I look at Mitch with a silent, *who is this person?* He explains to me that she has come from a group of photographers who volunteer to take photos for families who have a newborn in crisis.

I nod. Ruby is handed to me. I do my best to look natural holding her for the first time in the face of a camera. Photos are captured.

We are left alone.

∿

Evening turns to night, and I am wheeled back to my room on another floor of the hospital. I start pumping right away for Ruby, and I work hard at it. This is one way that I can connect with her from a distance.

I ask Mitch what is going on with Ruby medically. He relays that some tests have been done, and others are scheduled. He mentions a few things that go right over my head. I can't seem to comprehend what he is saying, but I do hear him say, "Results are inconclusive." I feel the sting of hearing about her condition secondhand. I missed the first few hours of her life. I wonder if I will ever recover them.

Throughout the night, I shake in and out of restless sleep. I am in a lot of pain from the C-section. I have to keep telling myself in waking moments that I am not pregnant anymore, and that the baby I held earlier is mine. I feel disillusioned by her abnormal physical features, ashamed that I care. At last, I sit up and quit trying to sleep.

My eyes stare out the dark window. Twenty-four hours ago I was 39 weeks pregnant with a seemingly healthy, full-term baby. One late-term ultrasound, an emergency C-section and here I am.

A ragged transition from pregnancy to birth.

"Morning!" I hear Mitch's voice and question if he has slept at all. "Katie, she woke up last night!" He kneels down next to my hospital bed and pulls out his phone. He flips through pictures of Ruby that he took at 3:00 AM. Her eyes are wide open.

I grab the phone and widen the screen. *There she is!* A grin spreads across my face, and I get a warm feeling inside. *She's going to be just fine.* "Look!" I show Mitch the phone as if he had not already seen her. The sight of Ruby awake strengthens me. I stare at the photograph, mesmerized. *She's here; she's alive.* Later that evening, we send out a birth announcement.

Announcing RUBY JOY LUSE. 4lbs, 4oz, 17 ½ inches long.

Born on July 10, 2009 at 1:30 PM in the afternoon.

She is a priceless, precious, adorable bundle of life

who has arrived on mission to teach us about love.

Chapter 2

The medical reports begin pouring in like an endless pitcher of bad lemonade on a hot day when all you want is water. While some things have been defined (congenital heart defects, cleft palate, hearing loss, vision impairment, polydactyl, and so on), the root cause of Ruby's medical issues remains a mystery. Doctors think she has a genetic disease. They seem anxious to give her a diagnosis; I wish they would not. It's one thing to have a list of problems; its quite another to be given a prognosis. My internal dialogue reels. *One day at a time, people. Ruby has never lived before. Don't go looking in a book to find out who she is. Look at her. She's a miracle. I know it.*

The day comes when a neonatologist visits us. She seems to know something concrete about Ruby. Her steps into the room are careful, her demeanor solemn. I feel an odd tension between wanting and not wanting to know what she is about to say. She shuts the door and stands before us. She tells us that the medical team thinks Ruby has an incurable genetic disease. They think it is Trisomy 13. They have sent out a chromosome test to confirm it. I ask a few questions. She reluctantly responds, "Ruby is incompatible with life. Her life expectancy is seven days."

"Seven-day life expectancy" crashes into the room like a bomb.

And, like a bomb, all things are shattered before there is time to think.

But in our case, the bomb is emotionally destructive. We are left with maddening silence and no signs of visible change. In the face of white, sterile hospital walls, weeping ensues. Our tears are the only tangible sign that we have been hit with an explosion.

In our tears, we are left alone.

⌒

Mitch and I make our way down to the hospital lobby. For the first time in a week, we step into the sun. It's a hot afternoon in July, almost identical to the day we were admitted. We've made it to seven days. Ruby is still with us. The sliding doors open, and we inch toward the curb. That curb, still within earshot of critical care, is as far as we dare to go. The sun hits my face, and I recall that life is still happening. The sun is rising and setting; traffic still fills the streets; people are going about their routines. I have not experienced these things in days. I suppose I somehow assumed that all had drowned with my own loss of "normal."

I sit down on the curb and stare at the asphalt beneath my feet. X-ray images from that morning run through my mind. I glance at Mitch and wonder what an X-ray of our souls would reveal right now. A thousand throws against a concrete wall and our spirits, souls and bodies have had enough. We are living in a life-and-death battle with Ruby.

Mitch takes hold of my hand. "We need to decide what we believe, Katie. We are not going to survive this time if the medical reports continue to rule our internal lives."

I frown. I know he is right, but I sincerely hoped a miracle would occur so that we wouldn't have to make any decisions. But here we are. Ruby is very sick. The question is, *what are we going to do about it?*

On one hand, we could continue to ride the medical reports. This seems intelligent: accept reality and utilize our faith in God as a comfort and support in the hardship. On the other hand, we could believe God to heal Ruby in spite of the medical reports. This seems foolish: deny reality and utilize faith as an intervention against impossibilities.

Our conversation continues, and we find that both our hearts are drawn to the faith journey. We fear it; we could lose credibility quickly if we choose a public faith journey. Wholehearted faith is foolishness to those who do not understand the height of God's goodness. It will appear to be insanity, the fiercest form of denial.

Something about that cost stirs my heart, draws it closer to faith.

And what if we are labeled crazy? Is it worth it to us? I pose the question to myself as flashes of ridicule pass through my mind, some already having occurred.

"I would rather have a bold, whole-hearted, public, unashamed faith than put God, who I have declared is Lord of my life, on the sidelines as insufficient in my time of need," Mitch declares.

"Good point," I respond.

We spur on each other.

I dig deeper into my own heart. Honestly, I am afraid of accusation. I do not want to be accused of being a bad mom who cannot embrace reality and who uses faith as an excuse to live in denial. I evaluate. It would be much easier to forfeit this fight for Ruby. But the thought of Ruby interrupts my retreat. Reactions aside, what do I believe about *her*?

"Ruby is more than they think she is," I speak out loud. "She is already shattering the initial report over her life. The most honest thing I feel is that Jesus wants to heal Ruby. He is fully capable and He already paid for her healing."

"Let's believe God, Katie," Mitch hangs his proposition in the air before us. "Let's choose faith for Ruby. Let's fight not only for her life but also for her complete healing. What do we have to lose?"

As soon as I hear "believe God," joy hits my gut like a bullet. Something on Earth just aligned with heaven. I'm in. *I would rather take the risk of believing God than miss the opportunity to see where the road of belief leads.* I nod with a fresh smile.

"What about internet updates announcing to the world that we are believing God to heal Ruby completely?" Mitch's posture perks up.

"Yeah!" I respond. "What about responses to doctors and therapists who demand the atmosphere of faith be protected and the current of hope released?"

Release sweeps over us. We laugh. Then, we cry because laughter has found us. Bizarre expressions of faith grow in our hearts, and we bounce them off of each other with joy. One thing we can tell already: this approach is definitely more fun. Hope and joy dance an inseparable tango. Where hope finds space to move, so does joy.

Mitch solidifies the conversation with a sign, "So...we are on the same page? We are choosing to believe God for Ruby's complete healing?"

"Yes," I smile.

He picks up a worn leaf from the gutter of the curb. Holding it up like a trophy, he exclaims, "This is our memorial: our reminder that today we made a decision to wholeheartedly believe God to heal Ruby. No Plan B."

"No Plan B," I whisper in support.

The leaf is tucked into his wallet, unknowingly a heavy anchor for the days to come. Goodbye, passive faith. We are setting out to discover just how radical faith can be.

～

People in bright-red T-shirts come into the room, pack up Ruby, and take her away. Mitch and I stand shoulder to shoulder watching her roll down the hallway. She turns the corner. She is out of sight. The room deflates upon her exit. The monitors are off. The wires hang dead. Ruby is the only thing that kept us here. We are free to go. But free to go where? We will go where Ruby is going, of course, into the heart of another hospital. Ruby is being transferred to Children's Hospital.

I watch the streetlights as we drive away from the hospital and fall into a heavy sleep. Traces of Mitch trying to wake me up pose as a dream. He's lost? Needs directions? Needs help? I cannot wake up.

The car stops. My body is too tired to move.

"Katie, we are here. Katie! Ruby is in this hospital. We need to get to her."

I hear him, but I cannot respond. I wonder if I am too tired or perhaps debilitated. Mind over matter is not working.

"Katie! Wake up, we're at Children's Hospital and we need to find Ruby!"

My body feels like a whale washed up on shore: stuck. I thought I knew what exhaustion was, but apparently not. I thought I knew many things, but real experience overshadows expectations.

Car door opens. Car door shuts. I still cannot move. Quiet.

Car door opens again. "I brought you a wheelchair."

Mitch lifts me out of the car and into a wheelchair. At that moment, I realize I am in pain. The incision from the C-section rears its ugly head. Sliding doors open and a bright light catches my eye. *Angels?* I think to myself. We are now in an elevator. I stare at the number of floors represented on the elevator buttons. This is an enormous hospital. Ruby is somewhere inside.

Ruby.

The thought of Ruby sends a surge of energy back into my body. I wake up and feel in my right mind. "We need to find Ruby," I speak out loud. "Mitch, move faster!"

Elevator doors open and I see color. I smile. Mitch grins. The lady at the front desk tells us to go to Floor 11, NICU. I fear that we might somehow lose Ruby on our way there. Anxiety drives. We are escorted down the hallway. This NICU is much bigger than the one from which we came. Critically ill babies fill the rooms. Heartstrings are real; mine are pulled. We are here for more than Ruby; I can feel it. We have a mission. Mitch turns my wheelchair around a corner.

There she is—Ruby Joy!

A bedside nurse attends to her. One nurse, compared to a full medical team, is good news. I am relieved. Upon seeing Ruby, love erupts in my heart. I stand up from the wheelchair and run to her bedside. I stop short. I place my hand on her tiny body and peace zips through my soul like an electric shock. Ruby is at peace. She just drove alone in an ambulance to a new hospital and yet she lies here at peace. Internal rules the external. Settlement of the heart can settle any storm. Maybe I need to take a lesson from her.

I turn around. Mitch is watching me. I would not have made it here without him. I think Ruby got her peace from him. He is wearing it too. Mom is the anxious one. Mom is willing to give up that role. I repent, and, in doing so, find stillness.

Stillness.

All three together again.

Peace.

$\sim$

I hear the sound of heels clicking in the hallway. They are coming toward our room. A chill runs up my spine. *Genetics*, I think to myself. Sure enough, a women turns the corner and steps into our room. She is wearing odd pointy shoes, grey stockings and a mid-length woolen skirt that looks like rotten upholstery. Her hair is knotted and pulled back, her face colorless and tough.

"I am the genetics doctor. Is this Ruby Luse?" She peers over Ruby's hospital bed and I find myself wanting to protect Ruby. I'm not sure why, but I sense negativity.

I nod.

Through a thick German accent, she presses me with personal questions about Ruby's condition. Behind her, two students peer over her shoulder as if in a museum. This Genetics Team is fascinated by Ruby's anomalies; they stare at her oddities. These people bother me.

I suppose this is what people call bad bedside manner. It's when someone is bedside and everyone else in the room is worse off. I feel hurt, which quickly turns to anger, and then to hatred. *Can I fire this person right now?*

"We'll be back later." The doctor concludes her evaluation and, with a cold shoulder, turns to the door. I shudder as it shuts behind her. She and her curious students are gone. *Thank God.*

~

Later that afternoon, I hear the clicking of those odd shoes nearing our room again. This time I grab anointing prayer oil and slab it unto the doors, Ruby's bed, and the gloves the doctors will likely use. I plead the blood of Jesus over everything in the room before the doctor gets to the door.

I see her foot in the doorway. Next, her scraggly frame comes around the corner. Her face wears the same invasive demeanor as it did this morning. She picks up the gloves and puts them on. I smile. She has no idea that I just prayed over them.

She is alone this time. She tells me that she has a genetic diagnosis for Ruby and asks if my husband is here. I feel anything but excited to hear her prognosis. Information is always affected by its deliverer. Always.

"No," I respond. "My husband is on his way back from work. Can you wait until he is here? I would rather have this conversation with him present." I do not feel safe allowing this woman to unload on me alone.

She looks at her oversized watch and grunts. "Well, it's the end of the workday. How long do you think he will be?"

In a trembling voice I respond, "Half an hour?"

"Okay. I'll be back in a half hour."

Door shuts. Every muscle in my body is tense.

Wow, I think to myself, *my first true nemesis.*

I do not like this person—*at all.*

~

Mitch arrives moments later and greets Ruby first. He folds his two hands under her body and gives her a gentle squeeze, "Missed you today, Rubes." He turns to me. My body is still gripped with tension. He asks me how I am. I tell him about the genetics doctor and that she will be returning shortly to give Ruby a medical diagnosis. Mitch offers to take the conference with the doctor alone. No, thank you. My heart rate is already up. I'm not going anywhere.

Minutes later, the pointy-shoed, matted-hair, ugly-skirted doctor appears again. When she sees Mitch in the room, she lets out a sigh. Without any personal introduction, she delves into the most dreadful prognosis over Ruby's life.

"Ruby has a fatal disease.

Smith-Lemli-Opitz Syndrome.

Severest case I've ever seen.

All abnormalities Ruby has are consistent with this disease.

The disease is caused by a gene mutation that results in the inability to synthesize cholesterol.

Cholesterol is necessary for all normal human development.

We checked her cholesterol, and it is at a 9. It should be 100."

She moves right into prognosis:

"Severely deformed.

Mentally impaired.

Unable to walk.

Unable to talk.

Unable to eat."

Pounding blows.

"Her mental capabilities will probably make her very angry and you will have to institutionalize her at a young age. You will not be able to handle her yourselves."

The doctor continues to draw out worst-case scenarios, and I feel I could vomit at the fierce contradiction I feel between what she is saying and what I believe about who Ruby is. Despite my certain disagreement, her words pierce. I can feel her plastering scenarios in my mind that I will have to fight tooth and nail to disintegrate.

She finally pauses, let's out a sigh, and then says, "It's too bad you didn't know ahead of time." She references that we could've terminated the pregnancy. This is *not* okay.

I object. "Our perspective on Ruby's life is different. This may sound crazy to you, but we have faith in a God who heals. We believe that God has His own prognosis over Ruby's life and…that His prognosis is good."

She looks at me with the first softness that I've seen since meeting her this morning. For a moment, I think she is feeling empathy. She then shakes her head and looks at the ground. It's not empathy, I realize. It's pity. She pities my inability to accept her report.

In an effort to make me understand, she takes a deep breath and starts all over. She repeats the diagnosis and the prognosis, line by line. Twice, I interrupt her. Twice, she repeats herself in harrowing detail.

Mitch takes authority. "We understand what you have said. We don't need you to repeat it anymore. Stop."

She stops talking and makes her way to the exit. As she walks away, I notice that her head is hung low. I wonder if this was somehow hard for her too.

Do I care?

We are left facing the door like two soldiers on the front line of Ruby's hospital room battlefield, wounded, but unmoved. In the face of the report, I felt strong. But right now, within seconds of her departure, I can feel the piercing of her words like arrows in my heart. *Severely deformed? Mentally impaired? Unable to eat? Unable to walk? Uncontrollably angry?*

Clicking shoes.

Matted hair.

Ugly skirt.

Oversized watch.

Emotionless speech.

Insensitive release.

Unhappy face.

Pitied gaze.

Meet my nemesis—the scraggly-framed geneticist. What a day. And, as a result, Ruby is now medically "diagnosed." *So what?*

⁓

"Egg yolk," the geneticist orders. An awkward silence falls on the medical team. We all wait for her to retract, or at least explain. She adds nothing.

"Egg yolk?" the dietician at last responds. "For a two-week old, tube-fed infant?"

"Yes."

The geneticist explains to the medical team that Ruby's diagnosis, Smith-Lemli-Opitz Syndrome, is caused by a cholesterol deficiency in the body: a missing enzyme that helps synthesize cholesterol. *Cholesterol,* I think to myself, *that substance of which the rest of the world has way too much.*

The question is raised to the geneticist. "Could Ruby assimilate and utilize supplemented cholesterol? Would it make any difference for her?" The geneticist goes on to explain that the abnormal development that occurred in the womb is not reversible, but there is a chance that supplemented cholesterol could support her growth and development now. The research to date is…non-conclusive. This *might* help.

Her explanations fall on inquisitive ears. The medical team's curious reactions are a blaring sign to me of the disease's rarity. I watch the discussion continue among the medical professionals. On one hand, the geneticist says that "this child" (she never uses Ruby's name) cannot live at the level of cholesterol with which she was born. On the other hand, the neonatologists object to the thought of putting a newborn in critical care on an egg yolk diet.

The discussion runs its course and lands at a decision that egg yolk is not about diet for Ruby; it is her "treatment" and must be given. Egg yolk: an attempt to supplement Ruby's cholesterol.

This whole discussion has tangled my gut into a tight knot. I'm her mom. Can I really allow them to feed egg yolk to my 4lb 7oz two-week-old baby? It doesn't take a scientist to figure out that this will make her sick. The heart-wrenching nature of treatment presents: choosing for someone you love to suffer more now in the hopes that they will suffer less later. *Arctic.*

Later that afternoon, two hard-boiled eggs are delivered to our room in a Styrofoam bowl. A plastic spoon is placed in the bowl with them. The attached instructions read, "Prescription: 2 egg yolks per day. Instructions: crush the egg yolk until smooth, add liquid to form desired consistency, and feed through the NG tube."

I peel the eggs and pit the egg yolk. I wonder how these smelly balls of yellow will fit into the belly of a little girl whose body is currently the size of my forearm. Reason pressed aside, I take hold of the spoon and start to obliterate the egg yolk. Every speck needs to be flattened so that it will not clog the feeding tube. I work at it for an hour. When it is finally blended, I add liquid and pull it back into a syringe.

The egg yolk is then slowly administered to Ruby though the NG feeding tube. It goes in. Shortly after the feeding, Ruby gets violently ill, throws up the egg yolk, chokes from vomiting with a feeding tube in her throat, and then whimpers with aspirated breathing.

The next day, I explain the vomiting episode to the doctors. "It is unfortunate," they tell me, "but there is no other option." Egg yolks are ordered again.

When I see the eggs arrive, my patience begins to boil. It takes everything in me not to dump the eggs into the trash and report that we fed them to her. "Egg yolk or no treatment?" I ask myself. I feed them to her again.

Again, Ruby gets terribly sick: whimpering, crying, vomiting, and aspirating within hours of getting the egg yolk. *Insanity.*

Egg yolks ordered.

Ruby vomits.

Egg yolks ordered again.

Ruby vomits again.

Ruby's body lashes out and she starts losing more than egg yolk; she is now vomiting her full feeds.

I become angry and blame the feeding tube. If she were eating by mouth, we could not force this yellow muck into her, and with good reason. It feels unjust for anyone to be force-fed through a tube. She has no control over what or how much she eats.

A few days into this egg yolk trial, I realize that the doctors don't have other options. Despite her sour reactions, the only part of the egg yolk prescription that changes is the amount. This is discouraging. The egg yolk is the best option they have, and it feels like a twisted solution that reduces her quality of life.

If this is ever going to work, I think to myself, *we are going to have to think strategically. How can I help Ruby tolerate this?*

I suggest to the nurses that we try administering small bits of egg yolk every hour instead of feeding it to her in a lump sum. I also suggest that we give her the egg yolk at different times than her other feeds. The doctors agree that as long as the overall volume remains the same, we can administer the eggs to her in parts. This seems to help. She is still vomiting, but not as much of her standard feeds.

The doctors, nurses and I spend ourselves on this egg yolk therapy for days. Eventually, it is time for Ruby's cholesterol to be drawn again. Everyone is hoping that her cholesterol number will be higher. The blood work comes back: 17. Her cholesterol has gone up.

The conclusion is that the egg yolks are working.

A number on a page makes everyone feel better, but I am too strung out from the process to celebrate. I look at Ruby. Her color is pale. She is not tolerating her feeds. She is sick, sad and hurting. I look at myself; I wear the wounds of participating in my child's suffering. I am exhausted, sad and hurting. We are not better; we are worse. Our routine has become more complicated, our experience of suffering deepened. And yet we are told, "The paperwork says you are doing better! Keep doing what you're doing!"

Treatment. Sometimes it feels like a curse I am forced to embrace.

~

Days later, my mom comes to the hospital to stay overnight. This means I can sleep for a few hours, and Ruby will not be alone. I drag myself away from Ruby's room and proceed down the hallway to the family lounge.

Stiff plastic recliners are scattered around the room. Many of the chairs are already full. They have been pulled into the four corners of the room by parents and family members who need to be alone. This is a strange place: a community with no community. We're all too tired for one another, and yet we are all here together.

I see a chair facing the window. It appears empty. I carefully move toward it and peek over the top. It's vacant. *Thank God.*

Hello, chair. Hello, respite.

My body collapses on the plastic cushion and I pull my knees up to my chest.

My eyes are drawn to the blackness outside the window. The sky is thick with night; faint flickers of light arise from sleepless spots in the city. The rest of the world lies drowned in darkness. *Night.* I haven't considered it for sometime; day and night are fused in this facility.

My thoughts turn to Ruby. One minute away from her, and I miss her. Memories of our time together flood my mind, memories unprocessed. I feel scared as I become aware of dormant trauma. The external stillness threatens to set off an explosion of internal noise. There's an army of emotional need waiting for space to lay siege. I wish I could hide from myself rather than face my internal reality. I consider returning to Ruby's room where her tender frame holds my attention hostage.

But what good is it, really, to run from myself?

An hour or more passes, and I wonder if I will sleep. My opportunity slips through the cracks of time. I set an alarm; I need to be up in two hours. I welcome sleep, drift off into it.

The sun hits my eyes, and I turn over. *Morning?* I sit up quickly.

Oh my gosh, I think to myself, *I fell asleep, hard.* I look at my phone. 7:00 AM. *Yikes!* I don't know what happened to my first alarm. I slept for six hours, a record by far. My first instinct is to run out of the room, panicked, to find out what the night held for Ruby. But something, Someone, taps me on the shoulder. I sense, "Read first."

My Bible seems to open itself to Psalm 23, and I begin to read.

The Lord is my Shepherd.
I shall not want.
*He **makes** me lie down–*

I smile. Maybe it was God who shut off my alarm.

He leads me beside still waters
He restores my soul.

I stop and ask my Maker, "What is it, God?"
"Is."
"Is…what?"
And then I see it.

Is. Present tense.

I read the psalm again. This time the present-tense verbs jump off the page.

Is.
Makes.
Leads.
Restores.
Walks.
Comforts.
Prepares.

Anoints.

Follows.

Dwells.

It's all for right now.

God always—*is*.

A veil begins to lift. Psalm 23 *is*—always—for *now*. My first glimpse of God in the darkness shines like one of those sleepless lights I saw from the window the night prior. God is here. God *is*.

He is my shepherd.

He is leading me.

He is comforting me.

He is preparing me, anointing me, feeding me.

He is here.

I begin to wonder, *What would it feel like to be shepherded by God in a time when I am lost? Or led in a time when I am confused, or comforted in a time when I have indescribable pain? What if my circumstances actually heighten the space in which I can experience these very things? What if Psalm 23 is mostly for now? What if it's application is here and now?*

Psalm 23.

I refuse to allocate its benefits to tomorrow.

It's written in present tense, which means it is for today.

I'm out to find it. Discover it. Experience it. Expect it. Walk into it.

Up from my plastic blue chair, I rise. Psalm 23 organizes my thoughts. They uncoil into a simple faith:

He is my Shepherd.

I am not in want.

He just made me rest.

It was really good.

Thank you, Jesus.

Chapter 3

A bright-eyed spunky nurse enters the room, draws the curtains and begins to handle Ruby. She is older than the nurses I am used to and seems more confident. I watch her, trying to decide if I like her or not. Her chirpiness rubs me the wrong way after a sleepless night.

"Does this child have any clothes?"

Clothes? I think to myself. *This is a first.*

I am accustomed to morning interrogations by doctors and nurses. Generally, it starts between 5 and 6 AM with the resident doctor and ends sometime before noon with the full medical team. I don't know who all the people are, but they come in and out throughout each morning with their questions. And, each time, I recount Ruby's medical history into the faces of strangers, reliving the shock and trauma I am still unable to digest. "Ruby was born through emergency C-section, has been diagnosed with a terminal disease, is unable to eat by mouth." I watch the medical professionals write down the facts as if they were...facts...and I envy their ability to fully process what I cannot. But out of all the professionals I encounter, this lady seems to be of another breed.

Instead of the usual questions, this nurse asks about clothes. I feel nervous. I'm the mom. I should know this answer. I shoot a glance to the side of the room where Ruby's diaper bag lies untouched. Two weeks prior, we packed it for her birth, anticipating simple needs such as clothes, diapers, lotion and blankets. The carefully constructed parcel has not been touched; it lies as lifeless as the dreams that are packed within it.

"Yes," I reply, "she has clothes. But I didn't know she was permitted to wear them in intensive care." Ruby lies quietly in diapers and wires.

"Bring them to me," the nurse responds.

I walk over and unzip the bag, along with the memory of total ignorance from a few weeks back. I unzip the hopes of bringing a baby home right after birth. I unpack the pure expectation of good. Neatly folded newborn clothes lie untouched, still waiting for their moment—which has come and gone.

Holding up a purple onesie, I walk over to Ruby's hospital bed and lay it down next to her, hoping it will work. It's a newborn size and at least two times her size. I let out a sigh and step back, "Maybe if we had doll clothes."

The nurse steps forward and begins rearranging the tubes that tangle Ruby's body. I watch her stick the feeding tube through the neck hole of the onesie, and pull Ruby's head up out of it. She is dressing Ruby for the first time. Wires relocate, monitors shift, pulse-ox is replaced, and, at last, there she is—Ruby Joy—in royal purple.

I look once at Ruby and feel happier. Look again and feel happier still. Look a third time and my heart starts throbbing with joy. She looks like a real person, and she looks *cute*. The scars from her blood draws and wires hide silently underneath the cloth. Something greater has just covered her.

Dignity.

Dignity transforms the scene so quickly I hardly know what has happened. In minutes, a pathetic little body has become a princess. The transformation hits my heart hard. I feel like a lion with a lioness cub who deserves to live. The power of dignity on a human life!

The nurse continues, replacing Ruby's feeding tube, and drawing a butterfly out of the NG tape for her face. I watch in wonder. *Wish I would have thought of this myself!* Or, if I'm even more honest, I wish I had known I had permission to think for myself.

For two weeks, I have lived as a first-time mom listening to reports on what is wrong with my child, while she lay nearly lifeless in an over-sized diaper and a hospital blanket. Day after day, people have come into the room pointing out her anomalies, trying to congratulate us through their fierce discomfort. Then this nurse arrives, pulls back the shades, lets in the light and dresses Ruby in dignity. She normalizes her needs to include looking pretty and dressing cute. I am uplifted and realize no one here is going to teach me how to live in the middle of this crisis. And yet without that skill, we are seriously missing out.

The lioness inside roars. *Find the things that make life worth living, Katie. Make room for them.*

～

Ruby and I are sitting in the chair next to her hospital bed. She is propped up on my left arm. My laptop sits on the window ledge behind us. This morning, Mitch and I sent out a mass online request for a week of twenty-four/seven prayer for Ruby's healing. We creat-ed an online form where people can type their name into time slots, committing to pray for her during a designated hour of the day.

Today, Ruby will have an MRI on her brain. I don't know what that means apart from it means more medical testing. I pull Ruby close. If I can help her feel safe in the "off" moments of medical care today, perhaps the "on" moments will not prove as harmful.

I reach over to the computer and push "refresh" on the blank docu-ment that sits on the screen behind me. It's only been two hours since we posted, but I am curious. I hold my breath. *Will anyone participate?*

I look up and into the empty spaces a few names appear. My eyes brighten, "Thank You, God." These initial names feel like streetlights on a dark night. They begin to crack my sense of isolation. Helen, Linda, Victoria…James? Who is James? I scroll to the left of the page. Wow! Three AM is filled. So is 4:00 AM and 6:00 AM.

Ruby is being called for her MRI. I help the nurse detach the wirings and reattach them onto the cart upon which she will be trans-ferred. A heavy blue jacket is laid upon Ruby, a shield for the pend-ing radiation. I look at Ruby and remember those few names that appeared on the spreadsheet. The radiation jacket reminds me of the need for prayer covering.

Ruby is rolled down to radiation and I am left in the waiting room. I have come to despise testing. Not only is it stressful for Ruby, but we have yet to receive a good report after a medical test. Test results have consistently yielded bad news that further complicate our lives.

The MRI is quick; we are escorted back to our room.

I decide to peek at the spreadsheet again. I push the refresh button on the computer. It's half full! People are gathering through cyberspace to contend with us for Ruby's healing. I close my eyes and a vivid scene passes through my mind. I grab a pen and the scene unravels onto the thirsty pages of my journal.

A father, mother and child are alone in a dark pit. The child is sick, dying. All resources in the pit have been exhausted. Hope runs dry. The light above their heads is the only sign that there could be more than the pit in which they find themselves. A decision is made to yell for help in the hope that someone—somewhere—will hear.

But even if someone does hear, would they come? For all those whose lives are still in routine, unscathed by tragedy, unmoved by pits, what reason would they have to respond?

Nonetheless, for hope's sake, hope is pursued. A call is released, a loud and specific cry for help, just in case someone within earshot will come. The echo of their cry billows back into their laps.

Silence.

Silence.

Silence.

At least they tried. And then...footsteps. The distant sound of someone coming. Someone? More than one. Footsteps. Many footsteps, hooves. pounding the ground. It's an army. People, many people, are racing toward the scene. People are exiting their routine to come and help.

This sound, these people—are they friend or foe? The first face arrives and they squint to see. Friend! From there, the rim of the pit fills with faces, many faces, friends, acquaintances, strangers, who have come to help. Ropes begin flying through the air and down into the laps of the family.

Hope builds.

Dad grasps a rope.

Mom looks down at child,

"We're going to get out of here."

Later that day, I refresh the spreadsheet again and it is two-thirds full. It's a sign to me that we are not alone. Isolation is breaking down like a melting glacier. The walls of loneliness split with glorious cracks. I recall my objection to prayer updates. *Do we really want our journey to be public? Do we really want everyone to know what we are going through? To know Ruby's issues, to know ours?*

I lean back to catch a full view of the computer screen and reflect. *I am so glad I stepped over the hurdle of sharing. This is so encouraging; we needed it.*

My phone rings. It's Mitch. He is driving back to the hospital from work. "Have you looked at the spreadsheet, Mitch? People are committing to pray for Ruby around the clock! Can you imagine what God is about to do? Maybe Ruby will be healed this week!"

Later that night, Mitch and I look at the spreadsheet together. The slots are nearly full. People have committed their Bible studies, prayer groups, and small groups to pray for Ruby's healing. A few have committed their whole church to a certain time slot. In addition, we have started to get e-mails from people who want to add their names to slots that are already filled. We need to add more slots; we make room for support we didn't know we had—until we asked.

Mitch and I look at the specific names of people on the spreadsheet and marvel at the diversity of people represented in this form. There are people on this list whom we did not know believed in God, let alone prayer, or healing. There are others who disbelieve in divine healing, and yet, for Ruby, will pray for it. The invitation to believe for a miracle is pulling people of all kinds into a place of faith.

Ruby is giving us a reason to believe. She is inviting us all into something bigger than ourselves, giving us a reason to champion a

God who is good. Together, we are daring to believe that our God will intervene.

> *"For Zion's sake, I will not keep silent; for Jerusalem's sake, I will not remain quiet, till her vindication shines out like the dawn, her salvation like a blazing torch."*

I pull out my pen and write in my Bible next to that verse, "*for Ruby.*" And next to her name I write "*God,*" with a smile. "*Thank You for our new radiation jacket.*"

A week of twenty-four/seven prayer for Ruby commences.

∿

My neck is stiff from dozing off in a chair most of the night. It's morning. I carefully shift wires out of my way and move Ruby to bed. At last, she fell asleep. If I could sleep now, I would, but unfortunately my day has just begun.

I pull my seat as close as it can get to the window and begin to daydream about life outside the hospital. Raindrops fall on the windowpane and I zero in on the dark clouds overhead. I am glad that it is gloomy out there today. It feels honest.

I watch the parking lot eight stories below our window fill with cars. Hospital employees. I watched them leave last night, and I'm watching them come back this morning. I wonder what it feels like to have the liberty to come and go from a place at will. That freedom feels foreign to me right now. Everything feels prescribed here, and we are not allowed to leave. I wonder what would happen if I asked outright about taking Ruby home? Would they consider me an irresponsible mom? If they knew I had escape plans in my journal, then what would they think?

The first doctor comes in and interrupts my thoughts. She asks questions, and I answer them, recounting the events of the night. As she leaves, I wish I could bolt the door behind her, providing a safe place to think—but I don't have a bolt or a key for that door. It is not mine and I remain at its mercy.

I walk back toward the window. On the other side of that glass is the free world. On my side of the glass are Bible verses we have plastered all over it—promises we believe will break that glass and provide an escape ladder down. It's just a matter of time. For the hundredth time, I stare down those scriptures and courageously declare them over Ruby.

A few minutes later, I collapse back into the chair. I want out of this place more than anything right now. I convince myself that the problem is not Ruby, or us, or God—it is the hospital. If we could just get out of this place, as a family, and create our own environment of peace for her, she would thrive. And from there, I set my face: we're going to get out of here. Call it a jailbreak, I don't care, we're getting out.

I see the full team of doctors coming down the hall and my stomach turns. I'm going to do it. Crazy woman? Whatever. I'm going to tell them—we want to go home.

The medical team concludes their normal rounds and then asks me, "Mom, do you have any other questions?"

"Can we go home?" I shoot straight.

They look at each other as if each one is waiting for the other to respond. And then, to my utmost surprise, the scraggly-framed, emotionless nemesis of a geneticist responds in my defense. "These parents have not left the patient's side [she still does not use Ruby's name]. I think they could do a lot of this from home. They are really committed. Why don't we have the nurses train them over the weekend and then start moving toward discharge?"

I stare at her in shock. *Is she really going to be the one to fight for Ruby to go home?* She continues, "A lot of this ongoing care could be done as an outpatient. They just need to learn the feeding tube."

Chitter-chatter, nods and it is done. The medical team has agreed to start working toward Ruby being able to go home!

And…it's thanks to the geneticist.

I shake my head in disbelief. Sometimes life is complicated. Like that moment when, out of nowhere, you want to hug your enemy. The medical team moves on to the next room and I catch the geneticist from behind by tapping her on the shoulder. She turns around. My timid remark tumbles out, "Thank you. *Thank you*," I repeat.

She nods and then clicks her heels on down the hallway. I turn around and look straight out the window on the back wall of Ruby's hospital room. The world outside that window just got one step closer.

~

We are down to the wire. If Ruby can sit for an hour in her car seat without her vitals dropping, we can go home. They call it the "car seat check."

I am not concerned about her vitals; they've been stable since birth. I do know, however, that if she has a vomiting episode during this hour it will affect her oxygen and we'll have to start over. The other concern is that she'll just get worked up and it will heighten her blood pressure.

Ruby's car seat is brought in from our car and placed on the floor next to her hospital bed in proximity to her monitors. She is lifted up and buckled into the car seat. The time is jotted down.

The test is on.

Ruby sits for about ten seconds and then begins to fuss. Her tiny body is slouched into a seat that is way too big for her. I sit on the floor and take hold of her hands. In a panicky voice, I try to release peace. "We're going home, Ruby, hang in there!" Despite my best efforts to keep her calm, her fussiness turns to sadness, which turns to frustration, which turns to raw anger and then…screams.

I look at her angry face and think, *Wow. She dislikes this more than the blood draw this morning!* I wish I understood life from her view. I can almost hear her thoughts: *I like being held. I like knowing that when I call someone will respond. I need to know that I am not alone. I need to know that my needs matter. My mom and dad are my favorite.* If this is an accurate description of Ruby's current lenses on life, than it explains why she hates the car seat check so much. It invades every one of those preferences.

The nurse recommends we roll up baby blankets to support her position. A blanket roll is placed on her left side, another one on her right side, and a third, circular one to support her head. I spend the next fifty-five minutes watching one minute pass at a time and working tirelessly to calm down a child who will have none of it.

At last, the hour finishes.

She passes.

I'm exhausted.

But, we're done.

Over the next few hours a host of medical professionals visit us: doctors, nurses, a social worker, caseworker. Their countenances are bright. We are getting a lot of praises. "Congratulations, you're going home!" I cannot hide my proud grin. This is a miracle. Ruby is now three weeks old and we are going home.

I notice sincere joy in the faces of the staff. I thought most of these people were enemies, but today they look like friends. I realize that I have needed someone to blame for my hurt and have often pointed my emotional pistol at the medical staff. There were times when that pistol was an appropriate response. But in this moment, I can see that these blue-gowned medical professionals have been caring deeply for our family.

Today, I seem to see them more accurately, and I am thankful for their expertise, years of schooling, and practicum to help kids like Ruby. This is Ruby's team. Together, we have fought hard for her, and together we celebrate her ability to go home.

A nurse brings our discharge paperwork and I give her a big hug. She hands me a huge stack of papers, and I wish I could take the hug back. It's an enormous list of specialists and outpatient appointments requiring follow up. Most of the specialists listed are in this building—which we have yet to leave!

"Not a problem!" I lie through my teeth.

Thumbing through the paperwork, I realize that there is no way we can meet all the expectations in the time frame expected. I glance up and wonder if "incompetent" is written on my forehead to the very people who are about to discharge us. I let the paperwork sit half-evaluated and choose to say nothing more. I flip to the last page of the stack and sign the discharge paperwork.

We are told that a home-based nurse will come to visit us within a week to make sure that we can handle Ruby's care at home. This eases my stress. Another nurse then helps me pack our bags with ample medical supplies and medication.

Stepping out of the hospital room with Ruby is surreal. I'm living the escape that I envisioned many times. And yet, we are not escaping; we're being released. This is joy: walking out of a hospital with a child who was not expected to live. Mitch, Ruby and I exit the hospital and enter a warm summer day. The three of us have survived a long, hard fight, and we're finally going home.

Chapter 4

I stand on the front porch, holding Ruby against my chest. The sun is shining and her eyes are tightly shut. I'm looking at our front door and cannot wait to get behind it. Mitch calls to me from behind, "Wait! Let's take a picture!" I turn around, and a proud grin spreads across my face. Snapshot. We are home.

The three of us begin climbing the two flights of stairs to our apartment. I am carrying Ruby. Mitch is carrying our baggage from hospital living. I reach the bottom of the second flight and begin running. I run up the stairs as if I'm being chased, as if we could yet get captured halfway up this staircase and not make it home. I arrive at the top and wait by the door. Mitch catches up and turns the key.

Home.

Door shuts. Huge exhale. Exhaustion meets gratitude. I look at the door. It is shut. I search for a way to close it even more; I would tape it shut if I could. It is hard to imagine that doctors and nurses are not waiting on the other side, ready to barge through it. This is our space; for the first time, we are alone as a family. Our need to rejoice, relax, collapse, give thanks, scream, sob, exhale, sleep and *be*—uninterrupted—collide simultaneously and we stand still, unsure of what to do.

Ruby makes a sweet noise. I draw my head back to see her face. "Ruby, come see what I prepared for you!" I carry her into our bedroom where we decorated part of it in preparation for her arrival. A co-sleeper, changing table, shelf and rocker are arranged for Ruby. Fabric hangs on the wall above her things; this is Ruby's space. Compared to the hospital, this small corner of a bedroom feels like paradise. I lay her down in the co-sleeper and take a step back.

I recall spending many evenings in this space, with my bulging belly, trying to imagine what it would be like to bring my baby home. I imagined a baby meeting her bed, cooing on the changing table, and wearing the clothes we bought for her first days of life. I notice Ruby's feeding tube hanging over the edge of her bed. *What would it have been like if we came home without her?* I shove the thought back down. *Hell.* A hell that some people know.

Mitch is watching from the door. Ruby is at peace. This is all very good. Good feels new. Good feels so new that it does not feel safe. Fear has been supervising us, and we just escaped. Now what?

All of a sudden, I feel ferociously hungry. I turn to Mitch, "I need to eat. Now. I feel like I haven't eaten in weeks." My own stomach has been the least of my concerns.

We walk away from Ruby and head into the kitchen. Our 500-square-foot apartment feels like a treasure chest of freedom. There is so much we can do here that we could not do in the hospital, like eat when we want!

Mitch and I enter the kitchen and almost simultaneously fall on our knees. I press my forehead into ground. He flattens out prostrate. Gratitude boils within, and the steam rises. Hunger steps aside. We open our mouths and begin thanking God. Together, we start pulling praise up out of our gut and releasing it like heavy weights into eternity. From the tile of our kitchen floor, we express thanks to God. A life spared.

Yes, we will make some noise.

Heaven attracts and suddenly we are surrounded by His Presence.

~

Ruby turns one month old a week after we return home. There is *much* to celebrate. And yet, coordinating her care feels like assembling an impossible puzzle. The home-based nurse who was supposed to visit us within a week has not shown up. We are scrambling to become what people study for years to become—medical professionals. In the meantime, doctors are calling, family members want updates, Mitch is back at work, and I fill my days pumping and feeding Ruby around the clock.

I flip through my journal and find scribbled notes from our first week following discharge. The pages reveal nothing; my voice is not there. I fear what my words might reveal. Instead, my writing contains one scripture after another, each promising a way out. I have been rummaging through my Bible like a starving child hungry for hope. Whatever good I find, I cling to it, believing it is for me, for Ruby, for us, for now. I make the Word my language; I prefer it to my own.

Yesterday, I needed to scream. I found this and screamed it: "To you, Lord, I call; you are my Rock, do not turn a deaf ear to me. For if you remain silent, I will be like those who go down to the pit. Hear my cry for mercy as I call to you for help, as I lift my hands toward your Most Holy Place" (Psalm 28:1-2).

The day before, I needed hope. I found this and embraced it: "I will not in any way fail you *nor* give you up *nor* leave you without support. [I will] not, [I will] not, [I will] not in any degree leave you helpless *nor* forsake *nor* let [you] down (relax My hold on you)! [Assuredly not!] So we take comfort *and* are encouraged *and* confidently *and* boldly say, The Lord is my Helper; I will not be seized with alarm [I will not fear or dread or be terrified]" (Hebrews 13:5-6).

Today, I need courage. I find this and declare it: "Have I not commanded you? Be strong and courageous. Do not be afraid; do not be discouraged, for the Lord your God will be with you wherever you go" (Joshua 1:9).

My journal is a line up of scriptures, like hanging ropes at a playground, like monkey bars overhead. I cling and swing from one to the next and refuse the ground, a mere foot beneath my feet. Whatever happens, I cannot touch the ground. The ground is, as reality is to many, a scary, bottomless, monster-filled pit. Whatever happens, do not touch the ground. *Is this faith or fear?*

I cannot be bothered to answer the question at the moment. I have found a tool that is enabling me to move through what would otherwise overwhelm me. Regardless of where it is rooted, it contains power and produces faith. My faith is growing and it gives me strength. Faith comes by hearing, and hearing by the Word of God.

I open the Word again, thirsty, and read:

> *"I am the Lord, the God of all mankind, is there anything that is too hard for me?"*

The current of His nature leaks into my heart and I like Him all the more for what I see. He doesn't limit Ruby in any way; this feels right to me.

I swing to this verse and hang on for dear life.

~

Today, I am taking Ruby to her first doctor's appointment, the first of many. We are happy to be home, but so many doctors want to see Ruby—now. There's the pediatrician, the cardiologist, the ophthalmologist and the audiologist. Then there's the gastroenterologist, the orthopedist and the urologist. And don't forget the physical therapist, the craniofacial team and the ear, nose and throat specialist. They're all competing for our time and they want it now. *Where do I start?*

We start with the pediatrician. The office is situated in a residential area and looks like a small townhouse: red brick, black shutters. We enter and find a square waiting room lined with young families waiting to be seen. All of them appear to be Middle Eastern. We chose this practice during the pregnancy because its practitioner shares our values, much of which are stronger in cultures outside our own.

I check in. Ruby's feeding tube dangles from her tiny face. Crisis won't hide. I sense tenderheartedness in the room toward us. I begin to talk with the people around me. They do not seem uncomfortable with Ruby, or with suffering. It makes me wonder how familiar they are with suffering themselves.

We wait for forty minutes. I have yet to see anyone taken back to see the doctor. Another forty minutes, and one or two patients cycle through. I look around. *Does everyone here wait two to three hours to see the doctor?* I ask one of the moms near me and, in broken English, she responds joyfully, "Dr. Morshed takes her time with every child. Yes…we wait. It…is good." She nods confidently and returns to her magazine.

I approach the office manager to explain that I didn't bring enough food for Ruby to wait much longer. The room is small. Everyone hears my dilemma. And everyone, like a true community, decides together that Ruby should go next. Ruby and I are bumped to the top of the list with nods of agreement, silent cheers heard through the women's hijabs.

Soon afterward, we are called back to meet the doctor. I bid farewell to my new friends, who will likely still be here when we finish, but I thank them all the same. They have made me feel like Ruby and I are part of a community instead of on the sidelines of it. It is healing to feel like a part of the whole. The gift of community.

The pediatrician comes into the room. She is a tall Egyptian woman with jet-black hair and heavy makeup. She carries a stack of papers that I recognize from Children's Hospital. Seeing the stack of papers brings fear that we will be dismissed from her practice.

"Good morning," the pediatrician greets us solemnly.

"Good morning," I respond.

I pause for half a second and then continue, preempting my feared rejection, "I don't know if you can still see us considering the challenges with Ruby's health, but we would really like for you to be Ruby's pediatrician…if you are willing."

"Yes, I'm willing!" The doctor responds. "Ruby is going to have to see many specialists, but I am happy to be her primary care doctor." She turns her back to me just in time to miss my visible sigh of relief. Getting to choose a doctor feels like a weighty privilege after hospital living.

Thumbing through the medical records, she continues, "I have looked through Ruby's chart, but will *you* also tell me what the medical concerns are?" She turns around, looks at me, and waits. Full attention. *Present.*

Her question hands me an unexpected honor. Papers do not always represent realities well, but few people in this field seem to understand that. She is interested in my version, my perspective. I proceed to unload Ruby's medical history. She listens intently. And then, with straightforward conviction, she puts order to the stack of chaotic reports.

"Okay," she pauses. Nods. Shoots straight. "You need to see the cardiologist first and then the ophthalmologist. Don't delay seeing the ophthalmologist. A quick intervention could save Ruby's eyesight."

She then takes Ruby from me and puts her on the scale.

"Five pounds!"

We both cheer.

Dr. Morshed smiles, bright-red lipstick widening across her face, jet-black hair flung over her shoulder, "Good job, Ruby! And good job, Mom! Keep doing what you're doing. Ruby has gained weight since her discharge from the hospital. That's fantastic!"

This "good job" burrows into my heart. I didn't know if we were floating or sinking with Ruby's care at home. I dare to be…*encouraged.*

Ruby and I finish the appointment and pass through the waiting room, still full of hijab-covered women with their children. We exit the office in high spirits. That "5 pounds" on the scale is a slice of happy news that we will gobble up and sing about all the way home.

Mitch gets home from work and I shout toward the door, "Ruby hit five pounds!" He stops in his tracks. His chin lifts. Eyes brighten. A smile appears. He walks over to Ruby and we observe her together. She does look a little bit chubbier now that the doctor confirmed it.

"Plumpscout Ruby!" Mitch lets out and swoops her up.

Five pounds feels enormous to all of us.

If commiserating and celebrating can exist in the same space, they do in this moment: our little girl is growing up!

～

I am up for the fourth time tonight with Ruby. Two hours more and the sun will be up with me, at which point we will need to be out the door. I lie back down and try to sleep, but my mind overpowers my body and I remain awake.

The stillness of the night seems to intensify the dread of the coming day. Today, we will go back to the hospital for a cardiology appointment. Every muscle in my body tenses at the thought of driving back toward Children's Hospital. We have not been there since Ruby's initial discharge. I am afraid of what the cardiologist will say, or do, or make us do. My biggest fear is that we won't come home. Walking into that facility feels like an unintended invitation to admit Ruby into the hospital and swallow our experience of home.

Time is exhausted in my anxiety, and I am forced out of bed at sunrise to prepare Ruby for her appointment. Feed. Medication. Clothes. Hair. Diaper. Socks. Shoes. Car Seat. Another diaper. New clothes. New socks. Shoes again. Bag packed. We're finally ready.

It's 7:15 AM and the doorbell rings. It is Victoria. She has come to help me take Ruby to Children's Hospital today. Our front door is two flights beneath us. She will have to wait. I rush to finish the task at hand while thinking about how much of a gift Victoria is to us in this time. She felt led to quit her job before Ruby was born to make room for something new God wanted her to do. That new assignment is Ruby. She has made herself available to help Ruby and me.

A few minutes later, I answer the door and greet her. Together, we pack the car. I drive. Ruby and Victoria are in the middle seat. Ruby starts to cough. The cough turns to choking. The choking turns to refluxing, and the refluxing becomes vomiting. I am at a loss, hands stuck to the wheel, heart thrown into the back seat. Victoria handles it well, because she loves well.

As we near the hospital, I start trembling. Familiar sights trigger memories. Flashbacks of our hospitalization are awake in my mind. I feel the impact of them as if I were still there, stuck inside of those crazed moments. I wonder to myself if I have a degree of post-traumatic stress.

My hands clench the wheel of the car as I work to keep myself under control. An angry driver honks his way across the street in front of me. *People never know who they are honking at,* I think to myself.

Unsolicited anger directed at a hurting mom on her way to Children's Hospital. I pull into the parking garage below the hospital. I force myself into a perspective of empowerment. *I am here for Ruby.* The thought strengthens me.

Diaper bag in one arm, car seat in another, Ruby and I enter Children's Hospital for the first time as outpatients. At the front desk, they ask if I've been here before. I look at the lady like she has four heads. *I was imprisoned here for weeks, doesn't she know?*

Name tags are given and we're directed to the second floor for the cardiac clinic. Internal fear is talkative. I want to go home. At the clinic entrance, I peer through the glass doors and see a room packed with people. Concern rises. I didn't bring another feed for Ruby. My lack of preparation stings; I feel like I'm giving them more reason to admit us.

Inside, we sign in and wait for a seat to open. The room is full of children, from infants to teenagers. One thing has gathered us all into one room today: the heart. I wonder what the other conditions are. I wonder if these moms feel like I do today, troubled with fear.

Time crawls as we wait. Ruby is getting fussy. I go to the front desk to ask how long the wait will be. I explain that Ruby is tube fed and I don't have another feed with me. "I'm sorry, ma'am, but you should always bring another feeding with you," the clerk rebukes me. "We have no guarantee how long you will have to wait."

I sit back down bewildered. *Is it ridiculous for me to expect this appointment to be less than three hours?* I learn my lesson. A single appointment can take all day. Two hours later, Ruby's name is called.

After a few tests, we're directed to the patient room to meet the cardiologist. He looks cheerful. Nearing us, he approaches Ruby first. Bending over her tiny body, he introduces himself, "Hi! I'm Dr. Davis, you must be Ruby." A warm grin spreads across his face. He seems genuinely happy to meet her. He then steps back and watches her silently. After a few minutes, he looks up with a smile. "Upon initial evaluation, I don't see any signs of heart failure. You look good!"

"Hi. I'm Dr. Davis, are you Mom?"

"Yes, Ruby's mom."

"And are you Grandma?" he addresses Victoria.

"I'm a friend."

"That's a good friend."

We both nod.

Dr. Davis pulls out Ruby's chart and begins to survey the reports with a peace and joy that are notable for a hospital. I realize as he browses the paperwork that he read Ruby before he read her paperwork.

"So…Ruby was in the NICU with us for almost three weeks."

I nod.

"During that time they did some evaluations on her heart. Do you understand what they found during those?"

I name off a few medical terms that I had been told, and then, in a moment of candid honesty, shake my head no.

Dr. Davis pulls out a piece of scrap paper and a pencil. He pauses for a moment, and then, with bright eyes and a surge of energy, sketches out a diagram of the human heart. "This is the heart," he explains. "These are the chambers; these are the main arteries." He breaks it down to the basics for me, and then proceeds to draw Ruby's heart with an explanation of how it is different. "This is what we are seeing," he explains. "Her initial diagnosis of *patent ductus arteriorsus* and *atrial septal defect* are no longer present."

"No longer present?" I ask. "Like a miracle?"

"Could be!" he continues. "However, I am still detecting an arch obstruction and mild coarctation of the aorta." The diagram and explanation continue.

I learn that Ruby's heart is shaped differently than most hearts. There is one major artery instead of four pumping blood into the heart (arch obstruction). There is also a narrowing, a coarctation, of the aorta.

"The arch obstruction does not seem to be interfering with her heart function," Dr. Davis continues. "The coarctation is currently mild but could warrant intervention depending on what happens as she grows."

That flimsy piece of scrap paper in the doctor's hand has become a distinguished chalkboard as Dr. Davis teaches me about Ruby's heart. He talks about the implications for her conditions and possible needs for interventions. He tells me how the heart is amazing in that it sometimes will reconfigure its blood flow to compensate for congenital anomalies like Ruby's.

This man is happy talking about the human heart.

A few minutes later, he looks at me to see if I'm still engaged.

"Thank you for explaining all this," I respond to his questioning eyes. "It's helpful, and it makes sense."

"You are welcome. We can either proceed now with a cardiac intervention to widen the narrowing of the aorta, or we can wait to see what her heart will do as she grows." He pauses and then continues, "The danger in waiting to intervene is that the coarctation could result in heart failure if it doesn't widen with her growth. If we choose to wait, we will have to watch her closely for signs of heart failure and commit to regular check-ups."

"We would like to wait." I feel relieved it's an option.

"That's what I would recommend too," he responds. "She looks healthy to me. I feel good about waiting to see what this little one can do on her own before we choose to put her through surgery."

This is the first doctor who has called Ruby healthy, and I know he means it. I'm guessing he has more experience with childhood disease than most people we have seen.

Dr. Davis rises and, with a smile, says he will reevaluate Ruby in two weeks. The door shuts behind him and I find myself scrambling to pack up our stuff. Underneath my skin, I am still in fight or flight mode and want to get out of the hospital as soon as possible so we will not be admitted. Irrational? *Rational.*

We race down the hall back to the parking garage. As I put my foot on the gas pedal, the thought catches up with me: *That appointment was actually good. We were not admitted to the hospital or informed of heart failure or kidnapped by the genetics team. We were in and out, and we met a very kind man in the midst of it.* As distance between us and the hospital grows, I think even more clearly. *That was actually real-*

ly good. Two of the main cardiac diagnoses that Ruby had are no longer present. The other two presenting conditions are mild and non-critical. I dial Mitch.

"Mitch! Good news!"

~

It's evening. The tape that holds Ruby's feeding tube is peeling off of her face. It needs to be replaced. When the edge gets loose, it leaves a small loophole, just large enough for her finger to get stuck and pull the tube out. If the tube comes out, we have to replace it. It's an event we work hard to avoid.

I go over to our medical supply bin and pull out some new tape. I call Mitch over to help. Mitch holds Ruby down. I soften the tape on Ruby's face with adhesive remover. Once it softens, I gently pull it up to replace it. As I am pulling up the tape, Ruby starts to thrash and her finger gets into the loophole of the tube. *Yank.* The tube comes halfway out. I panic, try to stuff it back in. I fail. She gags and the job needs to be finished. I pull the tube out completely.

Despair.

Mitch and I sit on the floor silently with the feeding tube next to us. That dark familiar feeling plops into my gut. *We're all about to suffer badly and there is nothing I can do about it.*

Placing the NG tube is a waking nightmare. Somehow, we have to get the tube through Ruby's nostril, down her throat and into her stomach. It can easily go into her lungs by mistake, which cuts off her airway. To Ruby, the experience of having something shoved down her throat feels like being gagged. *Unwelcomed suffering.*

Without words, Mitch goes back over to the medical supply bin and pulls out a new feeding tube, tape, adhesive remover, and a syringe. Here goes.

He sits on the chair with Ruby and I organize his supplies. He prays and asks God to heal her mouth. I hand him the tube. He leans Ruby back and begins to the push the tube into her nostril. Ruby cries. He pulls it out and tries again. Ruby cries harder. A third time, and she gets so upset I think she may vomit.

I try not to intervene as my motherly instincts scream. I contribute some suggestions, which frustrate the scene further. Mitch tries again. This time the tube goes in, but something is not right. Ruby has stopped making noise. She is now turning blue.

"It's in the lungs! Take it out!" I cry.

"No, I don't think it is. I think I finally got it! I don't want to have to do it again."

"Mitch!" I scream. "Take it out!"

Mitch gets angry, ignores me and continues, as if my interruptions are the hard part of the task. I watch Ruby's color drain.

I scream again, "It's in her lungs! TAKE IT OUT NOW!"

Mitch shakes in frustration and then yanks the tube out.

Ruby is convulsing.

I am crying.

Mitch is fuming.

The tube is still out.

We are thrown violently back to the start line.

I storm out of the room, crawl into bed, and pull the covers over my head like a child. Hands clenching the sheets, I pull my knees into a fetal position and cry. Groans of sorrow awake like sleeping monsters that have just been woke up. From the other side of the door, I hear Mitch trying again to place the tube. Ruby sounds like she is being choked. I know this breaks Mitch's heart too. I try to tune it out, but I cannot. I can still hear. I can still feel. It's as though I haven't left the room, and at the same time I hate that I have.

At last, the noise dies down. Ruby stops crying. I hear Mitch walking around with Ruby in an attempt to comfort her. I wonder if the tube is in or out. In time, he opens the door to the bedroom where I am hiding and talks directly to me, as if I were not under the covers.

"The tube is in."

I do not respond. He leaves.

Hours pass and tension rules in the air of our home. I am going to have to come out. Ruby needs to be fed. Mitch and I need to reconcile. The beauty and sting of marriage: no one is going anywhere. We have to work this out. I come out. Mitch is in the chair with Ruby and now he is the one crying.

"It was in the lungs, Mitch. You wouldn't listen to me!" My need to defend myself overrules his need for comfort.

"I know, Katie. I am so sorry. I didn't want to have to place it again if it was right, because she suffers every time. I'm sorry. I was not listening."

We sit in silence. I look at Ruby. The tube is in. I could not have done that, and without *that*, she cannot eat. "You did a good job, Mitch. I don't think I could have done it."

"Thank you. It was awful."

Pause.

"Katie, are you okay?"

"No. Are you?"

"No."

"I hate this feeding tube."

"Me too."

We leave it at that. We both hate the feeding tube. We can agree on that. It's not right that Ruby has to pay such a high price to get food she cannot even taste. We agree on that too.

I attach Ruby's feed to her tube that night. I consider praying, but I feel too angry. I have nothing to say to God tonight. I feel as though He is on vacation. I don't understand why He is not intervening. A few minutes later, the feeding pump starts beeping.

It's clogged.

Here goes another long night.

Chapter 5

I look around the room; it is full of children who have challenges with their eyes. There are infants with thick glasses, babies with patches, older kids with lazy eyes, toddlers running around with an inability to focus, and more. There is a mom with twins who are smaller than Ruby. Their eyes are shut; perhaps they have yet to open. Welcome to Children's Hospital Opthalmology Clinic. I sign in. I feel delight writing Ruby's name. She's healthier than she was at discharge. I am a proud mom.

We wait a long time.

At last, a door opens and a petite Asian-American woman with straight, dark, shoulder-length hair steps out and calls, "Ruby Joy Luse?"

I pick up my three bags, car seat, coats and child and head back into the patient room. The room is small. It contains one chair, a few specialized lights whose faces stare at the chair from every direction, a table with magnifying glasses, flashlights, unusual metal utensils, and a big tethered diagram of the human eye on the wall. *The eye*. Ruby, Victoria and I enter. Our wait continues.

The doctor comes into the room. A cordial exchange and then straight to business. She recounts that in the NICU, Ruby was diagnosed with severe congenital cataracts in both eyes. Then, in a hushed tone, she explains, "Ruby is currently blind. She may never see. She may never see you."

Her words feel like daggers. I am not sure how to respond, unwilling to share in that belief with her, and yet forced, in some way, to interact with respect. The doctor turns my attention to the diagram of the eye on the wall. She continues her explanation. The visual helps me understand.

Ruby has severe cataracts on both eyes. At this point, she is blind, her vision blocked by the cataracts. They can attempt surgery, but it would be risky. The doctors are uncertain whether or not surgery is worth pursuing because the function of her optic nerve is in question.

I pry a little bit, "Why do you think the optic nerve may not work?"

"Given the rest of her challenges, we would guess that her brain function is not normal, which could affect her optic nerve."

"Oh." I frown. *That's not enough for me. I would rather err on the side of hope.* "What about the surgery? What are the risks?" I ask more questions.

The doctor unpacks the risks of surgery and I let them fall to my side. If I let these statements sink in, I'll never be able to choose it.

The bottom line is that Ruby's eyes may have capacity to see. The doctors question if her optic nerve can or will function. If it is in fact working, the cataracts need to come off as soon as possible so that her eyesight will develop and not atrophy. This reminds me of the pediatrician's warning: "Don't delay on seeing the ophthalmologist; it could save her eyesight." The ophthalmologist will not officially offer surgery until she consults with the genetics team regarding the risks involved for Ruby's condition.

The options are clear. We either forfeit Ruby's ability to see, pursue surgery, or get a miracle. Ruby is five pounds and fragile. Surgery is a big decision. I need to go home and think.

The need for a decision hangs like a weight over my tired head.

I am with Ruby at a state-run therapy program for children with disabilities. In the midst of our hospital madness, someone told me that when we got discharged, we needed to make an appointment with one of their specialists as soon as possible. So, as soon as possible, we are here.

When we arrive, Ruby and I are interviewed to see if we "qualify." At one point the interviewer says, "Oh, she has cleft palate? That means you automatically qualify for services; we can end this interview now." I nod and walk out of the room in disbelief. *Cleft palate?* I think to myself, *That's the least of our concerns right now.* Care that is not centered on survival feels foreign to me after living in the NICU. I begin to wonder, *Do we need to be here? If this is not about keeping Ruby alive, why are we here?* I lay Ruby on the floor for her first evaluation with therapists. Four overly friendly ladies crowd around her. I can see tension behind their toothy grins. I would guess this is the smallest, neediest child they have evaluated in a long time.

They put Ruby on her belly; she begins to squirm, fight, and then rather suddenly lifts her head from the right side to the left. The happy ladies all cheer. "Overachiever!" the director calls out.

I stare at the director—she is awkward, but sincere. *Seriously? Did Ruby just go from "incompatible with life" to "overachiever" in eight weeks? That's my girl!*

When I get home, I place Ruby on her belly again. Her face plummets into the floor and she whimpers. I tuck my hands beneath my knees to withhold my mom impulse to rescue her. This is the first time I have put her on her belly. I am copying the therapists. I want to see if she will lift her head again.

Watching intently, I see the slightest strain of muscle on the back of her neck and I excite. "Ruby! You just moved yourself! Keep going, you can do it!" I continue to watch as she works tirelessly to pull her head up from her face plant and, suddenly, boom. She picks up her head and it falls to the other side. She did it again! She lifted her head! Unable to tolerate her whimpering any longer, I pick her up. I whisper softly into her tiny ear, "Ruby, you're a champion."

I then look her square in the eyes; her forehead is red from being pressed face-down against the floor. She is not happy with me—at all.

A forced performance, I admit, but one that shatters layers of impossibilities so recently spoken over her capabilities. I grab my phone. I will take a video of it for Mitch and text him. I put Ruby back on her belly and fail many times over to get her to do it again. She's not repeating it. Babies don't perform for cameras. I guess that's something we learn to do later in life. Sadly. Even so, Ruby lifted her head today! This is a miracle!

~

"God, I ask that You would heal Ruby's eyes so that she would not have to undergo surgery." My journal is littered with the same request over and over and over. Day after day I press my heart's cry onto the page in ink.

"Please, God, spare Ruby from needing surgery."

At five pounds, Ruby is vulnerable to many risks if admitted for surgery. Doctors don't know how she will respond to general anesthesia or if they will able to place the breathing tube needed down her tiny trachea. In addition, there is a pile of unknowns about how her eyes will respond or heal from being under the knife.

We are faced with the decision: surgery or no surgery. The choice feels like a curse. We have both been wrestling for days. In the wrestling, I unravel. *Why do I have to decide whether or not Ruby undergoes surgery? I'm her mother. Of course I don't want to darken her experience of life with general anesthesia, increased hurt and risks to her life! How can I choose this knowing that she will suffer from it? When Ruby wakes up with slits in her eyes, how will she know that we chose it in the hope of helping her and not harming her? She won't, she will just hurt, and at the sight of her pain, I will hurt too. But how can I not choose it when her chances of sight lie within its ugly grip?*

The internal cycle rages.

The decision point has to come.

It's coming.

It's here.

We have to decide tonight.

Mitch and I sit at the kitchen table, solemn. He looks me straight in the eye and says, "Sometimes the best decision is the one you never thought you would have to make."

I sit still. His words resound in the room as if they are the right words at the right time. Moments pass, a conviction silently grows in the both of us. Before another word is spoken we both know we will choose surgery.

"What are you thinking?"

"Surgery. You?"

"Same."

The word "surgery" causes chills to run up and down my spine. I hate it. I hate the word. I hate the risks. I hate the facts. I hate the costs. It's scary. Threatening. Beastly. Unknown. Choosing surgery for Ruby feels like choosing for her to suffer more. I am angry. *Hope should not come with a cost, but today it does. Today, it really does. And the cost is so steep we can barely reach out to choose it.*

I clench my jaw and, through hatred, grab it. Choose it. Take hold of it.

Hope that costs.

We choose surgery.

 ∼

A TV is on; no one is watching it. We are in the Surgical Waiting Room for parents at Children's Hospital. The atmosphere is tense. I find it hard to breathe in a place where everyone is holding their breath. I stare at my feet. My eyes peruse the other feet in the room. These are all feet of parents whose children are in surgery, feet of people walking their own road of suffering, feet that are stepping into risk today for the sake of hope. None of us knows for sure what is happening with our children and none of us knows the future. We are just here, feet planted as firmly as possible, hoping to walk out of this day with more and not less than we entered.

I consider trying to be friendly, but I have no words. Neither do I have any true desire to lift my eyes from my feet. Mitch says he feels peace. He thinks Ruby is going to be okay. This is of some comfort to me.

I watch some medical feet come into the room and approach a set of parents. I dare to look up. The medical person shares something with the couple. The mom bursts into tears; the dad's posture collapses as he wraps his arms around his wife. They leave the room, hearts breaking—broken. Something awful has happened to their child.

A half hour later the scene repeats. This time, the parents' tears are clearly joy. Something good has happened, something very good, to their child. I sigh in relief.

I don't know how much more of this I can take.

The unfolding scenes in the room continue and I grow weary; experiencing surgery as a parent and observing others go through the same is exhausting. It doesn't feel normal to witness even one of these dramatic scenes, let alone ten in a day.

Three hours pass and we have heard nothing about Ruby. I'm getting nervous. The repeated drama of surgical updates blasting anxious parents undermines my confidence. We were told we would receive updates on Ruby, but we have heard nothing. I hope we did not make a mistake. I keep looking at the floor.

A new couple enters the room and something about their presence causes me to lift my eyes. They appear to Middle-Eastern, middle-aged, and from my view, clearly parents of a child in surgery. The mom catches my eye and says hello. She is trembling, and yet seems to have a fierce resolve through her brokenness. She asks me about our child. I talk for the first time in hours. A broken verse:

> *Ruby.*
> *5lbs.*
> *2 months old.*
> *"Blind."*
> *Cataract surgery.*
> *We hope she will see.*

She wishes Ruby her best and then proceeds to tell me their story.

Her family has traveled from Egypt for a specialized heart surgery for their baby girl. Their daughter has a heart defect that was detected during pregnancy. They came to Children's Hospital for a specific neonatologist who offered hope for an otherwise fatal condition. They explain that this doctor invented a machine that simulates a heart function by force-circulating the child's blood. The machine pumps blood out of the child, through the machine, and back into the child to keep her blood flowing. The mom explains that the machine has been sustaining their baby's life, but their daughter cannot remain on it indefinitely. Today, their baby girl is undergoing heart surgery in the hope that her heart will beat on its own. All of their hope hinges on this operation. It's why they flew to the States. It's why they chose this hospital. It's the only reason they are here.

Today, they sit a few seats away from us, waiting to hear if their baby's heart will beat on its own…or not.

Our conversation dies down. I think about the parents' love: outrageous, beautiful, whole, persistent, relentless, strong. I don't know if there's anything more powerful than the love of a parent. Love that flies across nations and forces its way into the hands of top specialists and risks everything. It is awesome to behold.

Their story helps me gain perspective. We live ten miles from this facility. I'm angry to be here, and I hate the operation. Perspective. *Conviction.*

Our silent wait continues. Minutes feel like hours, hours like days. I wonder why everyone else seems to be getting updates on their child except for us. It's unnerving. Time is crawling. I wish something would distract me. I wish for something to consume at least five minutes of this time.

"Please, God. Do something. Speed this time."

Gazing at the floor and praying for help, I hear Ruby's name coming from the television. "Ruby, Ruby!" a cartoon character is calling. I look up. Mitch looks up. We smile at each other. It's the cartoon, Max and Ruby. "Maybe we'll have a little boy after this and name him Max," I say to Mitch. "Yeah!" We laugh at the thought: Mitch, Katie, Ruby, Max. That's certain to be a quirky family.

For thirty minutes, we watch the cartoon and, in a strange way, draw comfort from it every time they say her name, "Ruby." The TV eats thirty minutes of my wait and I sincerely thank God for helping me pass time.

A medical professional comes and approaches our Middle-Eastern friends. I wish I could excuse myself to give them some privacy, but they don't seem to mind. They're too eager to care. In low tones some updates are shared, and the mother bursts into tears—tears of joy. They embrace and start thanking God over and over again, bowing their heads to Almighty, loudly and publicly.

Their baby's heart is beating, on its own, for the first time.

They exit the room. Our wait continues.

At last, a gowned professional comes in, "Parents of Ruby Joy?" We raise our hands and she comes toward us. As she walks over I peer into her face for information. She looks unhappy. I hope I'm wrong. She pulls a seat up next to us.

"Ruby is okay," she starts out. Obviously, she has experience updating parents; we needed to hear that first. "However, we had a very difficult time intubating her. It has actually taken the surgical team this entire time to successfully intubate her, and the surgery has not yet started. Ruby's airway is very small and it made the intubation very difficult and dangerous. The anesthesiologist is not certain he could do it again. The good news is, she is currently intubated, which means we can proceed with surgery today."

I realize it has been five hours and surgery has not begun. *They have been trying to place a breathing tube for five hours? Ruby needs to be intubated before anesthesia can be administered. She's been awake this whole time?* My heart breaks. Ruby is suffering. Alone.

The nurse practitioner continues, "I was sent out to talk with you to update you on Ruby's status, but also to ask for your permission for the doctor to operate on both of Ruby's eyes today instead of just one. The surgical team is not willing to intubate Ruby again in the near future due to the difficulty presented by her small airway. It's too dangerous. With your permission, we would like to operate on both eyes today."

She keeps referring to the intubation as "difficult" and I wonder if Ruby was near death and what really happened. "What do you mean difficult?" I ask outright.

"The doctor can share more with you, but it proved life-threatening." I realize she is not going to give me details now unless I press her or create a scene. I do not have the strength to do either. My mind becomes a battlefield and I feel the attacks within. I feel awful for not knowing what happened with my child and that, whatever occurred, I was not there.

"The doctor has begun the first surgery. Generally, we only do one operation at a time in order to limit the surgical stress on the body. As you know, Ruby is scheduled for surgery on one eye today, and another one in two weeks time for other eye. We now recommend doing both eyes today due to the difficulty of her intubation."

Mitch and I discuss the option of surgery on both eyes. We know it increases risks and there's no turning back. Ruby's eyes are precious; it doesn't feel easy to surrender them both to surgery on the same day. Fears aside, this somehow feels like a grace. The thought of consolidating our surgical stress into one event instead of two is a good one, and we are okay with it. We sign the papers and the nurse practitioner exits the room.

Soon after, we receive word that the family scheduled for surgery after us has graciously given Ruby their time slot in the operating room. They are willing to have their child's operation postponed so that Ruby can have double surgery today. We bow our heads in gratitude and bite our lips with fear.

The doctor is set to perform cataract surgery on both of Ruby's eyes in one day—a rare medical endeavor.

Our wait continues.

$\sim$

Hours later, the surgeon comes out in her operating gear and invites us into a private room to debrief Ruby's surgery. She tells us that the intubation was difficult, but she was able to successfully operate on both eyes. She reminds us again that there is no guarantee that this surgery will enable Ruby to see. I look into her tired eyes and feel thankful inside. *How many people actually have the skill to do something like this? How many years did she work to be prepared to operate on my daughter's eyes?*

She then recommends that we stay in the hospital overnight so that Ruby can have her initial recovery under specialized care. If all goes well, we can head home tomorrow to continue her post-op care from home.

The doctor continues to talk. I try to listen to her but my mind is with Ruby. This is the longest that we have been apart. I don't really care much about the report at the moment; I just want to be with Ruby.

Our conversation with the doctor ends. We are directed to the hospital room where Ruby will spend the night. It is empty. We wait for her for a long time. Finally, I see a rolling bed turn the corner and I run down the hallway, knowing its Ruby, and it is. I peek over the edge of the carrier. Ruby is lying flat and does not seem awake. She has eye patches over both eyes.

Then, we wait for her to wake up.

Cough.

Gag.

Vomit.

Ruby's awake, and she is not well. She vomits with a severity that I have never seen or heard before from her, or anyone for that matter.

The nurse asks me, "Is this normal for her?"

"No. She has had reflux, but nothing like this."

Doctors evaluate. They determine that her airway is traumatized from the difficult intubation. We are assured that the fierce gagging will cease as time distances her from the event. It never does.

Overnight care.

A handful of eye drops.

Strict instructions.

Discharge paperwork.

We're back home.

～

The first night we are home post-surgery, Ruby vomits fiercely throughout the night. She cannot tolerate any of her food, and the gagging noises are severe. Hours pass, and it becomes scary.

She is trembling. Trembling hard.

"I'm so sorry, Ruby." My heart aches.

I'm looking in the face of trauma.

Mitch and I place our love for Ruby into one pot and devise a plan. We decide to take turns so that one of us can physically hold her until she stops trembling, even if it takes days. We begin a cycle of one person sleeping while the other rocks Ruby and sings songs of deliverance over her tiny frame. We will not put her down until she knows that she is safe. Until that moment, we are committed to demonstrate tangible love.

Hours into the night, I see the trembling begin to decrease. Pressing her body into mine I keep telling her, "Ruby, you're safe now. I am right here." I pray to reverse the effect of trauma. To remove fear, to break off panic. I try to erase the experience.

The trembling decreases, but the vomiting is relentless. Later that night, the vomiting becomes dangerous. She is losing everything and seems to be stuck vomiting. I fear for her life. We end up in the ER where they support her with fluids to protect from dehydration.

When we are released, we continue our rhythm at home, trying to comfort our trembling little girl. The ER did not help with the trauma recovery.

The holding continues.

Mitch holds her for hours; I hold her for hours. We take turns, and press tangible love into her every way we know how. We will not let trauma have our little girl. We will not let her go until love has convinced her that she is safe again.

Three days later, she is still for the first time. Peace is finally on her. I can see it. Like innocence restored. Sun after storm.

I wait.

Her stillness remains. She has finally come home.

I lay her down in her bed...

...and then collapse.

I have never been this tired in my life,

And I have never witnessed a victory so beautiful in my life.

Love chased trauma down and overcame it.

Ruby is *free*.

Part II

Learning to Love

Chapter 6

It's 6:00 AM. Ruby was sick throughout the night. I quit halfway through and Mitch took over. Apparently, he has yet to quit. I am in bed with my eyes open and can feel the resonance of Mitch's life verse in the house, *"Like a champion rejoicing to run his course."*

I inch out of the bedroom and find Mitch in the living room sitting in our brown recliner with Ruby. I evaluate Ruby first. She is at peace, locked into Daddy's arm. I look at Mitch. His eyes meet mine, and mine widen fast. I stare into his eyes and think, *I have never seen love with my physical eyes, but today I am looking straight at it.* Mitch shifts his body, obviously in pain from poor positioning overnight.

"I need to go to work," he says. Mitch carries Ruby to her crib, puts her down, and, after a short clean-up, is out the door.

I sit down in the brown chair where Mitch was caregiving for Ruby overnight. Love lingers here. I can feel it physically. It's that charged atmosphere of care, the nature of God, somehow manifest in our living room. *I wonder if heaven feels like this.* I close my eyes and imagine a place where the air is love. I then open my eyes and realize that place is here, and that place is now. Ruby has brought us an invitation to experience love, the oxygen of heaven.

I feel an unseen spotlight hit me, *"You, in the brown chair. Want to become great? Here is your opportunity. Her name is Miss Ruby Joy. Lose everything for love."* My head jerks back and I stare wide-eyed at nothing with a sudden internal clarity of an opportunity.

Ruby is an *opportunity*. She is an access point to a rich life on this side of eternity. She is an invitation to become what we could not become without her. Ruby can teach us how to be lovers, where love costs us something.

I think about my experience of love to date. The love that I feel for Ruby is unlike any love I have felt before. Most parents will relate. What is the difference? What is it that unlocks deep love?

"No greater love has any man than this,
that He lay down his life for his friends."

Sacrifice.

For all those I have "loved," I have loved, at least in part, for what I got out of it. Most people I have loved, I have loved because they loved me first. Others I have "loved" out of obligation. My love has danced sweet circles around my sweet self. I have loved where it was safe, and given where exchange was imminent.

With Ruby, it is different. I love her for *her*, not for me. I thought I knew what love was. But this?

Career.

Time.

Sleep.

Money.

Hopes.

Dreams.

ALL.

There is no debate whether to give or withhold. Any such debate would feel outrageous. For Ruby, it is no sacrifice. *Why?*

Where there is love, "sacrifice" would better be described as a "blessing" because there is *so much joy* in having something of value to give to the one you love.

Yes to the brown chair invitation to learn to love.

A thousand times, yes.

~

My life has been hospital to home for weeks. I need to emerge, but I don't know how. Today, I have one single goal: to get outside. Outside our apartment door there is a closet for outdoor things. In it is a stack of baby carriers, untouched. Today, I will pull them out.

"Ruby, we're going outside!"

I put the first carrier on and slide Ruby into it. She is so tiny that I fear she will fall through the foot hole. Awkwardly, we progress until she is inside. I wait a moment. Her body slumps to the bottom like a ball. She whimpers. I rescue her. Comfort her. Frown. Sigh.

Next carrier. This time I wrap Ruby in a stretchy fabric, following close instructions on a computer screen in front of me. We get tangled together in a piece of cloth, and, for a moment, it is fun. Until her feeding tube gets tangled in the fabric and yanks. I grunt out loud. *This is not going to work.*

Third carrier. I sit down and put Ruby inside a carrier that will go on my back. I lay it on the floor and strap her in. The horizontal view looks good. I take a deep breath and pick her up. As she becomes vertical, her head flies back. I then realize this carrier has no head support. *This is not going to work for her either!*

I sit for a moment in despair. Then the thought dawns on me, "Stroller!" Friends bought us a stroller. It, as well, sits untouched. Maybe it could work. I leave Ruby on her mat in the apartment and run down to the first floor where the stroller is parked with our bikes. When I see the stroller my jaw tightens, face crinkles. *I'm not sure. It looks really big. Maybe.* I place it by the front door.

Back upstairs, I bundle Ruby in warm clothes. Through a series of refluxing and diaper changes, we are finally prepared to go outside. Downstairs, I put Ruby into the stroller. She slides down immediately to the point of nearly falling out. I try to reposition her multiple times but without success. Her low muscle tone will not hold a position without better support. *This is not going to work either.*

I look at the front door of our building, three feet from where we stand. I look at Ruby. I already told her we were going outside. *Hello, determination.* I take my one free hand and fling the front door open. I put Ruby up over my left shoulder and march out unto the front porch, down the steps, and into the street.

We are going for a walk. Period.

Ruby and I walk down the street together for the first time. I feel very awkward. I have a limp child hung over my shoulder with a bright orange feeding tube dangling from her face. *Oh well. Sometimes, you have to soldier on, even when you don't match your world.* At the end of our block, I turn the corner and fear that someone will be waiting to arrest us and send us back to Children's Hospital. But no one is there, just another block of concrete.

In time, my nerves die down and my attention shifts to Ruby. She has been silent the entire time, deeply content. *Content.* This makes me smile. Like mother, like child: get us outdoors and we will be fine. I watch the wind brush over Ruby's head out of the corner of my left eye and catch her pressing her eyelids shut. *I wonder what wind feels like to someone who has never felt it before.*

Then, I begin to ponder. *What if wind is medicine of its own kind? What if the silent ingredients of the outdoors contain in themselves something of value to the weak body, the struggling soul? What if fresh air is in itself a healer? What if what we are experiencing out here is just as important as what is prescribed in there? What if it is more important?*

A growing pain in my back and neck interrupts my thoughts. "Shut up," I remark to my own pain. "You are the only carrier that Ruby has." A few minutes later, my pain increases. Left shoulder held stiffly upward begs for release, retreat.

Reluctantly, we head home.

Inside, I lay Ruby down and look at the clock. We have missed a feed, a pumping cycle, and my time for cooking. We are late on meds, overdrawn on energy, and entirely off-kilter with her prescribed schedule.

And, we are cradled in contentment and covered in happy.

We were outside.

∿

A few weeks later, we are back in the ophthalmology clinic. Dr. Johnson tells us that Ruby's eye patches can come off. It's time for her to get fitted for glasses. During Ruby's eye surgery, they removed the cataracts and her lenses. Ruby now has no lenses in her eyes and needs artificial ones to be able to see. This is something that is often surgically implanted, but at her age, with a lot of potential growth, we start with glasses. *Thick* glasses.

There is anticipation around Ruby getting glasses, because once she has lenses to see we will learn what she can do. Uncertainty still rests on whether her optic nerve functions normally, whether her brain is able to process sight. I am probably the least enthused about the glasses. My hope is not in them. I prophesy new lenses into Ruby's eyes daily. I believe Ruby's eyes will be healed.

And yet, the medical journey continues.

I have written, rewritten, called, appealed and nothing short of fought for these glasses to be paid for by insurance. "She has no lenses in her eyes," I tell the insurance representatives over and over again. "These glasses are medically necessary." The surgery that Ruby had on her eyes is so rare in children that I have to create a precedent for it with insurance. Setting a new precedent with an insurance company is complicated, exhausting, but possible.

I watch Dr. Johnson examining Ruby. She begins to write out a few prescriptions. "Do you know where your nearest Opti-Shop is?" I try not to giggle. She's an ophthalmologist, and the way she says *Opti-Shop* is quirky.

I tilt my head to have some fun responding, using her tone, "No. What's an Opti-Shop?"

"Oh, they're wonderful!" she exclaims. "It's a store all for the *eyeszzz,*" she says, elongating the word to emphasize her favorite subject.

Her eyes bug out like living creatures. I wonder if the Opti-Shop is Dr. Johnson's candy store. She continues to talk about it and my thoughts trail off. Dr. Johnson reminds me of an eye. She looks like an eye, acts like an eye; she even shifts back and forth rapidly, just like eyes. I suppose it makes sense that years of study in any direction is bound to rub off on one's personality. This eye doctor personifies the eye.

She continues, "Where do you live?"

"Alexandria."

"There's an Opti-Shop not too far from you, Bowman Optical. They should be able to get you these glasses."

She hands me a prescription with a smile. I take it into my hand. This thin slip of paper feels like a weight, another detail demanding attention in our already maxed-out routine. *I wish Ruby could see without glasses. I'm afraid of how thick these glasses are going to be.*

My sorrow is interrupted as I recall, "Opti-Shop." The left corner of my lip curls up into a smile. If that shop is anything like the light on Dr. Johnson's face whens she talks about it, it can't be that bad.

"Field trip, Ruby!" I peek my head into the car seat as we leave and press my cheek against hers. "We're going to the *Opti-Shop* this afternoon!" Might as well make it fun. Thanks, Dr. Johnson, for loving the eye.

~

I drive up to a tiny optical shop in a large shopping center. I can barely see the sign on the rugged storefront. I take Ruby out of the car seat and we go inside. Inside, the store walls are lined with frames and lenses. It's a library for glasses. Many of them are peculiar—shapes, sizes and colors too weird for faces. The shop is narrow. No one is in the front room. I make intentional noise. A man comes out from the back to greet me. He stares at me over the top of his own thick frames. I hand him Ruby's prescription. He evaluates it.

"Wow, this is a really strong prescription.... rare..." His voice trails off in wonder, as if we just brought a gem to a jeweler. "But," he interrupts himself, "we can fill it for you." He then leans forward and looks straight into my eyes. I realize he is checking for contacts. I preempt his questions and explain that the glasses are for Ruby, who recently had cataract surgery. "They are not for me."

"Oh my God!" he replies with no filter. "I've never heard of that surgery being done on a baby! How old is she?" I remain quiet. He comes out from behind the counter and takes a hard look at Ruby. "Miraflex!" And then with an honest reserve adds, "They're the closest thing we have to something that will work for her." I realize in this moment that finding frames to fit Ruby's face will be no small feat.

Miraflex frames are brought out. They are designed for babies, made out of a flexible plastic and hard to break. There is a string around the back that holds them onto the baby's head. The design is cute and they come in multiple colors. The only problem is that even the smallest frames look like they will be huge on Ruby. The store owner puts the frames on Ruby. They extend beyond on the sides of her face, barely balanced on her nose. She shakes her head. The glasses fall off. He puts them on again. She shakes her head. They fall off again. The cycle continues. Meanwhile, no one is mentioning that the glasses look ridiculous, her face swallowed in plastic and thick glass.

The shop owner is watching my facial expressions, which reveal more than I intend. "This is the best we have, ma'am. We're not used to putting glasses on a baby this small. But she'll grow into them. I don't know of any other shop that carries more specialized glasses than these for babies."

"Okay," I nod with pursed lips and telling wide eyes.

Ruby and I choose pink.

We leave the prescription with the man and head home.

We'll deal with the challenges of glasses later.

~

The next morning is Saturday, the day when Mitch agreed to take the lead on Ruby's care. I wake up early, excited for a pocket of personal time. *Time.* I start by making Mitch a list. He and Ruby are still asleep. I write out Ruby's schedule from 9:00 AM to 12:00 PM. The list is dense: feeds, medications, stretching, special lotions, nebulizer, taste trials, changing, and so on. I write out every detail and can feel myself trying to gain sympathy for my life in the way I write the list. I catch myself and stop the sympathy hunt. *The only thing that sympathy adds to my life is resistance, resistance to owning my own state of being and making something beautiful out of it.*

I finish the list and decide to start my personal time with my Bible. The house is quiet. The Word comes to life. I am thirsty for it, very thirsty. I drink deep. Good start.

It's now 9:00 AM. I want to go outside. Nine AM: time for Ruby to eat. Nine AM: Mitch is still asleep. She is going to get her feed late, which means her whole schedule will be off today. I decide to do it myself. I go into the kitchen and prep the feed. *It's okay. I'll just do it myself.* I attach the feed to Ruby and then step back.

"I can't believe she's still sleeping," I mumble under my breath. "She never sleeps this late for me." I look at Mitch, who is out cold. It's as if Ruby knows that it is Daddy's turn and they are both sleeping in. *Why does this bother me?*

I stand there for a moment and try to decide what to do next. This is my time off. Mitch is asleep and Ruby's to-do list is growing on my back. Medications are due in the next fifteen minutes through her tube. I start to get angry and I decide to wake him up.

Anger wakes him up.

"*I am going outside, Mitch!* You're supposed to be watching Ruby. I just started her feed myself. Her meds are due soon."

He turns over irritated, "Why are you mad at me? I just woke up!"

"Ruby needs help, Mitch. It's my one time off in the week! I don't want to do it all for her! Please get up and help!"

"She's sleeping; Katie; she's fine!"

"She's sleeping; she's fine?" Tension swells in my voice. "I wish that sleeping meant we were all on a break, but Ruby's care is not that way. Disease doesn't sleep. Don't you know this? If I could put this feeding tube or medical prescriptions to sleep, I would. If I could command the disease to take a sabbath, I surely would, but that's not our reality. It all presses relentlessly—all the time."

I walk out of the room and put on my shoes. The difference this morning is that I can leave. Mitch is home for a change. I walk out the door: angry, frustrated, unhappy, disconnected from my husband, and stubbornly defensive. In my mind, Mitch ruined my morning. *This sucks.*

Outside the door, I have no idea where to go. I get into the car. I sit behind the wheel and think, *Why do I feel alone in the responsibility of Ruby's care when I have an amazing husband? Why do I feel like it's all on me? Is there something wrong with me? Am I the problem? Why doesn't Mitch take initiative with her? Is it my fault? Once a week for three hours, seriously, why doesn't he get out of bed and help?*

I start the ignition and drive nowhere for an hour. I can't settle on a destination. I don't know what to do with myself. There's no one I want to see. It's my only time off in the week, and it's swallowed in a lonely anger. I kick myself for walking out of the house angry. I suppose *that*, if anything, is not Mitch's fault.

At last, I decide to return home. I assume my to-do list for Ruby will be untouched. Mitch and Ruby will both probably still be in bed. I let out a sigh and open the door.

I am wrong.

I see the back of two heads at the kitchen table, two bedheads, two beautiful, messy bedheads sitting side by side having breakfast. Ruby's meds are measured out in syringes lined up on a paper towel. A bottle of baby food is open and there are flexi-spoons there for taste tests that are obviously underway. Ruby is not dressed, but her diaper has been changed. The list I made Mitch is sitting on the table, half crossed off.

"Morning, Mom," Mitch says, no eye contact.

"I'm sorry I left angry," I respond.

"Katie, I feel like you don't trust me. If I say I am going to take care of Ruby, then I am going to take care of her. I don't need you managing over my shoulder."

"But, Mitch, it was time for her to eat and your head was still under your pillow!"

"I'm sorry I slept in."

I pause. That *is* what I'm angry about—he slept in. *Is that really such a crime? On a Saturday morning?* I watch Mitch dunk his cheerios into his milk. I don't like the way he eats his cereal; it's messy and slurpy and gross. And I don't like that he slept in this morning. He's still not looking at me.

I look at Ruby. She is fine. She is more than fine. She looks happy to be a scraggly bed-headed little girl with her dad on a Saturday morning. I look at Ruby again and consider, *What if the care that Mitch has for her looks different but is also needed? What if she needed not to be disturbed with things through the tube this morning? What if she likes not having her hair done for a day?*

He may not do things the way that I do them, but she is his daughter too. I cannot sustain full responsibility for her care, which means I need to relinquish control and let him in, on his terms.

I now recognize that I have a problem.

My problem is that I scream for a break, and then I refuse to take it. I've not been able to let go and find out what his care for her looks like. I've not fully trusted him. I've been too scared.

The moment I realize this, I let go. I don't want to be in this alone. I cannot. We reconcile. "Go take your time, Katie; we're fine. You need it." He is right. They are fine, and I do need it. And, you know, it's possible that Ruby needs a day with a dad-constructed ponytail too. Could be.

Partnership.

God, help us.

～

It's evening. Mitch is at a band rehearsal. Ruby and I are home. Traces of our day are scattered throughout the house. I have no reason to clean up. It's just the two of us into the evening hours.

I hear a knock at the door. I freeze. Perhaps, if I don't move, this question mark of a person will not know I am here. The knock taps again, gentle, determined. Ruby makes some noise. We're obviously home. I reluctantly get up and answer the door. Our neighbor Jeff is standing outside the threshold.

Jeff lives in the apartment below us—second floor. He is a Midwesterner who moved East with a dream to work for the government. He got a government job and now rides his bike all over D.C. pressing his community-oriented Midwestern self into the world around him.

"Mitch said I could come up sometime and meet Ruby. Is now a good time?"

I hesitate. It's not, but what do I have to prove it? "Sure," I back up. "Here she is." Ruby is sitting in her seat propped up against the living room wall. She is tiny, sickly, and has a tube hanging from her nostril.

I feel the awkward swell happening. Unanswered questions dangle. Jeff crouches down and looks at her. I share a little of her history. It's quiet. *This is why I don't let people in*, I remind myself. *Relating through our circumstance can feel like scaling a brick wall.*

He looks up at last. "I was 4 ½ pounds when I was born too."

"Seriously?" I ask.

"Yes. I was born early and mom says they didn't know if I would make it."

"What happened?" I'm intrigued.

"I don't really know. I just know that I was 4 ½ pounds, premature, and fragile at best. I've never really cared about it much—until now."

He looks up at me, "This is the first time I've ever seen what 4 ½ pounds looks like. She is very small." I watch Jeff consider for the first time how far he has come, perhaps seeing for the first time the miracle of his own life.

"Hang in there, Ruby," he lets out. "You're going to be fine."

He then stands up. "Thanks for letting me meet Ruby." I like how he says her name. *Ruby*. She's a person to him.

I lead him to the door and welcome him to come back again sometime when Mitch is home. He nods. Door shuts. I sit quietly. It is hard to believe. Jeff Miller, 4 ½ pounds, preemie baby? He is a full-grown, healthy man. I never would have known.

I echo his words, "Hang in there, Ruby; you're going to be fine." I had no idea when I opened the door that a miracle testimony was knocking to come in.

Good thing I opened it.

Chapter 7

Door closes. Mitch is off to work. We just had an awful night, a night I hope to forget. Vomiting episodes plagued the dark hours as we fought to keep Ruby breathing. This morning we are drenched in exhaustion. And, yet, time rolls on, relentless. Mitch will work. I will continue with Ruby's care.

Ruby's care has intensified since eye surgery. In addition to tube feeds every three hours, we are administering medications and eye drops at various intervals of the day. I am learning to administer the medications carefully at times of the day when she is less likely to reflux and lose them. Ruby is still vomiting a lot, something that started post surgery.

I sit down in the corner of the room and pull my knees up to my chest. Face buried in my hands, I glance at the clock through my fingers. Ten minutes until I have to pump again. This cycle feels maddening: pump, feed, vomit, clean up. Herein lies my perpetual heartache of seeing Ruby's nutrition dripping down her face as waste.

Guilt is present. Speaks. *You're Ruby's mom. You can't even successfully feed your own daughter.* I cower under this accusation regularly. I think of other new moms I know whose babies are healthy and growing normally. They are doing their job well, which must mean that I am failing at mine.

I manage to stand up, pressed by the clock for the next feeding. As I walk into the kitchen, I feel a strange sense of disillusionment. On autopilot, I prep another feed. I carry the feed toward Ruby and do the only thing I know to do—keep going. Try again.

Ruby's care somehow happens for the remainder of the day. The feeds, the medications, the vomiting, the cleanup—it all happens from the odd and yet effective autopilot of a mom who's hurting. Laced with tears and in a frightful daze, the two of us make it through another day.

At the end of it, I sit down and write, "Disease is like a million-ton brick that sits on people until they are crushed to death." Tears fall on the page. "I am fighting with everything to keep it's weight above our heads, but its strength is overpowering me. My arms are tired and, with deepest sorrow, I admit this disease is crushing me. So long, wholeness, I am breaking."

$\sim$

It's the night before Ruby's first Thanksgiving. We create a scene on the street as we unload our house into our van. I look at the packed vehicle and wonder how in the world such a small child could need so many large things. My crockpot is duct-taped shut with beef stew leaking out both sides. Our pillows are squished in on top of luggage. We are bursting at the seams, in more ways than one, and yet determined to go somewhere for the holiday.

Thirty minutes down the road and we arrive at the home where we will stay. A friend offered this place to my family for Thanksgiving. They wanted to give my family a place to gather for the holiday near Ruby, near Children's Hospital.

Ornate single-family homes stare me down as we enter the neighborhood. Up the driveway, I wonder if we are in the right place. I grew up in a row home in Philadelphia. This breed of house feels like TV-town to me. We confirm the address and get out of the car. Glass windows encircle the door and I peer inside. The door opens in my face. My family is all there. A loud welcome happens in the foyer and my eyes drift up. There is a high ceiling and elaborate staircase. This house is really nice. I fear we will break it.

Mom shows us to our room: the master bedroom. Bronze pillars raise a king-size bed, and a full bathroom sparkles off the corner of the room. I wonder why Mitch, Ruby and I are being put in the finest room. One thing is for certain: it has nothing to do with Mitch and I both being middle children.

Something is different. *My role? My place in the family?*

Time proves that the hearts of our family members are tender toward us. We're given special treatment. I had no idea they felt so connected to us in this time. I think they needed to see us this week. I suppose I forgot that we are not Ruby's only family. I unload the crockpot out of our van that will smell of beef stew for months. We sit around a large table and eat it together. Ruby is one of ten people around the table. As I watch connection happen, I wonder where we have been. I think of the medical "isolation" signs that hung on our door in the hospital. Conversations buzz. I hold back tears. Behold: lives unmarred by disease. Funny stories are shared. Laughter attacks bellies.

People eat food, a lot of food. One pie per person. That's how my family rolls.

Ruby sits next to me. She seems content. I think she and I are both relieved that the attention has dissipated from us. Tonight, we get to watch others. I return to my food. The other kids have already finished. Wild and free they chase each other around the house. They run to and from Ruby's highchair with a "Hi, Ruby!" just to run away again, sift through the feet of aunts and uncles, pop their jittery heads out of the other side of the table, and then collapse on the floor on top of one another.

Family.

Tonight, Ruby is not a patient, a research agent, a diagnosis or a crisis. Tonight she holds her place as a daughter, a granddaughter, a cousin and a niece. In the context of family, her life normalizes for a moment. And so does mine.

Happy Thanksgiving.

One week later, it's the night before my birthday. I don't want to celebrate. Depression has been building in me like a steady snowfall piling on its weight.

I tell Mitch that I want to skip my birthday. He resists. I get angry. In my hurt, I unravel. "I have nothing to celebrate. I wish I were never born." Mitch's eyes refuse to leave mine. I look him in the eye and tell him I'm serious: I mean it. He resists softly. I react loudly, "I don't want to celebrate my birthday. Period." Tears, frustration and despair trail behind me as I storm off to bed.

I crawl into bed alone. Sadness is sitting in the house. Ruby is very sick. I am cursing my birthday. Mitch retreats at a loss. In the darkness of our room, I hide behind my eyelids and work hard to escape into sleep. Sadly for me, there is no good sleep when anxiety has put one to bed.

As I toss and turn, I notice that I am still alone in bed. It's 1:00 AM, he is not here. Three AM, he is not here. Four-thirty AM, he is still not here. Six AM, I lie in bed alone. There is a light on outside our door. I wonder if he is there, or gone. I wonder if he has left, driven out by a woman who has declared herself unhappy and wishing she were never born.

I get up slowly and inch my way to the door. The thought crosses my mind that empty may be on the other side of these walls. I peer through the crack of the door and find something unexpected. Through the living room corridor and into the kitchen, I can see my husband. He is sitting at the kitchen table cutting out birthday decorations, half of which are already hung up around the house.

I freeze. Like a deer in headlights, I find myself caught.

Across that corridor is a man who is refusing to let me quit. I watch him hammering away with scissors and tape, and his value for me begins to attack and overtake my poor value of myself. *How can I refuse a celebration that Mitch stayed up all night to prepare? It's 6:00 AM? He has not slept!*

I dare to emerge from the room. Mitch looks up and catches my eye. In his eyes, I see a love so deep it makes me feel sick. His gaze burrows down into me and I am shaken at the core by his silent plea, *Please don't go away.* We stare for a moment, and then he smiles.

"Happy Birthday, Katie."

I stare back at him with no words.

"You don't have to celebrate, but I love you too much to skip it. I am celebrating you today whether you participate or not. Consider yourself invited." He looks back down and continues his work.

I feel a smile emerge from my heart, and it reaches my face. I stop. I'm feeling a smile—a *genuine* smile. It just appeared on my face. Ta-da! No permission given—it just came. Happened. Is.

Mitch looks up and his own grin begins to emerge as he sees mine. I stand there awkwardly with a smile I cannot hide. And then… in a moment of conviction, I duck under my pride and race through the birthday décor and into his arms. Mitch holds me tight. I allow his embrace to swallow me whole.

Eyes perusing the dangling signs, I at last remark, "I would like to celebrate with you, Mitch." I stare at the ground embarrassed, and yet certain I have changed my mind. I want to celebrate my birthday.

"Oh good," he says lifting his chin slightly with concealed emotion. "I'm so glad you will be joining me. Your birthday would not have been the same without you." I shake my head in unbelief. *He was seriously going to celebrate my birthday with or without me.*

My birthday happens. Disease doesn't quit on it; the pain, disappointment, sickness, hurt is all still there. Some of it feels worse in the light of a day we ache to be good. And yet, we choose to celebrate, and in that choice we find one of the most important tools for living in pain—the discipline of celebration. Without it, celebration gets lost. And without celebration, life loses its spark. Without that spark, life is simply not what it ought to be.

The discipline of celebration.

～

Rough morning.

Outburst of tears.

Ugly thoughts.

Crazed emotions.

Rattling frustration.

Embittered grief.

I'm angry.

I'm angry with God.

Ruby's condition is worsening, and I am disheartened. Our hope is resting on an unseen reality that is not delivering. I don't know what to do or where to turn. The feeding tube came out this morning after a violent reflux episode. It took me almost two hours to replace it, every minute of which was a waking nightmare. Ruby is shaken. I'm shaken. The tube is finally in.

I begin pacing the house, holding Ruby tight. "It's going to be okay, Ruby. You will be okay." I release comfort until she settles. Then I lay her down and am left with my own shaking to deal with. *Where do I turn?*

I curl up in the corner of the bedroom, hide my head in my knees, and fight hard to organize my thoughts. Over the last few days, I have felt fierce internal wrestling to maintain faith in God. I cannot wait any longer for Him to deliver on His word. I don't understand the wait. It's awful. Is He? My world is darkening, and I fight hard not to be overcome by it. The current of daily disappointments presses me to give up my faith. "Forget Him. Look at life and make a rational conclusion about Him. He doesn't care. He's not good. He's gone."

Still in my corner, I cry out against these voices. *I don't want to give up. I love God. I don't want to forfeit this fight.* I use the name "Jesus." I hang on tight. I shut my eyes and cry, "Jesus, please show up. Give me a reason to continue to believe."

Silence.

The phone rings.

Good news?

It's Ruby's pediatrician. Bad news. Her blood work has come back with abnormalities that require hospital follow-up. Disappointment strikes again. My grip on Jesus loosens almost against my will. I hang up the phone and return to my corner. *I can't handle any more.* I said that last week and more is piling on. My thoughts turn back to God. Skepticism stretches its arms out of my spirit toward heaven. *Are you on vacation, God?*

Ruby begins to stir. My time in the corner is over. Nothing good came of it. I am still shaken, uncomforted. Prepping Ruby's feed, I gather myself to be with her. I will spend the next ninety minutes pressing one cc at a time down this tiny tube into her stomach. Ninety minutes with a grump is a long time. I try to shift my mood for her sake.

As I feed Ruby, my anger subsides, and I can feel the pain that is fueling it, the sadness. I am sad that I am unable to do more for her. I cannot heal her mouth. I cannot enable her to eat, or digest, or walk or talk. It has to be God. The stakes are too high for God not to intervene. Ruby's life is not a disappointment I can step over; it is not a loss I can bear. This is not a fight we can lose. I need God to be real. I need Jesus to be Healer. We are doomed if He is not experientially who He says He is. And yet, I am watching Ruby suffer and watching God not intervene. *What am I supposed to do with this?*

I refuse to believe, like some do, that Ruby's illness is divinely intentional: designed by God for a greater purpose. *What kind of Father would cause His child to suffer for the benefit of others?* These views, in my opinion, are twisted attempts to reconcile what cannot be reconciled at the expense of truth about His nature.

Truth.

But truth is not delivering today. It's beginning to feel conceptual. Unrealized. Not true. Mitch comes home an hour or two later. Anger masks the hurt that is sinking me today.

"What do you need?" Mitch looks me in the eye.

"I need to scream."

He pauses and then responds, "What about Theodore Roosevelt Island?"

I look back at him surprised. He's serious. I suppose I should be too.

"Okay. I'm going to Theodore Roosevelt Island—to scream."

~

Next thing I know, I'm in the car, down the road, over the bridge, and into the thick woods where there is space to scream. And I scream. I scream for a long time. I scream until I cannot scream anymore.

True expression finds it's voice in these blood-curdling screams. At last, my pressure valve is opened, raw emotion released. I can feel the weight lifting and the last of my strength draining out of my voice.

In the dirt on my knees, I lift my head to the sky and cry, "God, hear me! If You are real, if You are there, if You ever deliver me from anything my whole life, please let it be this! Let it be Ruby's life and health!"

The sound of my voice echoes through the trees. If ever a prayer reaches heaven, this one will I am sure. I cannot imagine a more earnest expression. I shudder at the thought of it not being answered. I am afraid of finding out that God is not there.

I walk out of the forest and drive home. I'm exhausted. Entirely poured out.

Few words are exchanged that night in our home. Among them is my whispering gratitude to Mitch for taking my need to scream seriously. I collapse into bed. There I lie awake for a long time and wonder what will become of us. My voice is gone, my strength is gone, my resolve to fight—all gone. I roll over and half expect this to be my last night on the earth. I've got nothing for tomorrow. Nothing.

~

The next day, I'm at the river at the edge of town and my head is hanging low. I feel like a failure. I have come to the end of myself and have nothing left to give. My sense is that God is angry with me for wearing out. I feel far from Him. I fear that as I drift from Him, He drifts farther from me. I fear I am losing my only anchor: faith in God.

I sit down on the hill overlooking the water and raise my head to peruse the scene. I am here because I need to hear from God. Out of the right corner of my eye, I see a big boat. It is tied to the dock. I look closer. It is drifting with the water away from the dock, but then stopping short of going too far. I stand up and walk toward it.

As I near the boat, I see a thick rope holding it to the dock. I watch the boat for a few minutes. I watch it drift, and I watch the rope pull it back. It's not going anywhere. And I realize, the boat cannot leave the dock, because the boat doesn't hold the dock; the dock holds the boat.

I then hear God's voice: "Faith is not all about you holding on, Katie. I am holding onto you. I promise that I will not let you go."

I hear this one phrase, and a sense of relief sweeps over me. I feel joy for the first time in days. I sit and watch the boat for longer, whispering to my own soul, *He is holding you. He will not let you go.*

A bird flies above my head, and I follow it to a nest hidden high in a tree. I recall learning about eagles as a kid—how the babies are pushed out of the nest in order to learn how to fly. It feels like a free fall for the eaglets, but the mama is there all along, ready to swoop them up from beneath.

Later that evening, I journal, "I am so grateful, God, that You are not angry with me for running out of steam." I sketch the dock, the rope, the water and the boat in my journal and then write, "Keep me as the apple of Your eye; hide me in the shadow of your wings. Don't ever let me go."

I wonder if the end of ourselves is where we discover what true faith looks like. I cannot hold on any longer; I am far too tired. Today my journey changes from being about my faith to being about God's faith for me.

Hold me, God. Hold me now.

Boat tied to the dock.

∼

I hear him coming up the steps. Ruby and I scramble to get everything in place. Door opens. "Welcome home, Mitch!" I race to the door. From the door, I follow Mitch around the house and then into the bedroom. As I follow him, I talk rapidly about our day, Ruby's day, the good, the bad, the ugly. My lack of adult interaction explodes on him. I know I should stop to listen to him too, but I can't. I just can't. My mouth keeps rattling. "Dinner! I made you dinner. It's ready right now, are you ready for it? Are you hungry?"

Fifteen minutes of intense chatting, and then I get tired. My excitement plummets into the reality of my exhaustion, and I collapse on the floor. I could sleep, here and now.

"Are you going to bed?" Mitch asks innocently as I lie in the middle of the living room floor. "Come eat dinner, Katie. I have good news for you."

Good news? I drag myself off the floor and into the kitchen where adrenaline has prepared food and set the table moments before his return.

"Damien called me into his office today. He said he was thinking the other day, 'What else can I do for Mitch?' The thought came to him that perhaps he could help coordinate things for me to work from home occasionally."

I feel tears start to well up.

"Are you serious?" *This is kindness. This is goodness.*

Damien is Mitch's supervisor at work. He is a kindred spirit, a friend to Mitch, and an empathizer to our circumstance. Damien and his mom, Ms. Peterson, have been primary caregivers for his brother with Down syndrome for almost thirty years. He gets it.

Mitch continues, "Katie, he proposed that I work from home every morning, getting to the office around noon. This would allow me to support you more with Ruby! There are a few approvals it needs to get through with management, but he wanted to know if we would be interested."

I stare back at Mitch, speechless. There's nothing quite like an act of kindness released into a graven space. Perhaps God *did* hear my scream from the island. Perhaps the dock is strong enough to hold that boat. I divert my attention to Ruby, "Ruby, I think you're going to be seeing more of Dad!"

In the following days, the details are hammered out and Mitch is approved to work from home each morning. During those times, I am able to get outside for an hour or two depending on his workload. Outside, I chase the river, and in the beauty of nature delve into an intimacy with God that saves my life. Conversations with Him build a foundation of friendship from which the whole scene of life changes. I echo the psalmist, "He has become my salvation."

Two weeks into this new schedule and I am renewed. Exhaustion is backing off. I'm dropping things less, forgetting things less, feeling more energy, and thinking more clearly. I'm not exploding on Mitch when he gets home, and he is not feeling detached from our journey.

That rope held my boat and held it well. Provision has found us. God's provision, deposited through the hands of a friend.

I wonder, is God's provision for someone else in my hands?

~

The doorbell rings. I glance at Ruby, and then at the apartment door. Do I carry her down two flights of steps right now to find out who is out there? Sigh. *Okay.* As I descend the second flight of steps, I peer through the glass to see who is there. I can't tell. I open the front door and am greeted by—no one. Empty space. Quiet Street. *That's weird,* I think to myself.

My eyes drift down, and then I see it: a pink package at my feet. I look at the package, and it looks back at me, all kinds of sparkly. The label is polka dotted and in large print it reads, "RUBY JOY."

I step out onto the porch and crouch down next to the package with Ruby on my hip. "Ruby," I pick it up and hold it in front of her eyes, "it's for you!" I take her arm and put it on the box, and then shake it for her. "I wonder what it is!" We sit on the doorstep for a few minutes together and guess what's inside. I throw out an idea, and then press my forehead against hers to sense her response.

One thing we know without checking is that the return label will read Jasper, Indiana, sent by Linda, Mitch's cousin. Every few weeks, Ruby receives a package from Linda. Without fail, these packages contain things that we need. They arrive wrapped in pink and butterfly print, always an answer to a need we didn't know we had.

After Ruby was born, we got a package from Linda with her first preemie clothes. They were quality garments that actually fit Ruby. Next she sent us a pile of burp clothes that had silk décor sewn into the center. Little did she know how these adorned rags would dignify our daily task of responding to severe reflux. Next, she sent a dress and tights, at which point I realized Ruby had no reason to dress up. The dress motivated me to bring her to church.

I scoot the new box inside the front door with my foot and shut the door behind us. I then hold Ruby at the center of my body, pick up the box and balance it behind her while climbing two flights of stairs to our apartment. Ruby's low muscle tone requires me to do all of the supporting work for her, which in a moment like this calls for more limbs than I have. But I am learning to do what seems impossible.

We reach our apartment door, and I am out of breath. I shut the door and sit down. I prop Ruby up in her seat so that she can see, and we open the box together. Bright yellow tissue paper pops out first, and we take our time with it.

Inside the box I pull out a thick fleece pullover for Ruby's car seat. "Oh, this is so helpful!" I remark out loud. Ruby has just started whimpering when we go outside due to the cold. "Thank you, Linda!"

I decide to leave the box out so that Mitch can see it. Ruby is celebrated all over the way it is wrapped and addressed; I think it will make him happy too. It's a wonder to me how this woman has instinct for what Ruby can use even as she lives halfway across the country. The gift of giving. Linda's family definitely has it.

Visited by a package.

Visited by a bundle of no expectations but to receive.

Chapter 8

I watch the mountains grow on the horizon, and my heart is glad. We are driving out of the city, away from the hospital, and into seclusion. Sometimes, I feel like we are mice and the hospital is a mousetrap. The farther away I get, the safer I feel.

Twisted reality. True emotions.

There is a camp in the Pocono Mountains where my family spent summers growing up. On one side of the camp, there is a retreat center directed by a family friend. This friend invited Mitch, Ruby and me to get away in one of their apartments for a few days without cost. We said, "YES!"

We pull into the camp and up to our designated apartment. We unload our things. It took me two full days to pack for this trip. I wondered at times if the work of traveling would be worth it. But as we cross the threshold of a new space this evening, the question is quickly answered. I feel a sense of renewal within minutes of being in the fresh space.

Ruby seems interested in the new environment. She lies on a mat while we unload the car. *I wonder what it will be like when she can eat by mouth. Easier to travel, that's for sure. I wish she were eating by mouth now; maybe this weekend she will start. No better time for a miracle.* We finish unloading the car. The load we live with, the load we carry, the load we can't escape, the load that travels with us in our oversized van, is unloaded in a new space. There are some things, like the hospital, we can escape. There are others, like the feeding tube, that we cannot. And so we arrive—with them.

Behind closed doors, we sit silently. There is a vast world outside these four walls. It's a world of majestic nature, a world of times and seasons, a world of growth, a world of life. Acres of woods surround us. Tucked within them, we find our peace.

Quiet sleep.

First thing in the morning, I tiptoe out the door. In the open air, I run until I am out of sight and find an old beaten trail to carry me away. It leads me along the lake and then cuts into the woods. Off the trail, I dive into the forest and hide myself there. Surrounded by silence, I sit. Beauty sits with me.

Crouched on the ground, I follow the height of the trees with my eyes. At the top, I find patches of sky where freedom reigns above this thicket of woods. I bow my head. The grace of solitude has found me. Hidden in the forest, it unlocks my soul. Solitude held a key for which I've been longing. It's the key to feeling like me.

I give myself permission to feel and in that permission begin to unpack my own heavy load before God. *Why, God? Who are You, God? Why me, God? Where are we, God? When will we see promise? Ruby is hurting, God. She doesn't deserve to suffer. Why are You not intervening sooner? Do I have to live through this? God, do I have to live?* As I share my heart with God, I sense Him nearing. I feel Him closing in on me, infusing the nature that surrounds me. Divine Presence thickens and I am inclined to duck farther into the ground. I press my face into the dirt and begin to worship. I can feel the eyes of heaven on me, like peering light shooting through eternity toward me. I hide; He finds me. Nature becomes His mouthpiece, and, in the hiddenness of the forest, I encounter the God who sees.

In this thin place between heaven and Earth, I feel loved, and the more I feel love, the less inclined I am to hide. The wind hits my face and I dare to look up. Light is towering around me. I peer through the trees to the lake ahead. Racing across the water toward me, I hear the voice of God: "I am My beloved's and she is Mine." At the sound of His voice, I rise. And when I rise, I begin to dance.

I dance in the garden of God.

When I am done, I have a new internal reality. Something changed. Needs shifted. Hopelessness moved out. Strength returned. I am different. He has fortified my heart with His love, and, rather suddenly, I feel that I *can* go on.

Wisdom speaks, "Let your internal reality govern your external circumstances." I nod and dare to press further, knowing that outside these woods is the circumstance from which I just ran.

"God, how will I get through this?"

"Surrender and trust. They are two sides of the same coin. Let that coin hold you on one side or the other until you land again on the banks of freedom." I hear Him. I believe Him. I take these two tools and begin to practice. Walking back to our house, I consider what they mean. *Surrender* and *trust*.

On the doorstep, I pause and consider if I have to go back in. Yes, I must. Running away from my life is as absurd as trying to run away from myself. Neither are true options, only circular madness. I would rather continue to face my life, to go through it, and perhaps learn to love it.

I reconnect with Mitch and Ruby. Ruby was sick while I was gone. Mitch managed it. Mitch notices immediately that I am different. "You seem lighter, Katie." I nod. Holding the encounter close to my heart, I share simply that I met with God. Eyes on Ruby, I begin to interact with her with a newfound strength. She lights up.

In her own way, I can see Ruby celebrating my breakthrough. I realize in this moment that much of Ruby's life experience is me. I thank God for changing "me" into something more enjoyable. Mitch seems to be doing better after my time outdoors too. I think we all needed this: Mom finding herself in God again.

That night, I journal the encounter in the woods: the wild dancing, the hiding, the worshiping, the resonance of His voice. I softly tuck those two new tools into the pockets of my heart: *surrender and trust*.

Tonight, I feel like we're going to make it to those banks of freedom. All of us.

~

The glasses did not work. We abandoned them and pursued contacts. After ten days in the contacts, Ruby is starting to fix her eyes on things for the first time. The blank stare that she has worn since the beginning of her life is fading like a dissipating cloud. I am beginning to see Ruby in her eyes.

As a result, I have added eye stimulation to her daily routine. I spend a lot of time waving things in front of her face to help her learn how to track. I start by holding a bright object in the center of her face until she focuses on it. Then, I slowly move it to the side. She tends to track for an inch or two from the center, and then her eyes wander aimlessly again, at which point I start over.

Fascinating journey. Focus takes practice.

It's Christmas time. On a whim, I pick up a strand of Christmas lights and try using them for Ruby's visual tracking exercise. I am stunned. She tracks with them all the way out and back. I cheer. She does it again. I cheer. She does it again. *Christmas lights.* I recall shining a light directly into Ruby's eyes in the past, and she did not even blink. Something is definitely waking up in these windows to the soul!

When Mitch gets home I tell him about the Christmas lights, and we decide to lean into it. We start with the Christmas tree. Woven through its green, the tree is lit. Ruby sits and stares. Awake. Engaged. We sit and stare at her, stunned. Her visual attention on anything is a waking wonder. With minimal activity in her senses, it's a challenge to find stimulation for her. *Could it be that we found something she likes? Christmas lights?*

Mitch and I catch each other's eyes and without any verbal cue stand up and start on the same task. Ruby likes Christmas lights. We will smother the house in them. S-m-o-t-h-e-r.

Christmas lights on the mantle.

Christmas lights on the tree.

Around the windows.

On the bedpost.

Christmas lights…everywhere…for Ruby.

We prance around the house and string Christmas lights wherever they will go. Ruby is waking up to the world around her, and we choose to decorate it for her, wild and bright. Ruby's first impression of the world will be a bright, colorful, explosion of Christmas day. For days, we get caught up in the miracle of Christmas through the experience of something wonderful. Ruby is beginning to see.

And onto this glistening light-bulb scene, Ruby's two eyes open for the first time. Weeks of increasing vision release her soul into a whole new dimension: life with sight.

Merry Christmas, Ruby Joy.

~

I watch snow tumble out of the sky. It's so thick I can barely see through it. Someone up there is dumping bags of sparkly white confetti on us, and it's making me really happy. *Happy.*

Evening radiates white. Morning sparkles bright. Snow day. Mitch is home from work. I cancel Ruby's medical appointments. We are together.

In the afternoon, we bundle up and venture outside. I put Ruby's snow suit on her. It's a white, fluffy, full-body suit with pink bunny ears that dangle off of the hood. I pull the zipper to the top and cup my two hands around her body. It fits her well. It used to be that she didn't fit into anything. She is growing.

Outside, Mitch carries Ruby. I walk by his side. Piles of snow have blown up over the cars, burying much of what was parked. Neighbors gather in the street with their shovels. It doesn't take long to discern who loves this and who hates it. There are some bright faces out here, and others are plastered with frowns. We are all victims of this historic invasion of frozen white fluff. My face is a happy one. I like this. My neighborhood feels more like a community today instead of a stack of isolated boxes. Here we all are. No one can go anywhere except by foot.

Ruby is bundled up so well that people are not noticing she wears the marks of a genetic syndrome. Instead of the usual questions we get about her condition, people are adoring her fuzzy coat and commenting on her sweet eyes that gaze out into the cold. We nod as our gratitude for her eyes is much deeper than any of these people realize. All the same, we don't go into it. Normal talk is refreshing. Our trials are hidden behind a snowsuit today. We'll take it.

Mitch, Ruby and I trample down the street together in the snow. When we reach the major cross section, we find a number of people wearing cross-country skis. It is nothing short of amusing to watch these high-strung professionals running out of their houses to play.

The snow is bright white and has lit up the world on which it lies. I could explore out here for hours, but, thankfully for Ruby, Mitch is sensitive to her being in the cold too long. He has a special empathy for what I seem to be born without: dislike of the cold. In time, Mitch's and Ruby's cold noses lead us back home.

Inside the threshold of the apartment, we take off our layers and begin to defrost. I hang Ruby's snow suit next to ours to dry. Warm drinks come into our hands, and under blankets we sit together to watch what others are saying about the storm.

On the television, newscasters report with dramatic flare that this "storm of a lifetime" holds the record snowfall in the last hundred years. News anchors report the inconveniences the storm is causing around the city. I wonder if anyone else watching is as grateful as I am for this "inconvenience."

Mitch turns off the news after some time and checks his work e-mail. "Surprise!" He comes running back into the living room. "No work tomorrow either!" I start jumping around the house, thanking God, and then feel the full impact of tears of joy tumbling down my face. You would think we had just won the lottery.

Mitch laughs. "Wow, Katie. Thanks for being so happy to have me around!"

I wonder why I am so happy. While everyone loves a good snow day, I do seem to be overreacting. And yet...

I consider Ruby's and my life together. We are happy, we share love, we are optimists in the midst of suffering. And yet, we are also stuck indoors a lot, controlled by a medical schedule, and very limited in what we can do together. Our daily routine is monotonous and includes very few things we truly enjoy. Somehow, that makes us prime candidates to fully appreciate the power of a surprise.

I stop.

The power of surprise.

A prime candidate for surprise?

If Ruby and I are prime candidates for surprise, this means that prime candidates for surprise exist.

What if anywhere there is a monotonous life, there is also a person who is a prime candidate for a surprise? What if we can't fix their problems, but we can break up their routine? What if breaking up an oppressive routine is like releasing dynamite on an overpowering structure that no one thinks will come down?

I think of an elderly woman I know who lives alone, a family who has been struggling for months to make ends meet, a friend of mine who just lost her father, another who was recently laid off. All of these people live with daily hardship—and suddenly *they seem like people who are primed for a surprise.*

I peer over the ledge of the window to the piles of snow beneath us. *God is good.* He surprised me today with snow. Someday, I want to be someone who can strategically dump sparkly white surprises into the laps of those who least expect it and most need it.

The power of surprise.

A prime candidate for surprise.

I wonder, *Who can I target?*

Ruby has acquired eczema, badly. Her skin is very dry and a rash has developed in multiple places, causing her significant discomfort. Her hand coordination is such that she is unable to scratch it, so she just cries. Tiny bright-red bumps bubble from her skin; the worst spots are the back of her calves. In response, we add a thorough dose of lotion to her morning and nighttime routine that includes prescribed topical cream.

Tonight, Mitch is getting Ruby ready for bed. I stay in the kitchen, washing dishes, thankful for a break, happy to give those two some time together. Happy, until…ten minutes turns to twenty minutes, which turns to thirty minutes, and Ruby is still not in bed.

I tiptoe across the living room to peek into the bedroom. Ruby is still lying on the changing table, and Mitch is still there getting her ready for bed. *What in the world is taking so long?*

I consider barging in and decide against it. Five more minutes pass and I cannot help but stare at the clock. I watch the minute hand roll right past Ruby's closely guarded schedule, and then I sit on my hands to keep them from being thrown up in exasperation. As I sit, I consider my options. *I can either go in there and take over so her routine is done my way or accept Mitch's help on his help's terms.*

I wrestle. It's a wrestling match I have had before, and yet I have it all over again. Taking an objective view, I'm able to talk some sense into myself. *She's okay, Katie. Let it be.*

My curiosity builds, and, after a few more minutes, I find myself springing out of the chair and moving toward the room where they are. I enter the room with as little drama as I can muster. "What are you guys up to?" Mitch looks up at me entirely unaware, as if time is simply not a factor in life.

"I'm buttering up my breadstick," he says with a proud grin. "She's not going to have dry skin anymore!"

My lips press straight sideways with a toothless, hold-in-your-emotion grin.

Mitch proceeds to explain to me that he is covering Ruby in lotion, allowing her skin to soak it up, waiting for it to air dry, and then repeating this cycle, multiple times. His plan is to repeat this routine, as many times as is needed, until her skin will not soak up any more lotion.

"Oh my gosh, Mitch! What about her bedtime?"

"I'm pushing it back."

I swallow hard, exercise self-control and choose my words carefully. "Okay!"

There goes our schedule. There goes our sleep. There goes my hard-earned routine. And here comes a proud dad.

The next morning, Ruby's skin is as shimmery as it has ever been. She was dripping with lotion by the time she was put to bed last night and this morning is as soft as can be. Mitch kisses her on the forehead before leaving for work, "My little breadstick!" Ruby smiles back at him. I don't get it. But what I do get is that these two bonded.

The truth is, most of the time I do barge into the room and take over, assuming that I know better and controlling what does not need to be controlled. What if Mitch wants to learn from Ruby, instead of only from me? What if his direct care creates a bond that I could never create standing between them? This morning I evaluate the outcome when I let Mitch lead.

I got a break.

Ruby's skin is…moisturized, to put it lightly.

Mitch is proud.

Lesson learned again. Make space for Dad to do his thing. *His* thing. And just…be okay with it. The value of having him involved is priceless.

And plus, how else would Ruby have ever experienced the delight of going to bed in a bath of lotion? Far be it for me to derail a train that is headed straight for a good memory. I tap my head with my own index finger, *Remember this, Katie. Mitch is a good dad. Let him be. Please, let him be.*

～

Today is a quieter day. I am feeding Ruby for the fourth time. She has only vomited twice. My brain scrambles to determine what the difference is so that I reproduce it tomorrow. I am left with no answers. Today, she is just doing better. I have no idea why. I sink back into the rocker and take a deep breath. I may not be able to press this peace into tomorrow, but the least I can do is count it as respite and embrace it today.

Outside the window, leaves are dancing with color. I have watched their journey from bright green to crinkled brown, many already fallen to the ground. I think of process, letting go of that which I cannot control. I am exhausted from my own inability to control life, efforts running me into the ground. The trees urge me to let go, to be in the process, facing what I am—even if means discovering myself in the crinkled brown or already on the ground.

I glance over at Ruby, who is tucked into my left arm, as the feeding pump cycles. She is dozing off, and the feed is almost complete. I allow her weight to sink into mine. We feel as one. She in me, and I in her. We belong together.

A moment later, my opportunity has come: I must lay her down before my only break of the day is behind me. Carefully, I rise. I rise with the most precious cargo in the world, my daughter, weight sunk into mine. Carefully, I move. I move with a grace that only a mother can know. Carefully, I lay her down. Release the one that I love more than life.

And then, I wait.

Stillness.

Success.

She is asleep.

I begin to walk out the door but am stopped. I turn around and look back at her. Ruby is at peace. I let out an exhausted sigh and then stand still. This moment is precious. For a small child who suffers most of the time, respite from suffering is more precious than gold. I wish I could freeze time and keep us both here. My soul lets out its cry, *Oh, that life would soften and allow us to live from peace instead of this relentless turmoil of disease!*

I lie down next to Ruby. *To-do list—to-shmoo list—who cares.* I move my body forward, landing an inch from hers. I close my eyes. Between my body and Ruby's I feel a flame, a passion for Ruby, a furious love. *I love her.*

The heat of love continues to rise, and things inside of me begin to burn. *Good-bye prestige, good-bye need to succeed, good-bye appearances, performances, achievements. Good-bye career. Good-bye aspirations, entitlement, need. Good-bye.*

I begin throwing things into the flame of love. There is nothing I want to preserve.

I let it all burn, and burn, and burn. I don't care anymore. I don't care. I don't want it. I only want to live in love. And right there, bedside with my daughter, I lose my life for love.

The flame recedes and this simple verse is what remains in me:

I am in love with my daughter,

And content to remain, right here, by her side

Forever.

Chapter 9

I woke up early this morning to pray. There is something precious about the "fourth watch of the night" as my Bible calls it: 4:00 AM.

These days Ruby is consecutively vomiting, coughing up mucus, and eventually coughing up blood. When I see the blood, I know there is internal breakdown, and it breaks my heart. This morning, I sat with God and poured out my heart. *From the ends of the earth, I cry to You for help. Lead me to the rock that is higher than I.* This verse has become one of my favorite prayers:

Lead me to the rock that is higher than I.

Lead me to the rock that is higher.

Lead me to the rock.

Lead me.

Lead.

I am so proud of Ruby. She is a miracle child. And yet, I never imagined she would still be this sick months after her birth. I live with conflict. This morning in prayer I felt a nudge to "remember."

I choose to remember Ruby at 4 ½ lbs.

I choose to remember that doctors gave her 7 days to live.

I choose to remember that she is beginning to see.

I choose to remember that her heart was healed.

The laundry list of persistent health issues float to the top of my mind and fight for a voice. These matter to me, they matter to God— and yet today is not their day to shine. Today, I am drawn by the Spirit to take up residence in testimony, remembering what God *has* done.

Testimonies are anchors for the soul.

We must not forget.

~

I lay Ruby on a mat in the living room and sit beside her. I begin moving her legs in a bicycle motion. Back and forth her knees bend, legs stretch. I start slowly and then speed up. I can tell it feels good to her. She is alert and enjoys being moved. Ruby can move her arms by herself, but she rarely moves her torso, and never moves her own legs. Her legs hang limp until I move them.

Movement is necessary for life. Sometimes movement looks like change, sometimes it looks like a small shift, sometimes it feels like an overhaul. Sometimes we fight movement in life, we fear it, but in movement there is momentum and momentum is needed to remain healthy. Some of this I know from studying dance and watching the effect of movement on people over time. But I am learning much more about it through caring for a little girl who requires a third party in order to move.

If I don't move Ruby, she becomes stiff and suffers throughout her body. No movement means digestive complications and potential damage to her bone structure and internal organs. On days when I have not had time to move her, guilt sits on me. It's a lot to be re- sponsible for the movement of another. This is another quiet and yet demanding factor in Ruby's care.

On my knees, I bend over Ruby's body and begin to pray as I move her limbs: "Legs function normally in Jesus' name." "Muscle tone be restored." "These legs were made for walking," and so on. I continue working with Ruby's body, letting my focus climb to her neck and head. I gently cup my hands around her head and stretch her neck, back and forth, up and down. I pray for her mind: "Brain, develop normally." "Neuropathways be formed." "Mind, you are not limited."

Music plays in the background and I hum along, releasing subtle praise into the air as I enforce movement. In time, I lie down next to Ruby, stop the movement, and become still. When I am next to Ruby, I feel very close to God. Together, we rest in the Presence of God and I allow hope to fill my vision of what will be. I hold her small hand and dream, "Ruby, someday we will both be up off this mat running, wild and free together." I turn my head toward hers and repeat softly, "Someday....you and me...wild and free."

Timer goes off. I need to prepare another feed. I roll over and then roll Ruby over. I put her on her belly. She whimpers and I pat her head. "It's going to be okay." Her belly is her least favorite position, but one of the most necessary for her back muscles. Sometimes pain is necessary for gain.

As I walk out of the room, I feel a notable lightness of heart. That time was refreshing. Movement breeds joy, release. The distinction of movement makes stillness all the more precious, all the more accessible, to *really* enter in.

Call it an exercise routine, therapy, or medically necessary—but I call these times "hanging out with Ruby." This is our life, this is what we do, and I'm beginning to enjoy it. I suppose almost any experience can become enjoyable when it is soaked in faith, hope and love.

Faith, hope and love—an invincible marinade.

$\sim$

We drive back to Virginia Hospital Center where Ruby was born. Nearing the building, memories flash before my eyes, reliving scenes. I fight to keep my eye on the road. Today, we are scheduled to see Rhonda Fraser, an occupational therapist who works in the outpatient clinic.

Two weeks ago, I quit on the government-funded therapist. She arrived in our home chipper, but nervous, which made me nervous. When Ruby started vomiting, as she often does, this girl's face turned completely white, and I found myself trying to comfort her and keep her from panic. By the time she left, I was exhausted from trying to care for the therapist as she fearfully handled Ruby. I don't think a therapist who is afraid of Ruby can do much for her.

I contacted a speech therapist whom we met in the NICU and asked for a recommendation. "Rhonda Fraser" was her confident response. "Rhonda," she shared, "has been in the practice for decades. She's the best." I picked up the phone and made an appointment.

Ruby and I circle the hospital parking garage to find a parking space. It's packed. At last, we find a space and pull in. I shut my eyes, *Oh, God, please don't let this be a waste of time and money.* I take Ruby out of the car and click her car seat into the stroller base. We ride the elevator up out of the parking garage until its doors open into the hospital lobby. A few months ago, we were living here with little hope of escape. I step off the elevator and feel a sense of pride, proud of Ruby. She is with us. While the NICU is physically a few floors away, it is experientially far from the therapy where we are headed today.

This distance is a journey that Ruby and I have taken together.

We circle the hospital hallways and take another elevator up to Outpatient Rehab. The waiting room in the rehab clinic is full of elderly people. Ruby is the only child there. Sweet smiles from elderly women follow me as I roll Ruby toward the window to check in. I feel weird about being here with a child. *It's not fair. Ruby should be at a playground today, not sitting in a rehab waiting room full of seniors.* I check in and sit down.

In time, a middle-aged woman comes out and calls our name. She has loose fitting clothing, tousled hair, and a spark of life in her eyes. We follow her down the hallway into a small room with a single mat. At her heels, I feel a familiar sense of incompetence as a mom, following a specialist into a small room so that she can teach me about my child.

Rhonda does an evaluation of Ruby. She puts her on her belly, pulls back her shirt, and watches her back muscles. Next, she checks the range of motion for each of her joints: elbows, wrists, knees, ankles. I didn't realize how limited some of Ruby's range was until she was under evaluation. Next, she begins to check her mouth. I warn her that Ruby will vomit if she puts anything in her mouth. Thankfully, she heeds my warning and asks me questions instead. I tell her that Ruby is entirely tube-fed and has suffered severe reflux since a difficult intubation with eye surgery.

As the evaluation continues, I notice that Rhonda is not only evaluating Ruby; she is evaluating me as well. She asks me questions to reveal the nature of my connection to Ruby, my perspective on her life, my willingness to be involved in her care. It doesn't take Rhonda long to realize that I am entirely invested in this little girl, and it doesn't take me long to realize that this therapist is not out to micro-manage that connection but to support it.

Relief.

I don't have to fight to have a voice with this person.

I watch Rhonda interact with Ruby. She stretches, stimulates and interacts with her in ways that I have not known how. She feeds me ideas through example, which breed more ideas. My creative wheels spin.

Toward the end of the evaluation, Rhonda talks to me about Ruby's ability to eat by mouth. She is willing to help us work on it. I tell her in a moment of transparency that one of my great dreams is that Ruby will eat by mouth. I feel deeply moved that she brought it up and believes she can and will. Rhonda nods with a solemn hopeful look.

Rhonda shares that we have to teach Ruby that stimulation to the mouth is good. Ruby's experiences with her mouth have been negative; the feeding tube down her throat, intubation with surgery, reflux, vomiting. Slowly, we have to help heal this trauma and strengthen positive associations with her mouth.

"Start at the cheek," she instructs me. "Move toward her mouth, but stop as soon as she shows signs of discomfort. We'll start with facial massage and slowly move toward the mouth as she tolerates it. Don't push it.'"

"Okay," I answer respectfully, sincerely.

Ruby and I are given a little handout of homework and asked how frequently we would like to come.

"You're asking us?" I remark out loud.

"Yes! You're the mom. How often would you like to bring her?"

This blows my mind. *My choice?*

"Honestly? We are really busy with medical appointments; we're hardly home. What about every other week?"

"I have a feeling you're the type of mom who is going to work with her at home. Therapy is much more effective when there is consistency, but you don't need me for that. If you're willing to work with her, it's fine with me if you come every other week."

I have to refrain from hugging the woman.

She actually trusts me with Ruby's care.

Back in the car, Ruby and I head home. I'm excited to tell Mitch about this appointment and teach him some of the things I learned. I think Rhonda can teach us how to play with Ruby, how to interact with her, and how to think outside the box in stimulating her. This is an enormous gift and not as innate as one might think.

Behind the wheel of my car, my mind strategizes on how to incorporate some of these new things into Ruby's routine. Jaw clenches at the thought of Ruby's schedule. *There really isn't any time in Ruby's schedule for…anything…and yet we've got to find time for this.* Rhonda's trust in me to work with her at home motivates me to make a way. *I think I'll just call our therapy "playtime" and we'll do it first thing in the morning. That sounds fun to me.*

Fun?

The thought of fun exhilarates and I smile.

⌇

Ruby and I are in Philadelphia to visit family. It took me two full days to prepare for a two-day trip. A bag full of feeding pump supplies, a carton full of medical care supplies, a bag stuffed with baby supplies. Here we are.

Our guest room has yellow walls and pale blue curtains. It is a fresh space, a gift to us. I decide to put Ruby in bed next to me. Mitch and I rarely do this because of all the props it requires to position her well. If Ruby is lying too flat or interrupted at a certain stage of an overnight feed, we are certain to awake to severe reflux.

But tonight, with Mitch away from us, I feel that this spot on the bed belongs to Ruby. There is something about being near her that makes the world feel right side up. If there is one place I belong in this world, that is next to her.

I begin to organize Ruby's care for the night. We are in a big house. I map out an overnight plan and in it realize what a gift it is that we currently live in a tiny apartment. Tonight, I will have a 12:00 AM, 3:00 AM, and 6:00 AM feed to administer in a house where the kitchen is on another floor.

I lie down facing Ruby. There it is. *Bond.* I feel it with such definition it's nearly tangible. I don't know if it's physical, spiritual, emotional, or all of the above. But I do know that it is real. I inch closer. The feeling of love and connectedness draws me into her like a magnetic force.

Ruby Joy.

Her presence is like a heater for my heart. The closer I am to her, the warmer my heart feels. Hard things melt off my soul as I lie in proximity to her. I let that happen and wait for my own mind to dial down from the day.

At last, I shut my eyes and sink into sleep, wrapped in the thought that I don't mind so much getting up throughout the night tonight. I know why I am doing it. In the warmth of our bond, I know clearly.

I do it for Ruby.

Stairs.

Feeding.

Pump.

Up and down.

Down and up.

Throughout the night.

For Ruby.

$\sim$

We finish dinner. Mitch offers to do dishes. I sit at the table and pull out my calendar to see our schedule tomorrow. *OT with Rhonda.* I smile. The smile is rare and notable; I catch it, freeze it, and walk over to Mitch.

"See this?" I point to my plastered smile. "I just caught it while thinking about seeing Rhonda tomorrow."

"Noted!" Mitch responds.

I sit back down at the table and continue, "I really like Rhonda. She's helping us." He turns around and nods, a sense of relief on his face. I wonder if his relief is about Rhonda, my smile, or a pause from my complaining about medical appointments. I decide not to ask.

I look back down at my calendar. We have multiple medical appointments throughout the next few weeks, with therapy squeezed in between them. I catch myself wishing we could balance out the scale of care, taking some time off the hospital commitment and putting more time into things that actually support Ruby's day-to-day life, like therapy.

I look back and forth on the calendar page to consider which appointments I could move if I wanted to. Cardiology—too critical. Ophthalmology—too critical. Pediatrics—mandatory. Audiology—we've already rescheduled twice. Orthotics—critical...

"Oh forget it," I let out a hefty sigh.

Mitch turns around, "What?"

"I just wish we had more flexibility in our schedule. We spend so much time in waiting rooms at the hospital outpatient clinic, and I have yet to feel that any of these appointments are helping."

He listens.

"Rhonda has been pressing me to consider more therapy for Ruby, physical therapy, speech therapy—we just don't have time!"

I flip my calendar around so he can look at it right side up.

"None of these doctors are going to tell us not to come. They all prescribe appointments as if they were the only doctor in our lives. Little do they know there are 18 of them—eighteen. Eighteen, eighteen, eighteen. *Eighteen!* Somehow, we need to create more space in this."

"You're the mom, and I'm the dad." Mitch says bluntly.

I wait for him to explain.

"We can make changes, Katie. We're paying every one of these people. If they're not helping, we don't have to go—especially not at the frequency they demand."

"But they're specialists, Mitch; what do we know?"

"We know Ruby." A pause hangs in the air. "Why don't you ask Rhonda for some referrals for other therapists tomorrow and we can go from there?"

"Because it would cost us more money and time, neither of which we have."

He leans forward and fixes his eyes at mine. "Katie, Rhonda's occupational therapy appointments are the first appointments in this journey you have actually enjoyed. It is worth the time, money and effort. Let's explore it. After all, what do you think would be best for Ruby?"

My lips purse, eyes drift up, and I craft my response.

"To be healed."

"Agreed. Second best?"

"Less time with doctors, more time at home."

"Third best?"

"Honestly, Mitch, if we can find more therapists like Rhonda, I think therapy can help Ruby."

He found what he was looking for. "Well, then, let's do it for Ruby."

～

The next day Ruby and I go to occupational therapy with Rhonda.

I ask Rhonda for referrals for other therapists. "Can you recommend a speech therapist and a physical therapist?"

"Yes!" She names a few and warns me that they are expensive. The word "expensive" draws out and I breathe deeply.

For Ruby.

A few weeks ago, the thought of therapy was just one more appointment on the calendar: one more stranger with whom we were forced to share our lives. Another four hours out of the house and I wanted none of it. That has changed. Rhonda has helped me discover that therapy is not just more medical care. It has a different approach. It addresses different things. It actually balances out the care. I stand corrected, and I own that for Ruby's sake. Ruby needs therapy. Therapy helps Ruby. It is worth the time and money.

Rhonda concludes the appointment and I pack up our things. I walk out of the door and then turn around. "I really appreciate you." Rhonda looks up intently. I continue, "Thank you for listening to me, and teaching me about Ruby. I realized last night at my kitchen table, with my full calendar looking back at me cross-eyed, that I actually look forward to these appointments. That is a miracle in this season. Ruby is progressing under your care."

I watch Rhonda's heart melt. I realize partway through that I am probably giving her what would be considered a therapist's gold medal. She doesn't answer me, but instead looks down at Ruby.

"Ruby, when you get better, tell your mom that she should go back to school to become an occupational therapist. She would be really good at helping other kids like you." Ruby stares back at Rhonda, as if giving her word. I smile, turn the stroller around, and we head out the door, down the hallway toward the exit.

Walking away I find that Rhonda's comment about my future has my brow furrowed, mind active. I haven't thought about my own future for months, forgot that I had one. It's an interesting thought—that I would eventually put my hands to something associated with this journey or that there could ever be a chapter in life after the one that I am in right now.

Presently, I have no file for this thought.

~

A thousand decisions to run *into* God instead of away from Him in the midst of our hardship have yielded consequence, good consequence. What was birthed out of need is now producing blessing beyond need. I can see the unexpected sprouts, the blooms, and the garden that is growing in our lives as a result of hours upon hours spent in prayer.

Initially, my discovery was that God is alive. He is really there. When I call on Him, He hears me. When I cry to Him, He answers. When He touches me, I become okay.

A touch from God can solve absolutely anything. He is alive.

Then I discovered that God is not only alive, He is a *place*: a safe place where I can run when trouble comes. Touches from God become visits with God. When I visit with God, I become strong, which sustains my faith.

And then, after months of running into Him as a hiding place, I began to hear His still, small voice: "I am more than a hiding place, Katie. I am a home. Will you move in?"

Unexpectedly, I found myself with a divine invitation to move into God, to discover what it means to make a home in Him, to live from His Presence. I knew that an invitation to move out of crisis and into home is one that I needed to take. My yes came quickly.

And right there, in the middle of my own pain, that has not yet left me, I moved out of it. In hindsight, I can see that Mitch, Ruby and I were actually in this transition for months. We spent months moving our things through the process of prayer, piece by piece, into God as our home. As we moved, our anxiety decreased, our peace increased, and I dare to think that we uncovered a simple secret to thriving in crisis: *Get out of chaos, move into God.*

Jesus says, "Abide in Me."

To abide means to remain, be held, be kept—and not to depart.

I choose to abide in Him.

Where peace rules.

Panic runs out of breath.

Anxiety is swallowed up.

Abide in Him.

Because His laughter sinks depression.

Because His perspective stretches into eternity.

And because the outcome ultimately rests in His hands.

I abide, live, dwell and tarry—in the God who is my home.

I find that there is ample room in God to move fully in, to unpack, spread out, and to be authentically at rest. He is not concerned with what I bring or what I will do there; He just wants all of me in Him. Because, when I am all there, He gets to be Lord to all of me. This means He can cover all of me with peace. This is His heart for me. For all of us.

Returning after an eleven-day trip, my heart longs for the home of His Presence that we have cultivated in our space. Before our suitcases are unpacked, or our things organized, our worship music is on and our voices are releasing holy noise as we return to this home of God's Presence. Although I am still at the tip of this experience, I can already say with confidence that there is no place like home.

That night I write:

God is my home.

God is not in a crisis.

I am no longer in a crisis.

I am now in God.

I have entered into the home I was made for,

The home I will always have,

The home that will always have me.

Welcome home.

That still, small voice reemerges, "I am not only a home for you,

I want to make my home in you. Now that you have moved into Me, can I move into you?"

Abide in Me. I will abide in You.

Chapter 10

Today, Ruby turns six months old. Time is going fast. How is it that time crawls one moment and then races the next? It's strange how single days seem to inch by but in hindsight appear fleeting.

It's morning. Mitch has left for work, and I am rolling out of bed. Ruby is still asleep. I take a moment to sit on the edge of my bed and reflect. *Six months. This is definitely a milestone of some kind.* I recall our pediatrics appointment yesterday. The report was that Ruby is growing and "breaking the red tape of her diagnosis every day." Good appointments are never taken for granted in our house. *Ever.*

I shut my eyes and dare to feel my own heart. I am completely exhausted and yet entirely stimulated at the same time. It reminds me of crossing a finish line after a race, when strenuous work is suddenly made worthy and joyful satisfaction overrides painful process. And yet, the exhaustion of the process is still very present.

This day marks a milestone for me as well. I stand up from the edge of my bed and turn my head toward Ruby's co-sleeper. She is asleep. I still perceive her quiet breaths as miracles. I lean over and place my hand on top of hers. Ruby's hand is less than two inches long, a tiny remarkable treasure. She lifts her hand and places it over mine. Her eyes are still shut. My heart melts. These are the moments that I must remember, capture. I exit the room and dig for a small notebook. I have an idea.

Opening to the first page, I write:

January 10, 2010
Happy 6ᵗʰ Month Birthday, Ruby Joy!
I love you and celebrate your life.
Here's to these moments…
Love, Mom.

I turn the page and begin, one simple moment at a time…

I love when Ruby holds my hand, like she did this morning.
Her fingers are so tiny, but determined nonetheless. She likes
her hand on top.

I have heard Mitch on a number of occasions say to Ruby, "This
is still my favorite part," to look and find that he is holding her
pinky toe.

Last night, I slept with my head in Ruby's co-sleeper so that I
could be near her. My neck is stiff this morning but I don't care.
Ruby, you have won my heart.

Over the next few days, I catch the moments that we share and
jot them down…

Today, Ruby was sleepy and tolerated being up on my shoulder
for a long time. There is something wonderful about the feeling
of her chest against mine.

Yesterday, Mitch was kissing Ruby all over her face—as he
often does—simply overwhelmed with adoration. This dad is
smitten.

One of the things about Ruby that I love is when she wakes up
slightly, she tends to stretch all her fingers one by one and then
fall back asleep.

Ruby swallowed three times in a row today as I fed her drops
of milk with rice cereal! Way to go, Rubes!

I continue to capture moments, day after day, in this mundane
notebook with an old pen. Looking for the good causes it to float to

the top. As a result, desire awakens in me to discover and embrace the life I now share with Ruby. I have been afraid to fully embrace it for fear of loss. The original, seven-day prognosis is now months behind us, and yet the fear zone it created lingers.

Gratitude interrupts the fear zone.

In the wake of simple moments jotted into a small notebook, I find my way to a measure of acceptance: grace to appreciate who we are and what we now have. These moments, captured and expressed, convince me that we are no longer just fighting for life; we are now also living it.

Happy 6th month birthday, Ruby Joy.

~

I'm washing dishes after dinner. The sound of guitar strums leak into the kitchen. Mitch is finding time for music. This is a good thing. I peek my head around the corner. Mitch is on two knees with his guitar propped on his thighs. Ruby is lying on her pink mat in front of him. He sings over her; she gazes back, wide-eyed.

I hear the tension in Mitch's voice: the longing, the ache, and the need for relief. His heart cry is bubbling up and spilling out in the form of song. I can hear the sadness in his voice. It shakes me internally. This is the heart cry of a man with a broken heart, expressed through quiet tones, sincere noise.

Surely God is hearing this.

Mitch has been the stabilizer in our family unit, catching the emotional tornado of his wife and daughter under the pressures of disease. He has held on through this storm with unyielding strength, determined to limit its destruction as it moves through our lives.

In the whirlwind of my own needs, it's easy for me to forget how much Mitch is sacrificing for Ruby and me to be home together. He commutes every day to a job that he does not like, and yet never complains. He spends hours shuffling papers while Ruby and I are in and out of appointments that he wishes he could be in. His heart is at home with us, and yet he goes out every day to make provision for us.

As I listen to his voice tonight, sung so specifically over his daughter, I have to wonder, *When is the last time someone asked him how he was doing? Or offered him some personal support?*

He stops singing and looks over at me.

Love shoots from his eyes into mine, and I realize...

Mitch has laid down his life for me. Literally.

He may even be dying for me.

He definitely would.

I know this.

I read his eyes. They say, *Worth it.*

He's sinking and still giving. *How?*

I shut my eyes.

I must find a way to see beyond my own needs to care for Mitch. It's not natural, with my own bleeding heart, but I cannot wait for my pain to stop in order to see his. Somehow, I have to find strength that he can fall into, and soon. Otherwise my husband may bury himself in the name of loving me.

∼

Today, we go for an audiology appointment. Ruby failed her newborn hearing screen. A repeat test is long overdue.

Back to Children's Hospital we go.

Inside the hospital, we find the audiology clinic for the first time. I check in and the office administrator looks up. "Newborn hearing screen? She's over 6 months old!" I open my eyes as wide as I can, lean forward, and burrow my gaze into the woman's eyes. "We have been busy with other appointments." She peers over the ledge of her counter toward Ruby, who is in the car seat. Undoubtedly noting some anomalies, she leans back, let's her eyes drift down and asks no further questions.

I sigh and turn around. *I am tired of defending myself.*

Soon after check-in, we are called back to a patient room. A nurse dresses Ruby for testing. She sticks wires all over her head and attaches her to a portable computer. The computer, I am told, will read brain waves as Ruby's ears are stimulated. I hold Ruby on my lap. My job is to keep her calm, as if that were within a mother's control. "The test won't work if she is fussy," I am warned.

I look down at Ruby, "You can be what you want to be." I look back up. The technician is not impressed. What the technician doesn't realize is that medical appointments are Ruby's life right now. I am not interested in forcing her daily behavior into that which fits medical testing. They can test her while she lives her life, as any child can and should. I am not going to tie her down and demand silence every other day for some glorified machinery.

Despite my apathy on the matter, Ruby and I manage to sit quietly together. I watch the signals collect on the screen and feel scared. The nurse conducts the test silently. It takes time. I watch her reading the signals on the screen and wish I knew what she was seeing.

After some time, the lights flicker on and I am told that the test will be repeated. No further explanation is offered. My heart sinks. I just want to get out of here. *Why is the test being repeated? What is going on?*

After the second round of tests is completed, an audiologist with a grim demeanor approaches me. "I am very sorry to share with you, but according to these test results your daughter is deaf."

A dagger hits my heart. I can't speak.

What does this mean?

She can't hear me?

She can't hear Mitch?

She can't hear anything?

"We can try hearing aids to see if anything emerges. I'm willing to prescribe them if you're interested. However, she is not signaling any brain responses from audio stimulation."

I still can't speak.

"Deaf."

I hate that word.

The doctor continues, "We can connect you to resources for deaf children in the meantime."

"But Ruby's not deaf!" I let out with conviction.

The doctor stands quietly before me.

I pull Ruby close to me. "You're not deaf, Ruby."

Whispering into her tiny ears, intrusive thoughts crowd my mind: *She can't hear you. She has never heard you. She will never hear you.* I try to shake myself free of the torment, but it continues: *Ruby has no idea what your voice sounds like. She doesn't even know you. What you thought your relationship was with her does not exist. Your connection with her is not real. She can't hear you.*

I shake as the mental attack escalates.

Frozen by internal turmoil, I sit unmoved in front of the doctor, who is at a loss at how to handle me in this moment. I look down and under my breath cry out, "God, I told you I couldn't handle any more. What am I to do with this?"

Later that evening Mitch comes home from work. I can't speak. My heart is sinking in the sorrow of Ruby not being able to hear.

At last, he sits me down. "What happened, Katie?"

"I'll tell you after Ruby is in bed. I don't want her to have to hear it again."

Hear.

My stomach turns.

I hate the thought that she can't hear.

That all forms of noise are nothing to her.

This can't be.

It *can't.*

Mitch puts Ruby to bed. I can hear him talking to her, sharing with her about his day, asking her questions. I then hear him singing to her, humming, and rocking her to sleep. I can't help but think as I listen that if Ruby is deaf, all of this changes. If Ruby is deaf, our relationship with her as we know it disappears.

Mitch concludes Ruby's bedtime routine and joins me at the table. I pull out some papers from the audiology clinic and then share in a matter-of-fact tone, "Ruby had her hearing test today. They said she is medically deaf. The doctor says she can't hear—anything."

"That's impossible," Mitch responds. "Of course she can hear! How and why does she respond to my singing if she can't hear?"

I push the paper toward him. Inked report.

He reads it and I watch the dagger that hit my heart strike his. I still don't know if sharing with him is the best course of action.

We're both bleeding now. *What is the point?*

"Mitch, I've been grieving this all day. You realize that if we believe this report it changes everything. If people in Ruby's life believe that she is deaf they will stop talking to her. She will sit unaddressed and uninvolved in any and every conversation. Our interactions with her, everyone's interactions with her, will dwindle to insignificant. I'm not ready to give up on Ruby's hearing: there's too much at stake for her." Hours of internal processing finds its voice. "What if they're wrong? What if she can hear, or will hear, and us believing she can't hear nullifies what could be? I don't know what to do with this report. I feel like I'm being crushed." I throw the papers on the floor.

Mitch goes into the file cabinet and starts thumbing through paperwork. He pulls out Ruby's newborn report, "Seven day life expectancy." He pushes the paper toward me on the table. "It doesn't matter what they say, Katie; they don't know Ruby and they don't know Jesus."

He picks the audiology report up off the floor and throws it in the trash.

"There. Gone. We reject this report."

We sit in silence for a long time.

In time, Mitch shares something. "Katie, call me crazy, but I feel like Ruby *can* hear. I know her better than the medical machines, and I really feel that she *can* hear. I just know that she can! I honestly don't think this report is accurate."

I feel a sense of relief. Earlier today it felt inevitable that we would be losing this entire part of Ruby's life on top of all the other loss we currently have. I respond, "I'm with you. It doesn't feel right to accept this. It's not right."

We take each other's hands from across the table. Together, we decide that we have nothing to lose for continuing to interact with Ruby as if she can hear perfectly. This report will stay in the trash and not be shared, not even with family. Inevitably, this information would change how people relate to Ruby, and therefore it is information we choose to conceal for her sake.

We reject the *deaf* label and believe that Ruby can hear.

∿

Mitch and I are not getting along. We are drained from our daily treks to and from work and medical appointments. In between our daily commutes, we hold Ruby. We are sick with love for her. We are also hard pressed by the dizzying details of her care.

Tonight, our exhaustion collides and it's not good. Mitch wants to be more involved in medical decisions, but I feel too fatigued to recount enough details from our appointments every day that ensure he can fully participate. We each have strong opinions on Ruby's care, and they don't always match. We're in conflict and doctors await what we cannot agree upon to deliver: decisions.

I feel the pressure of knowing that Mitch is at the mercy of what I choose to tell him. Almost 90 percent of reports on Ruby's care come through me, and he receives them in the tone and viewpoint from which I choose to give them. Knowing this, I can't just vent as one friend would to another. If I do, he will likely hate the doctors unnecessarily and cut off much-needed care.

Herein our relationship is pressed into a *functional* mode. My function is to keep Mitch involved in Ruby's process. His function is to provide for us so that the process can continue.

Tonight, our medical discussion turns into an argument, which turns into fighting, which ends up in an ugly explosion of anger, hurt, and frustration. I don't even know the source of the initial disagreement, but it has opened up a can of worms in our relationship. In the middle of this explosive interaction, we both notice Ruby at the same time. She stares up at us as if her world of innocence is collapsing before her eyes. My heart drops to the bottom of my gut. I feel the weight of *parenting failure*. I pick up Ruby and remove her from the room. Getting her ready for bed, I try to hide from her what she already knows. Mom and Dad are not getting along.

After Ruby is settled, I sit still in the bedroom and wrestle. I should go out there and try to reconcile with Mitch, but I'm angry, hurt and unmotivated. I choose what I should not and quit. Without a word, I go to bed. I know this will make Mitch very angry. I do it anyway.

Flat on my back, my jaw is clenched, and my eyes gaze at the ceiling. I hate suffering. Mitch and I were in love before this crazy storm hit. I hate how pain screams for an outlet and ends up hurting the person closest to me. It's not fair. Mitch and I are both hurting, and we're taking it out on each other.

Emotional dynamite untamed explodes on whoever is closest.

I cannot help but wonder, *Is there any other option? Are we doomed to turn against each other through this?*

∿

An hour after pumping, I'm in a deep sleep. Ruby begins to cough. I shake myself to wake up and dart over to her bedside. Lifting her head, I tilt her to the side just in time to catch vomit, again.

Vomiting and suctioning continue as I work hard to keep Ruby from aspirating. Handling these moments has become an art. An unwanted but necessary art form.

Stillness at last settles in the air. She's done.

I pick Ruby up and hold her close. Pressing her body against mine, I rock back and forth until I can feel the shakes pressed out of her being. These are hard times. Trauma strikes like lightning and we spend an hour in recovery.

Mitch is now also awake and at our side. I ask him to change

Ruby while I change her bed. The laundry I had finally finished fills again. Ruby's breathing now carries heavy signs of aspiration. With few words, Mitch changes Ruby and I change the bed. We prop her head support up high and tuck her back in.

She looks up innocently ask if asking, "When will this end?"

I bend over and press my forehead against hers. "I don't know, Ruby. But it will. I promise it will." Tears fill my eyes. I pull her hands on top of her blanket and stroke her arms. "It will end." I try to reassure myself.

Our room smells of vomit. It's too late to care. Back in bed we manage to fall asleep in our tears. Hard-line prayers hit the ceiling of our room. "Please, God, don't let us be struck again before morning."

Two hours later the whole thing transpires again.

Coughing.

Racing to the bedside.

Vomiting.

Suctioning.

Aspiration.

Laundry piling.

Changing.

Crying.

Holding.

Comforting.

Fighting to fall asleep again.

Four times in one night, we live through this nightmare of disease.

This is our "normal" nighttime routine. We dream together of a single night without disease striking. It has yet to happen. What is commonplace to us is not so common. Our normal is not normal.

Goodnight…not good.

Disease does not sleep.

~

I've had a passing thought the last few days. *What if we took the month of February off from doctors' appointments?*

I dream.

Could we take off for a whole month?

I dismiss the thought. *Crazy talk. We see doctors because we must.*

The thought re-emerges: *What if **you** took the month of February off from doctors' appointments?* The question poses itself to me, as if it originates from someone else. I stop.

God, is this You?

Utterly worn out from months of intense care, I would take a break from medical appointments in a heartbeat if it were possible. It feels impossible. I can only imagine the doctors faces when I tell them, "We're not coming back until March," as if it were up to me. As if this disease could be paused.

Later that day, the thought presents a third time: *What if you took a month off?*

Okay. Something is going on. Repetitive thoughts like this are not normal for me. Someone is asking me a question.

I begin to consider it. I'm guessing it would mean taking a risk with a handful of high-level physicians and hoping for the best. I wonder if I have the courage to do this. I wonder if I would be perceived as neglectful.

Prayer hugs the idea until courage emerges from it.

"Mitch, I feel like we are supposed to take a break from medical care for the month of February. What do you think?"

With a surprising lack of reaction he states, "Sounds good to me."

I hold my tongue from responding with all the reasons why we shouldn't do it. After all, I am the one who just pitched the idea. I pull out my calendar. It is jammed full of appointments. I look from left to right. Maybe we can take off on Mondays, shift a few things. I look from right to left. Maybe we could block out Fridays and Saturdays. I think. I strategize. I survey the calendar from every possible view. And yet, I'm still wondering—about the whole month.

"There's no harm in giving it a try," Mitch breaks the silence. My lips purse down. He stands up and walks away from the calendar, and from me. He either has no clue how much work it is going to be to figure this out, or he is convinced that it is nothing more than a decision.

The next day, Ruby and I sit in the waiting room for Ophthalmology. I keep rehearsing my speech in my mind about the month of February. I am nervous to ask.

We are called back into the patient room and the doctor comes in. Ruby's evaluation proceeds as normal. Eyes are checked, questions asked, prescriptions written. The doctor puts her hand on the doorknob and says, "See you in two weeks." Then she walks out and shuts the door behind her.

My heart sinks. I missed my chance.

I could chase her down. Instead, I turn left toward the exit myself. At checkout, the secretary opens the February calendar on her computer to schedule our next appointment. I'm trembling. And then I stop trembling and lean forward.

"We can't do February. Can you schedule her for March?"

She looks down at the doctor's note. "Hang on." She walks down the hallway and knocks lightly on another room where the doctor is treating another patient.

Door opens.

I dare not look, but I listen like a hawk.

"Ruby cannot come in February: is March okay?"

Door shuts.

The woman returns to her desk.

And February disappears from her screen.

We are scheduled for March. I am more relieved than I dare to show.

One down.

Later that week, we show up for a check-up with Ruby's pediatrician. We stroll through her routine: weight checked, length noted, concerns discussed. At the end of the appointment, the doctor pulls out her little notepad to write a few prescriptions. My heart begins to race; it's time to speak up.

She gets the first word, "Okay, I'll see her again next week."

"We won't be available in February for appointments," I respond rather abruptly.

"Okay. Are you traveling?" she asks.

"Not exactly, but we are setting aside time as a family."

Dr. Morshed stops, aware that I am withholding information. She then leans in. "I'm willing to wait to see her if you promise you'll call if anything seems amiss."

"I will."

Smiles exchanged.

Another one cleared.

A few days later, we arrive at a cardiology appointment. The commute has been stuffed with silence, my thoughts racing. Tracking Ruby's heart regularly could be considered critical care. Should I ask that she not be seen in February? Maybe this is the one appointment we should keep.

The staff completes the echocardiogram, ultra-sound and blood pressures checks, and then it's time to conference with the doctor. Dr. Davis shares with me that Ruby's heart seems to be doing well. He turns around in his chair as if a sudden inspiration has caught him. "I have an idea. What do you say we wait to have our next appointment and I'll see her in a month instead of two weeks?"

Joy jumps off my face, "Seriously?"

He laughs.

He has no idea.

That means no appointment in February.

Done. Done. And done.

Watching this third and most crucial appointment transition to March convinces me that a month free of appointments is meant to be. I grab my phone to call the remainder of the doctors and therapists to reschedule all of Ruby's February appointments to March. In near disbelief, I cross them off the calendar.

When the last appointment is successfully moved, I get on my knees and bury my head between my thighs. Misty eyes release full tears. I am so worn out by seeing doctors. God is giving me a break. Gratitude pours out of my heart.

In the last days of January excitement brews. There is not a single medical appointment left on February's calendar, and every one of them was moved with approval from the physician. *What in the world will we do with our time?*

Hello, February.

Chapter 11

It's a new day in February. Ruby is up, dressed, and fed. *Now what?*

I feel like a novice at life. We are accustomed to living under the weight of disease's restraint: medical procedures, doctors' appointments and difficult decisions. February's freedom makes me realize how limited our other life choices have been.

I peer out the window; the pane is frosty. Not too frosty for me. Ruby and I will bundle up and go somewhere. Anywhere. Supplies packed, we get in the car and drive. Our direction is…away from the hospital. I can't help but feel like an escaped convict. *If a doctor sees us, what will they think?*

We make it to the riverside, unload, and venture toward the river. This is the same river that sat with me the night before Ruby was born. The same spot that held the promise, "I will uphold you with my right hand."

I pull the top of Ruby's car seat as a covering for her head and drape a blanket over the remaining exposed space. Despite the cold, this draped blanket will come on and off countless times over the next hour. I want her to see, feel, and taste the outdoors.

On the trail, we encounter other people, people whose lives are floating in ordinary. I wonder what that feels like. Strollers pass us with healthy babies. I wonder what that would be like. These moms likely have the liberty to come out here any day of the week. What would that be like? What would it be like to have a baby whose schedule was not prescribed by medical needs? I wonder if they know what a cherished thing they possess.

Outdoors, Ruby and I hold our own. A vomiting episode happens; we manage it in the grass. I realize that I *can* manage it in the grass. This means that if I am willing to manage it here, we don't need to be trapped indoors. I take some time to comfort Ruby on the sidelines of the trail after she gets sick and then we return to the trail together. She dozes off. I lift my eyes and drink of the scene.

The sun is bright. Bouncing off melting ice, it radiates from the water and barren trees. There is something about unadulterated sun in winter that seems to be the brightest of the year. Something about light in darkness that glorifies light brightness. Something about color on gray canvas that amplifies color's brilliance.

There is something really special about returning to the river where God promised to uphold me and, in that same space, feel the pulse of its fulfillment. I hold on to God's promise, believing His Word to be a river of living water for my soul. In the dreariness of disease, a simple walk by the river pierces the darkness. Despair dissipates in the shimmer of gratitude and grace.

He is upholding me.

He is good.

We are not at the hospital today.

Find us at the river.

∿

A small plate sits in front of me with a perfect piece of chocolate cake on it. Chocolate cake is my favorite. I grip the edge of the plate and push the cake away from my place setting.

I'm fasting.

We have devoted this month to prayer and fasting for Ruby's healing. I have always despised fasting. Don't like it one bit. Who does? And yet, pushing this cake away today I am surprised by what

I feel: *joy*. Something about this fast is different than any fast I have done before.

This fast is for Ruby, but it feels like a gift to me. Any parent will understand: it's a gift to me that I have something meaningful to give to her. In the world of an incurable disease, it is no small thing to have something to give. Every time I refuse food, my joy increases because of my love for Ruby. I would gladly give up food for her any day of the week.

Could it be that this fast is not about what comes out of it, but the opportunity to sacrifice for love?

I feel like I am fasting for the first time. And perhaps I am. For what is a fast really if it is not motivated in love?

∿

One week into February and I find myself at a loss for what to do without medical appointments driving our days. It feels like we have been handed a new life.

The gift of time enables me to see Ruby more clearly. I begin to notice attributes that I hadn't seen before: nuances like how she moves her feet, where her belly button sits, and how beautiful her eyelashes are!

A preoccupied mind limits one's ability to see. February has brought many gifts, but the best may be vision. Sight renewed.

I learned this week that Ruby likes to be stretched. Pulling on her legs and lifting her arms seems refreshing to her. I also discovered that her hands are really expressive. I think she communicates more than we realize through her fingers. I also learned that she can swallow: small bits of baby food have been digested successfully.

A month ago, I could not imagine the joy of seven days uninterrupted by a medical appointment, but now we have it. February is respite for our weary souls.

After two weeks, I want to weigh Ruby. Mitch and I both feel that she is gaining weight like we haven't seen before, which would be a huge victory for all of us.

I stand on the scale and take my own weight: 127. I jot it down. I undress Ruby to a diaper and we get on the scale together. I maneuver Ruby to see my feet until I catch a glimpse a the scale's numbers: 140. I say the number over and over so that I won't forget it, which I have done one too many times. I dress Ruby, settle her and jot down the second number.

140.

I look down.

140 – 127 = 13lbs!

Oh my gosh! Ruby is growing! I can't help but run out of the room and take a good look at her. Stare. It's true. She's filling in and she looks good. My heartfelt whisper, "Oh, God, thank You."

When the disease is triumphing, Ruby loses weight. Her cheeks and belly sink in and it looks like she is disintegrating, going away. When Ruby is doing well, she grows. Mitch will often tell her, "We want more Ruby!" and we mean it. Literally.

I pick her up and give her a squeeze. "Ruby! Good job! You're growing!" I can feel her heart race a little bit. She can tell that I'm excited and we share in it. Toss the joy in the air like confetti. Thoughts reorder. This is the best weight gain she has had in her entire life—and it happened while we did not see a single doctor for two weeks. I wonder…

I wonder if all the medical appointments are stressful to Ruby? I mean, of course they are. But I never thought about needing to limit them for her sake. The thought lands like a brick. This weight gain gives me permission to put up some real boundaries on external care.

Not just for me, but for Ruby.

∽

Today is the last day of February. The calendar threatens to turn its page, back to the doctors, back to the same old crisis we left a month ago. Disappointment seems to laugh at my hope. I am caught between shame and disappointment for believing God that something would drastically change this month as a result of our prayer and fasting. How is it possible for nothing to happen when I have prayed this hard?

I dare not give up hope. She may be healed tonight.

It's Sunday and I ask Mitch for a break. I need to get outside and hear God. I find space and peace outside in a brief strip of woods. I begin to cry.

God, we haven't seen anything change.

I can't go back to what we were in.

Please, God, tell me that You are going to heal her tonight.

Tell me she is being healed right now.

I find a bench and sit down. My heart is in quicksand, and I need a rope, some measure of hope. That still, small voice comes, and, with the wind, I hear Him: "Get up, and leave this place. I am proud of you. You have done well. It's time to go."

He is asking me to step out of the position I have held—all month long—before I have seen one thing change. This does not sound easy. He speaks more. The sound of His voice awakens love in me, and I choose to follow Him because I trust Him. I stand up and begin to walk out of the woods, out of what is still entirely unresolved. Off of my contending platform, I walk.

Near the exit of the woods, I pause, and I hear Him again, "*Feast.*"

"Feast?" I ask out loud. "For all the fasting we have done without evidence of return, You want us to feast?"

"Katie, call a feast with you, Mitch and Ruby. Sit and celebrate what I have done."

I'm caught off guard. I've never "feasted" for God before. I choose not to question it further, especially after a month of fasting! Thinking it over, I recall that He did call feasts in biblical history, perhaps even more frequently than fasts.

Driving home, I feel excited. This is the first Holy Feast I have ever hosted and I've got ideas stacking up in my brain for it.

At home I tell Mitch, "I feel like God wants us to have a feast tonight, on this last night of February, to celebrate what He has done for Ruby and us."

"What He has done?" Mitch's view is as blank as mine. Ruby is still not eating by mouth. She is still vomiting. She is congested. Her muscle tone is unformed. She shows no sign of auditory responsiveness. She is still very sick.

I shrug my shoulders. "He said it; there must be something we can thank Him for."

"Okay, let's do it," Mitch says. He stands up and throws his hands up in the air, "I hereby call a FEAST!" We laugh. Our life is weird, but we love it. We're all in.

The menu is planned. The table decorated. I dress Ruby up. Mitch and I dress up. And we eat, and eat, and eat. We order out from three restaurants in one night. Thai Food. Pizza. Burgers and fries. Salad. Drinks. Dessert. We feast. For four hours, we eat. And for four hours, we thank God.

The first twenty minutes are slow. We can barely think of anything good for which to thank God. We are sitting with a table full of food in a desolate time of life. It feels weird, like throwing a party for a thunderstorm. We fight to make it work. Pulling on strings, we work at gratitude. Some of what we are saying doesn't even feel true or good. We press on.

After a while, goodness peeks its head out, like a guest who needed assurance he was welcome before making an appearance. And suddenly, we begin to see. His goodness is all over our lives. Like stars reappearing after a cloudy night has cleared, the goodness of God begins to shine until we can see it clearly. We have so much to be thankful for.

Talking about gratitude attracts more gratitude. Now that gratitude is a guest at our table, we notice joy as well. In the midst of our feasting, we've been unlocked by thanksgiving and out popped joy. Joy that we did not know we could possibly feel without circumstances changing.

By the third hour, gratitude pours out of us like a fountain, a faucet that refuses to turn off. Our view has cleared and we are literally in tears at the goodness of God in our lives. He is so good. We are so thankful. We feel like new people, though nothing has changed. Nothing…except for our ability to see.

I look over at Ruby. She is a star in our night sky. I am so thankful for her. And on this night she gets a new nickname, "Starlight." *Starlight Perfection Luse.* It sticks, sticks to her little life for a long time.

Gratitude has led us out where the sky is clear, and the darkness is no more than a platform to promote the most brilliant stars.

Goodnight, February.

You have been good to us.

Part III

Daring to Live

Chapter 12

A layer of chocolate cake.

A layer of frosting.

A layer of strawberries.

A layer of cream.

Another layer of chocolate cake.

Another layer of frosting.

More strawberries.

More cake…

This cake is so tall it is beginning to lean…

Quick, cover this cake in frosting!

I place a ruby-red ring-pop at the top.

A *royal*-red ring-pop.

Top and center.

Sprinkle the cake with coconut until

Everything in proximity is dusted with little white flakes.

Pray this cake stays upright…

Plate it. See it. Smile.

Now presenting…Ruby's 1st birthday cake.

~

The night before Ruby's birthday I tuck her in with grandiose gestures, exaggerated expressions of a normal night routine dancing around. "Tomorrow is your birthday, Ruby!"

I lie Ruby down, pull her arm out over the blanket and gently press her hand flat against the bed. I put my hand over hers and pray for her healing as I have a thousand times. My personal prayer resurfaces, persistent and sincere: "God, don't let this disease persist beyond her first birthday. Heal her before her birthday." I have never told anyone that I pray this, but I do, daily. It is my steady private prayer to God.

We stand at that threshold now. Ruby's birthday is in the morning. Perhaps she will be healed tonight. I check on the leaning tower of Ruby's birthday cake.

Lights out.

July 10th, 2010. It has been one year since Ruby was born. I crawl quietly over to her bed before she awakes and check her hands. I want to know if she's healed. She is not. I have a silent moment of deep disappointment: a year of a specific prayer lies unanswered before my eyes. *Unanswered.* Sun shines through the window and hits my left cheek. I look up. I have a choice today. I will either celebrate or grieve.

Realistically, I will do both. But I know in this private moment that the latter is a given; the former is a choice. I greet the discipline of celebration again. I sigh. Faced with an invitation to scale another emotional wall, I wonder if I have the stamina to do it. Do I dare?

I stand up.

I will try to scale this wall.

I am daring to live. Mitch and I approach Ruby's birthday as if it were the height of our career: the arch celebratory event of our shared journey. After all, when a child is given a seven-day life expectancy and makes it to twelve months, there is more than a reason to celebrate; there is a miracle to *enjoy.*

We celebrate.

Eat cake.

Play outside.

Open presents.

Share our space.

Praise God.

Hustle and bustle for Ruby. It's a hot summer day in July and the warmth is good for all of us. Hour after hour, we celebrate Ruby with accolades and noise. The sparkly red ring-pop is removed from the top of the cake and pressed against Ruby's lips. This will not fit through the feeding tube, and neither should it. It belongs in her mouth, and that's where it's found.

The day rolls in and out quickly; too quickly. The sun sets. We have spent ourselves in celebration for Ruby today. She seems to be done before we are, rubbing her little eyes. We relent to her cues and lay her down. She's soon asleep.

And suddenly, the day is over.

In bed with a single lamp left on in the house, I write...

Today was Ruby's birthday, her first birthday. I think Mitch and I both feel deeply the experience of the miraculous as we lived a day today that was once deemed impossible. We chose to celebrate, and I am so glad that we did because in the act of it, we found joy.

I had fun with my sister building Ruby's birthday cake; note the language, "building." It became a tower of chocolate with a ring-pop on top. It did not collapse until it was cut, and that was the second miracle of the day.

In the afternoon we bought burritos and ate by the river. We sat on the pier and Mitch prayed a startling prayer over Ruby, waves of power. We then shared a deep conversation over upscale sodas. Ruby napped.

In the evening we had a party with family. Our family showed up, which was special to us. My oldest sister drove in with her kids, which was a gift, a joy. Ruby wore a dark-green dress with embroidered flowers and a special birthday barrette. She was the center of attention all day. It was fun.

I would like Ruby's birthday to be longer. I didn't want to put her to bed because that meant her birthday would end. Cannot believe I debated capacity to celebrate this morning. A greater purpose of celebration I cannot imagine tonight.

Happy Birthday, Ruby Joy.

~

Inside the patient room, we wait for the doctor. He enters with a soft grin. He's an older gentleman with a kind demeanor. He introduces himself to us and to Ruby. I appreciate him interacting directly with her. He does an initial evaluation and then asks us about her medical history. He flips through papers as we share.

"She's gaining good weight," he remarks. He looks back at her chart and continues, "Tripled her birth weight in a year! That's remarkable! What are you feeding her?"

"Breast milk," I reply.

His eyes shoot up. "Exclusively?"

"Yes."

"So…you're pumping." He slowly puts two and two together knowing that she is fed exclusively through the NG Tube. I sit still and let him figure it out.

"You've been pumping for twelve months for her?"

I nod.

"You're a hero."

This catches me off guard, like a fly ball. I'm not accustomed to being anything but defensive in these environments. I give him a suspicious look.

"Well," he responds to my glance, "whatever you're doing is working, so good job!" I soften up. I think he's sincere. The thought of that makes me want to burst into tears, rather suddenly.

Mitch, Ruby and I are at the Genetics Clinic. This is the first time that we are seeing a geneticist since Ruby was born. Somehow, I have dodged the ball a thousand times, or more, until two weeks ago when Rhonda, Ruby's therapist, asked me if I had gotten her cholesterol checked recently.

"No."

"When was the last time you had it checked?"

"The NICU, birth."

Awkward pause. Ruby's condition is based on a cholesterol deficiency. Many would consider this paramount for medical attention.

"Why don't you want to get it checked?"

I pause and then honestly express, "Meeting that woman, our geneticist, is one of the most traumatic things that has ever happened to me. I cannot see her again." The thought of her puts her face before my eyes before I can blink.

"See someone else!" Rhonda responds quickly.

I hadn't even thought of that, twelve months later. I contemplate quietly.

"Katie, you're doing such a good job. Look at her! She's a chub! The cholesterol is just a number. Finding it out does not make or break her daily life. You may even get good news."

Okay, fine.

So, here we are.

"Do you guys have any questions?" The head of the Genetics Department looks me squarely in the eye as he addresses me. We are the "hard family" who fired their first geneticist, who happens to be another doctor on his team.

I ask him about Ruby's sacral dimple, about how I can wean Ruby off the breast milk and what I would feed her instead. I ask whether he would recommend that we draw her cholesterol level today. The doctor doesn't skip a beat. He doesn't even seem surprised by our accounts of reflux and vomiting. I experience a sense of relief talking with someone who has a grid for Ruby.

In time, he writes a slip for the lab to draw her cholesterol level today. She will have her blood drawn today, but it will need to be sent to another lab for results. This will take time. He seems impressed with how she is doing considering her condition. I wonder if a lot of my discouragement stems from comparison to normal, instead of comparison to prognosis, which Ruby is overcoming daily.

We are encouraged. The geneticist gives us his business card for any further questions, and we bid farewell.

And, just like that, it's all over. This appointment I have been avoiding and dreading for a year, comes and goes—painlessly. What a difference it makes to have a good doctor. All the difference.

A few days later, the phone rings. Ruby's cholesterol report is back. The number reads…99.

"What?!"

I shriek. Ask them to repeat it.

"Ninety-nine."

"This is such good news! Did you say 99?"

"Ninety-nine," a flat male voice repeats for the third time.

When I'm sure I've heard him correctly, a feeling of vibrant life erupts inside of me and I hang up the phone suddenly. I stand speechless for a half second and then skip around the house. I jump on top of the couch, fall back down, roll unto the floor, and then bury my head into the carpet to sob happy tears. *Ninety-nine, ninety-nine, ninety-nine.* I repeat the report to myself, again and again.

When Ruby was born her cholesterol was critically low at seventeen. We were told that one hundred is "normal," and we have been praying that number up for a year.

Ninety-nine?!? "Hello, miracle. Hello, hello, hello!" I shake my head in disbelief.

I am drunk in happy disbelief.

In time, 99 proves just to be a number. The chronic medical issues persist and Ruby remains sick.

⌒

I received an invitation to a neighborhood group for moms and babies, held across the street from our house. For days, I have been holding it over the trash, but I can't seem to throw it away. I want to connect with other moms. I want to feel a sense of normalcy in this new mom season. I want Ruby to be with other children. *But, what in the world would I say to people? How will Ruby and I relate? Can we relate? What will I do if Ruby starts vomiting there?*

Through the deliberation, I finally decide to go. I conclude that we have overcome worse things than social awkwardness. We can handle it. Maybe it will be good. Maybe. I dare to let hope lead me.

I can feel myself trembling as I leave the house. We are only going across the street, but I am so nervous. I decide to bring Ruby in her car seat, as she is unable to sit up on her own.

At the neighbor's front door, I stand still. I wonder if anyone has already seen us. *Is it too late to retreat?* I look down at Ruby. "We're here to try to make friends, Ruby; should we go inside?" She looks back at me, content to continue. I force my hand up and knock on the door. A nicely dressed woman with curled dark hair answers the door. She welcomes us inside.

For a brief moment, I feel glad to be here. I lay my cupcakes down on a table spread with treats and make an internal decision not to shy away from enjoying the food. We are one of the first to arrive. A pleasant conversation with the host lands us in the living room where we wait for more guests to find us.

People come in. Small talk happens. It pops around me like popcorn kernels breaking from their shells, but I can't seem to find anything of my own to share. My kernels don't seem to have any pop in them. They are stubborn and tight, transforming straight to charcoal instead of salty buttery sustenance. Simple questions like, "How old is your baby?" knock on doors I don't want to open right now. Apparently, crisis has killed my capacity for forming new connections.

Everyone gathers in the living room. We form a circle, to take turns sharing about ourselves and our babies. The other women talk about their experiences as new moms and I marvel at the things they call "challenges." Mental light bulbs illuminate as they share—revelation on how different our experience is from those around us.

I watch the babies crawling around, holding their heads, interacting with one another, and it's difficult for me. Ruby has made so much progress, but as our first child, we don't compare her to anyone; I hadn't realized how much she was not doing until I see the evidence running around in front of my face. It's sad.

Finally, it's my turn to share. *God, help me.*

I feel the curiosity of these women like laser lights all pointed at Ruby's feeding tube, her "special needs" features, her anomalies, her. I sit quietly, and consider sharing transparently. I decide against it. I choose to share nothing. "I am Katie. This is Ruby. We live across the street. Ruby was born at St. Mary's Hospital. She just turned one year old."

I look to the next person in the queue as though I'm handing off a baton. I maintain a smile and my internal dialogue speaks, *So sorry to rob you all of the entertainment of a dramatic story, but I'm done.*

Time passes, and Ruby and I seem to be shadows in the corner of the room. I wish I knew how to connect with people, make a friend, but it doesn't seem easy. I keep searching my brain for something relatable, but I come up empty. They are celebrating cloth diapers. I wonder if any of them knows what it feels like to celebrate your child coming off of oxygen.

Just when I feel the safety of invisibility, Ruby begins to reflux and then violently vomits. The whole room becomes quiet as six other mothers watch me handle an episode that is normal to me, frightening to them.

I tell them all she is okay.

They stare back at me.

Ruby cries in pain; she is hurting.

I tell them again: "She is okay."

I pack up Ruby's things. We are done. I walk out the door, cross the street, enter our house and barely make it up the steps, our things falling out of my hands.

We land. We sit. I cry.

"At least we tried," I commend Ruby through tears.

I let my tears fall, and then I speak to myself internally, an attempt at comfort. *At least we tried.* I believe in the value of trying. Trying expands territory, even when the try is a fail, even when it lands in tears. Really. It still expands territory every time you try. I pull Ruby out of her car seat. "Good job to us, Rubes, we tried."

Ruby and I sit for a long time and grieve the losses we share. We grieve that she could not crawl around with the other kids, that she got sick, that we didn't have a peppy baby story to tell, that we had to listen to people talk about "challenges" that reflect some of our best days. In time, I let my head drop down next to Ruby's and press my cheek against her face. I whisper into her ear, "You're my favorite baby, Ruby. I wouldn't trade you for anything. You're the baby I want. You're the best. I'm sorry today was hard."

I feel her press her head back into mine, and I know she is talking back to me through this gesture. It's as if she is saying right back to me, "You're my favorite mom. I wouldn't trade you for anything. You're the mom I want. You're the best. I'm sorry today was hard."

I receive it deeply.

We comfort each other.

Like only the best of friends can do.

~

Not long after our venture to the new-moms group, I decide to take Ruby out for a walk in the stroller. We walk to the small grocery store on the other side of our neighborhood. I've become somewhat of an expert at packing things into the little basket below the stroller.

Outside, I pull the top over Ruby's head to shield her from the sun. If I'm honest, I'm also shielding her from people. People ask difficult questions when they see her feeding tube. The forthrightness of strangers never ceases to amaze me. We take the side streets to avoid too much interaction. I take time to drink in the fresh air. Once again, it is a relief to be outdoors. Ruby seems to enjoy it too.

Around a corner we near the neighborhood playground. I watch from a distance as the moms and infants interact with each other there. Ruby's not holding her head, so there's nothing at the playground that she can do. *I could go join them, just to try talking with them, but I'm not up for "trying" today.* We circle the playground and continue to the grocery story.

Inside the store I tense up with hope that Ruby will not start refluxing while we are there. I rush through the aisles and pick up the things we need most to try to beat any episode she may have. In the checkout line, I am unable to avoid people.

The questions begin from the lady in front of me: "How old is your baby?" People have a hard time believing Ruby's age when I tell them, as she is so small.

"Thirteen months."

"What is wrong with her?" My heart sinks. I hate this question. It's the question I get most about her.

"She has a feeding tube."

"Oh, so it's not oxygen?"

The woman continues to pry with questions that frame Ruby as a problem. *I know she's curious, but doesn't she realize her questions are rude? What if Ruby is not a problem first and foremost, but a person to be seen?*

That woman finally checks out, and I am relieved.

Behind me is another woman, younger, who I can feel edging toward me to talk. I roll my eyes without turning around and stare at the conveyer belt of groceries. I then wait for the inevitable sting of her curiosity.

She leans forward and says to me, "You're baby is so cute."

I turn around quickly. "What did you say?"

"She's adorable! She—is—adorable."

The woman then steps back into her spot in line to assure me that she is done. That's all she has to say to us. I turn back around and continue to check out, impacted. Concealed tears drip down my face. I have never had a stranger celebrate Ruby like that.

All she had to say was "Adorable."

That night I am brought to 1 Samuel.

"Man looks at the outward appearance, but God looks at the heart."

In the streets of our neighborhood, Ruby and I have learned that man really does look at the outward appearance. For the hundreds of times we are asked, "What is wrong with her?" I realize that it makes me angry because people are defining Ruby by what they see without any sensitivity to what is within her story, within her history, within her.

People have no idea that this is a miracle child to be celebrated, a warrior princess beating all the odds. They don't know to whom they are talking when they ask their presumptuous questions.

I consider others with disabilities or physical anomalies. *How many interactions do they deal with that are centered around what people think is "wrong" with them, rather than who they are as a person?* This thought lands weighted in my soul. *Can I train my eyes to see past the outward appearance and into the heart? Can I learn how to celebrate people from the inside out?*

"Fix your eyes not on what is seen, but what is unseen. For what is seen is temporary, but what is unseen is eternal."

I suppose other moms are used to hearing that their baby is cute, or looks like them, or has a fun nose. But that's not my story. Today is the first time anything like that has happened to me in public. It was epic.

Adorable.

Pen to paper, I give accolades to the woman in the grocery store: "Kudos to the stranger in the grocery store who diagnosed Ruby correctly today with her decisive comment of 'Adorable.'" My tears resurface, and I continue writing directly: "I will never forget you. Your ability to see Ruby meant the world to me."

I then write to myself, and the whole wide world: "When it comes to relating to the disabled, learn to see the person. And, for God's sake, find something to talk with the person about besides the physical anomaly at which the world stares. There is a wealthy soul in there. *Wealthy.* Relate to the internal life of the person first, and that person will make you rich."

~

One thing that I desire greatly is to see a smile appear on Ruby's face. She's just over a year old, and we have yet to see one. It could be mental development, or muscle tone challenges in her face; we are not certain. The negative emotions have their expressions: crying, grimacing, aching, longing, suffering…but we don't get to see evidence of joy on her face.

Desire of my life: a smile from Ruby Joy.

I watch other parents. The pressures they endure with their infants dissipate in the face of their child's smile or laugh. Like a release valve, joy sucks the stress right out of their relationship. We don't have any such release valve with Ruby. No wonder we are overcome by sorrow. What else is there?

One smile. I long for it so much it makes me feel sick. *Could it be that she will never smile?* That thought is a dagger, best not to entertain it.

Almost a year without any sign of smiles feels like a lifetime.

It *is* a lifetime.

One thing I do know: I am not going to ask doctors if she will ever smile. I would rather wait and see. I wait. And I hope.

And then, one day, the moment comes.

"Katie! She's smiling! She's smiling! Come quick!"

Mitch puts his hand on Ruby's shoulder, and then begins to cause Ruby to smile more. She giggles, tumbles, into, sincere laughter.

I watch amazed at how quickly stress deflates in our house in light of Ruby's happy face. I wonder if this is how most moms make it through the hard parts of caring for a baby: ride the baby's joy. We drop everything and engage. *World, freeze. Ruby is smiling.*

I can feel my eyes glued to Ruby's face, trying hard to memorize quickly what her happy face looks like. I want that to be the face in my mind; I want that to override all the solemn, sad, pain-filled expressions that I often see. This happy expression is pent up most of the time, disabled, but in this face of joy I see the truest expression of who she is.

This is Ruby.

I don't know what started this joyfest today, but I do know that Mitch is playing a huge rule in keeping it going. From the belly, she is pausing, and then erupting, again and again. Mitch tickles. We wait. Ruby erupts in laughter.

A laughing Ruby turns our world right side up very quickly.

I grab the camera and get some shots of her smile.

She is finally laughing. Elated moments. Funny moments. Good moments. We laugh, laugh, laugh.

In the seconds between chuckles, I catch a deep sense of healing inside, perhaps the most healing seconds of this season to date. Laughter heals. I can feel the release of a thousand pounds of worry that she will never be able to do it. *Laugh, Ruby, laugh more!*

Ruby **Joy.**

Here she is—at last.

The joy spreads; we're now all in it.

Drinking deeply of the antidote to our pain.

Joy in the midst of it.

Chapter 13

Guests have arrived and they greet Ruby. She does not respond to them, at all. Her eyes stare unfixed; her facial expression remains blank. I know what it takes for Ruby to respond, and these people are missing the stimulation target epically. I wonder if our guests would mind some education.

I speak up. "You have to touch her. Saying hello from across the room is not going to work. Go over, touch her hand or her head; she'll respond."

We mingle, we chat, and we sit down for dinner.

Over dinner attempts are made again to interact with Ruby. Their attempts elicit no reaction; the whole table stares at her blank face. Individuals raise their voices. They try talking louder…and then louder. Soon there is near yelling happening in desperation to connect with Ruby. Respectfully, I remind them, "You have to touch her."

Mitch stands up from the table and walks over to Ruby's seat. Lifting her right arm he moves in close to her and whispers in her ear. "Ruby, someone is talking to you." She immediately responds to him. She reacts in multiple ways and there is a sense of relief at the table. We all exhale.

I ponder the experience. The difference in Ruby's response to Mitch is stark compared to her lack of responsiveness to our guests.

Mitch knew, like I did, that she needed to be touched. Talked to, yes, but also touched. To us it is absurd to think that talking louder to her will solicit a response. *But why? How do we know this?*

Over the next few days, I intentionally observe our interactions with Ruby. I find that we rarely, if ever, interact with her without physical touch involved. We don't do it intentionally, but apparently we have learned to speak her language: the language of touch.

Ruby's hearing is questionable, her eyesight limited, but her sense of touch is awake. I begin to marvel in observation at how Mitch and I can hold full conversations with Ruby through physical touch, not a spoken word.

The realization that we have a special form of communication with Ruby produces gratitude. I am so thankful that Ruby's sense of touch can be reached, radio signals on. *What if she could not feel? How in the world would we connect with her?* The acknowledgment of this inspires us to develop this form of communication further, with intention.

In the exploration I find that words, phrases, thoughts, and emotions can be communicated clearly through various forms of touch, and Ruby gets it. I find that once I repeat something a few times with the same intention, a pathway forms that can be revisited. It's like building road infrastructure for communication. Pavement is laid through repetition, which creates a defined and recognizable lane of access to say certain things through touch. I wonder if touch can be a full-scale language of its own? I wonder if we could develop a full language with Ruby?

I think it can be done. And if it can be done, we will do it.

～

I grab a fleece blanket and squeeze into a corner of our living room on the floor. I tuck the blanket under my knees, rest my back up against the wall, and sit. Ruby is in bed. Mitch is at a rehearsal. I could use sleep myself but need time to think.

Before Ruby was born I was succeeding in an international development agency. I traveled the world with a passion to change it. An advocate against modern-day slavery, I was teaching, training, carrying a heroic message from one nation to the next. Before that, I was writing and directing creative arts productions. Outpourings of grace wrapped in art.

Now? I don't know who I am, where I am, or what I am doing. But I do know that I am alone and no one is watching my life unfold. Who I once was seems very far away, swallowed up by a world I never anticipated entering.

I pull my knees into my chest and hold the tension there. White knuckles grip innocent knees as thoughts unravel.

Never in my wildest imagination did I think I would be here, administering medical care to my sick child. Never. What am I supposed to do when something happens that was never my desire? Something that would never be anyone's desire?

I stretch my legs out and cross them at the ankles. Here I am. I shake my head in disbelief. Memories come forward of dreams that I had as a kid.

Astronaut. I smile. Oh how I wanted to go to the moon! I wanted to go to space, see the earth from another view, and find something that no one knows exists. Then someone told me that going to the moon involves math. I changed my mind. I no longer wanted to go to the moon, at all.

Principal. I wanted to become a principal of a school. I didn't want to just teach. I wanted to be in charge of all the teachers and create a world inside of a world: an educational space laced with creativity and liberty. I pause. What does it matter? The point is that being a mom in my twenties with a sick baby was never in the line-up of my dreams. But here I am. A stay-at-home mom doing full-time medical care. Do I like it? Sometimes. And yet, I feel shocked by it. I feel like I have been put on a boat and sent far away from everything I knew about my life, myself. Lost at sea, lost in crisis. Uncertain if the land I come to will resemble the land that I left. Uncertain if I will see land again. Behind the curtain of shock, I sit on the floor of my living room and realize that life as I knew it is gone. I sigh and grab my journal from the end table nearby.

My dreams today:

One night without vomiting.

For Ruby to eat by mouth.

To trash this feeding tube once and for all.

To have a day off from medical care.

To get Ruby down to zero medications.

To learn how to love.

My dreams have changed.

$\sim$

I am at the toy store looking for a present for Ruby. Perusing the isles, I see a lot of toys. Toys that are useless to her developmentally. I imagine that all of this would be a lot of fun if she could push buttons, grasp things, hear sounds.

I stroll up and down the aisles. I land at an aisle of stuffed animals. This will do. I will pick something out for Ruby here. Something soft, something she can feel and appreciate through touch.

My eyes lift to the top shelf and peruse down. I see strange creatures; hard-headed, skinny-bodied, sequined toys with faces. Overdressed bears, dolls with plastic heads and hair, some other weird and creepy-eyed creatures. None of this will do.

I dig into the shelves. Don't they sell any sweet, soft, stuffed animals anymore?

I find nothing and continue walking down the isle.

Then I see it—thrown carelessly near the top shelf: a floppy gray kitten. My hand darts to it and I squeeze. Very soft, very fluffy. Pulling it down, it's tattered. The whiskers are bent out of shape, and its body is worn and flimsy. Maybe there's a newer one around? I search every nook and cranny of that aisle.

This gray kitten is one of a kind.

At last, I check the aisle for observers; finding none, I look into its plastic eyes and say, "You have weird whiskers, your body is floppy, you're tattered and worn. And I like you. You are coming home with me."

One beat-up gray stuffed kitten rides down the conveyer belt to check-out.

One tethered stuffed animal with dangly legs is on its way home, to Ruby.

At home I pull out the gray stuffed kitten and rub its soft fur all over Ruby's face. "Got you a present, Rubes!" I take its front paws and wrap them around her neck. "She's hugging you, Ruby; she likes you!" It's refreshing to see Ruby with a toy. A relevant toy is hard to come by.

I step back and see that the kitten is embracing Ruby's tiny body. She can't hold it, but it can hold her. I'm glad its flimsy body didn't deter me; it is just right for her.

Just right.

That night, I tuck Ruby into bed and nuzzle her new stuffed cat next to her side. A new friend for Ruby, rescued from the wildness of the toy store. I look at its tiny stuffed paw placed over Ruby's body and think to myself, *Sometimes we don't need something to hold; we just need something that can hold us.*

⁓

I can stand before physicians, spend the night in the ICU with peace, place a feeding tube at home, wrestle with insurance personnel…but I can't hold it together for a baby shower? *What is this?*

I kiss Ruby and Mitch good-bye and get into the car. My foot hits the gas with force. I'm tense. I don't want to go to this. I pull down the street and see pastel balloons rising from my destination. I park across the street and sit. Do I have to go in?

This is one of my closest friends; she's having a baby. Surely, I can pull it together to celebrate her. I force myself out of the car with the assurance that I can always leave early if I need. Gift in hand, I make it down the walkway to the door where bright faces greet me and show me inside.

Cupcakes.
Crazy straws.
Happy women.

Gifts.
Excitement.
Mommy talk.
Baby talk.
Pastel madness.

The house fills and we are instructed to sit down. One by one, we introduce ourselves, tell how we know the expectant mama, and share any advice we have. As I hear people sharing I squirm in my seat. I could tell her how to place a feeding tube, or how to love a child through the night when they're on oxygen. I could share about the balancing act of marriage in the midst of crisis, or the value of faith in the midst of disease.

But organic diapers? Baby bullets? Scheduling?

It's my turn. I share that I know the mom through church, and then I start to cry. Here, at a baby shower, where you would think my acquired courage of the season would conquer, it runs away, and I break down. I try to say something of value through my tears, but it's awkward because I'm not happy, I'm sad, and that is crystal clear to everyone in the room. I pause. The other women let me pause. Some know my story.

I look at the mom adorned in gifts and remember what it felt like to be in that seat. There was nothing but the pure expectation of good. At my baby shower, we celebrated boldly what would be. But... it turned out that none of us knew what would be. What happened to Ruby and me was a shock to everyone who knew us. Half the things I got at my shower are irrelevant because of Ruby's condition. No one knew what was coming. *No one.*

I sigh and realize the people are still waiting on me to finish. I dare not share any of *that*; it would be quite unfair. Instead, I lean forward and with all sincerity say simply, "Treasure every moment." I then wipe my tears and hand it off to the next person.

The circle of people sharing continues. I listen to other moms share their stories and advice. I wish that Ruby and I could share some of the experiences they describe. Most of these things have become fantasy to us as we wrestle with disease.

The circle breaks up. I see my opportunity to leave.

In the car I grieve. I grieve that I am not able to nurse my baby. I grieve that her schedule is largely determined by vomiting. I grieve that she will likely be in diapers for years. I grieve that we are not able to communicate through standard means. I grieve that Ruby and I have suffered instead of played.

I almost wish I had not gone. It is easier not to know the extent of the loss we have. Those women have so many things that we don't have.

A quiet internal voice responds to my thought: *And you and Ruby have so many things that they don't have.*

I pause.

I can't see it in the moment, but it feels like truth speaking.

Perhaps someday I will see it.

∼

We have one small window in our bedroom. It faces the street. The tree out front grows up into it. I consider the branches outside my window my personal property, messengers in their own right. They have become my view, my morning dew.

I have watched this tree closely from my third-floor view. The lifeblood of this plant has been working, pressing newness out of its tips. Barren for months, seemingly dead, buds have finally appeared —green buttons on the end of dead sticks.

I step toward the window and lean forward to get the best peripheral view. This is my morning news intake. What report has the tree for me today?

There, on the right, is the first bloom of spring. The sight of it pulls noise out of me. A happy, high, and loud squeal comes out of my mouth…and wakes Ruby up. *Oops.*

"It's spring time, Sweetie."

She rubs her tired eyes.

"I'll show you." I kiss her forehead.

After our morning routine, I dress Ruby to take her outdoors. On the streets of the neighborhood, we find blooms. One here, one there. They're coming. The ground was not so dead after all. It just needed time.

As we walk, I notice Ruby sneezes. The sneeze turns to wheezing. Congestion is appearing. By the time we get home she is sick. This is weird to me. Unfamiliar with it, it takes me awhile to realize… *allergies.*

Oh no, not spring!

But I love spring!

But not *spring*!

I resist what I love.

What I need.

What I've always celebrated complicates her disease.

What a hard thing.

I want Ruby to be able to sniff blooms and laugh. Instead, they make it hard for her to breathe. Over the next two weeks, I sadly resolve that we will have to watch spring mostly from the window, escaping to the outdoors now and again with dreadful consequence.

～

We are standing in the check-in line at the airport, nervous. I have no idea how Ruby will do on an airplane. Honestly, I feel afraid they won't let us on when they see her tube. Boarding passes are given. We roll our bags while holding our breath. We find our gate. It's for a flight out of D.C.

Just like that, we have decided to fly to Georgia for a week to visit a healing ministry. The ministry is purposed to create a place of respite for people in need. We didn't ask Ruby's doctors if she could fly, because we didn't want to hear no. There are some things you don't ask; you just do. The way I see it is, if there is breath, that breath is permission enough to live *fully*.

This is Ruby's first flight. I decided that it was important for her to get out of the region at some point. Living demands liberty for adventure. I felt great about it until we got to the airport. Now, I'm trembling. I am so nervous.

I have read and re-read what to do for babies on airplanes. I am ready with my chewing, swallowing and feeding strategies for ascent and descent. And yet…I have a re-occurring thought: *What am I going to do if she just screams?*

I turn to Mitch. "Do you think this is a good idea?" Practicality looks back at me. I smear a smile on my face. I know, I'm posing the question a little late.

We will take the risk.

On the plane, I see Mitch bouncing Ruby on his knee so fast it makes me dizzy. He's as nervous as I am. We are *so* nervous. There is nothing to say; we will have to wait and see what happens.

Here goes.

Engine starts.

Plane rolls down the runway.

And we're off.

In the air, I'm panicking trying to get Ruby to suck and swallow. It takes me a few minutes to calm down and realize—she is fine. I pull the stuff out of her mouth and tilt my head to examine her face. She's looking at me like I'm crazy and I realize…I am acting crazy. She is fine.

Ten minutes into the flight, and we let out a sigh of relief. Ruby has not reacted to take-off at all. As a matter of fact, she is doing better than we are. *Oh, thank God. Ruby is able to fly.* We soar over a few states and descend into a new land. *Georgia.*

Sunshine.

Friendly faces.

Uncharted territory.

We choose a bright-red rental car in Ruby's honor. The car seat is sorted. Papers signed. And we're off. Windy roads and green forests turn into small towns with scattered residencies. It's a different world. Our bright-red car sticks out like a sore thumb and we decide to accept it.

We chose to fly with Ruby.

We chose to rent a bright-red car.

We chose to visit a ministry for a week.

And we will own those choices. Wide-eyed, I think, *I cannot believe we are doing this.* Satisfied, I declare, *We are so doing this. Hello, Georgia!*

Some things are only experienced on the other side of risk, like a land full of peaches.

∽

There is a beautiful community pool down the road from our hotel. The water is crystal clear, revealing a bright-blue base. The sun beats strong and causes the ripples to dance their jitterbug. We decide to take Ruby swimming, another first for her.

Ruby in a polka-dotted bathing suit is a happy sight.

We pull the car up to the pool, and I exit first to swing open the side door and take Ruby out.

"Are you sure this is okay?" Mitch asks.

"As far as I can tell, if we keep her NG tube above the water she'll be fine."

Mitch seems unconvinced.

"It's worth finding out," I add with a smile.

Ruby seems to sense the nervousness and tenses up. I try to divert her anxiety. "We're going swimming! It's going to be so much fun!" Children are dangerously perceptive. I comfort myself with my remark, but that's about it. Mitch and Ruby both look at me with unfiltered, concerned gazes.

Mitch gets into the pool first, and I hand Ruby to him. He slowly lowers her into the water and her eyes increasingly widen as he does. We're watching a first. She's never been immersed in water before. We bathe her with sponge baths because of the tube and inability to sit up. Ruby whimpers as the cold water rises up her small body.

Mitch shoots me a glance. I raise my finger, *Just wait.* He waits a few seconds; she whimpers more. He shoots me another glance; I shake my head no and raise my finger again, *Wait.* This time I add a fierce look. *Wait.* He complies. Holds her body under the water, waits. And then…she adjusts.

Ruby adjusts to the water temperature and looks around in wonder. You would think we just lowered her into a whole new world. For one whose primary input comes through the sense of touch, I suppose it is that—a whole new sensory world.

Mitch holds Ruby under her arms and begins to move her gently around the pool to give her the sensation of floating. She seems to really like it!

After some time, I want to try. We switch. I hold Ruby on my hip and lower us both into the water with our heads and shoulders extending just above the water in the sunshine. We wade through the pool together. Playing with Ruby in the water, I think about how rare it is to find recreation that Ruby can enjoy. This is a prize.

The pool becomes like a basket of rare gifts and we rummage through it with eagerness to explore: swimming, floating, splashing, wading, dunking, chatting, laughing. I find the pool to be a sensory playground for our little girl who lives on sensory input. *At last, we found a playground for Ruby!*

It's a memorable afternoon in a hot pool in Georgia.

Wet bodies.

Sun-kissed noses.

Happy hearts.

Hidden far from home, we play.

Chapter 14

I wake up sharply out of a dream. *Ruby!* I jump out of bed. She is lying still, tube connected, body frail. It was a dream. I had another dream that Ruby was healed. In the dream I saw her rolling, pushing up, sitting up, standing up—and then walking. It was so real my heart is still racing. *Promise.* I cling to promise.

Ruby and I have been spending hours every day in worship and prayer. I have a 24/7 prayer room streaming live in the house almost all the time. Encouragement shoots off of the screen as we press our faces with those across the airwaves into the thin glass between heaven and Earth. We hope that Ruby will be healed any day now. As Mitch sings so often over Ruby, "May the best thing that could happen, happen—for Ruby."

I take a step back from Ruby's bedside and shut my eyes. Oh, how I wish today's revelation was more than a dream.

Someday.

Later that afternoon on the live-stream, the worship leader sings out, "I am the richest man in the world because I have your Word." It strikes me. Low on money, low on opportunity, low on community, but rich in His Word. *Man does not live on bread alone, but on every Word that proceeds from the mouth of God.* Proceeds—present tense. What God is saying to us, today, is our food, our sustenance, our life.

It may be a dream in the night, an age-old promise inked inside an old Bible, an inspired journal entry, a testimony flying across the airwaves of a live-stream, but it is all His Word. His Word is the gas in my tank; it's what keeps me going, keeps us hoping.

I take any encouraging word about Ruby's healing and gobble it up like food to the starving. A word, a promise, a testimony, a hopeful thought. I take it and digest it thoroughly.

My dream: *healed.*

I guard it tightly—the insight deep and the imagery profound.

I am the richest woman in the world, because I have Your Word.

$$\backsim$$

I hear the sound of footsteps slowly approaching our door. I race around the house in an attempt to perfect everything. Race, move, throw, toss, scurry—the doorknob twists and he's home.

This is a familiar scene. I hear Mitch slowly climbing to our third-floor apartment after a long day of work and race around the house too eager to see him. Interacting with Ruby all day leaves me craving adult interaction, and I tend to explode on him upon his arrival.

That's my routine. He has a routine of his own.

From the door, he calls, "Ruby! I'm home!" She sits still, just a few feet behind his bellowing voice with no sign of hearing him. I wait, watch, hope and then retreat. He moves closer and calls again, "Ruby! I'm home!" I watch her dull gaze stare straight ahead, and my heart breaks. Not even a blink, nothing. For all the children who go running to their dad when he gets home, our child shows no sign of knowing that someone just came into the house, let alone that Dad is home.

Day after day Mitch pursues Ruby in this way and eagerly waits for a response. Ruby sits unmoved, unresponsive.

This goes on for months, steady efforts to stimulate Ruby's hearing after that audiology report that we received and trashed. Sometimes I wish Mitch would quit trying. His efforts are sad to watch. I don't know if Ruby recognizes us. I don't know if we are any different to her than any other person. These bouts of trials feel like unhappy news reports. But Mitch refuses to quit. With unwavering hope, he continues in hopes that one day the same thing will produce a different result. It's the age-old definition of insanity in action.

And then one day, something happens.

Door knob twists, and he's home.

"Ruby! I'm home!"

Ruby's head turns around, and she lets out a noise. I freeze. Mitch freezes. *Did we just see her respond to his voice?* Mitch motions me to stand completely still, and he does the same. *Yes, factor out any physical stimulation, and try again.*

"Ruby! I'm home!" Ruby clearly turns her head looking around for the source of the sound. We are witnessing a miracle.

"Ruby!"

She turns and lets out a response.

And then, with no self-control at all, Mitch rushes to her with an embrace, and joy spreads across her face.

She can hear!

Over the next few weeks, we watch Ruby's responses to Mitch steadily increase. Mitch calls and Ruby answers. In time, she anticipates his coming and starts laughing and smiling before he even gets to her. Very slowly, she comes to life with smiling, laughing, little games and the ability to recognize our voices.

In this way, Ruby learns how to interact in response to sound.

I often wonder, *What if Mitch had not persisted? What if we had treated her as if she were deaf and forfeited this part of her life? What if we had no faith she would ever recognize or respond to us? What if we had not explored the limitation she was given?*

There is something powerful about belief.

It is not insanity; it is faith. Faith breeds miracles.

I salute Mitch. *Here's to a dad who was not afraid to talk to his daughter when she was labeled medically deaf. Here's to a dad who expected a response from her when he was told she could not respond. Here's to a dad who broke the sound barrier in his little girl's life and woke her up to a life of interaction that no one knew she could have.*

Here's to a love that refuses to take no for an answer.

Here's to the power of love.

∾

It was a long hard night. I hardly slept. It's 8:30 AM and Mitch is telling me to go to church. "Go. You need to get out." Church? Really?

I stand before the mirror on the back of our bedroom door, look down at my tattered clothes and then glance up at my matted hair. I feel like I haven't left my bedroom for months. I don't remember how to get dressed for church. I change my T-shirt and leave it at that.

Two strangers with plastered smiles greet me at the church door. They have no idea.

In the foyer, I stick out like a sore thumb. Hurting, alone and unknown, I slip into the sanctuary and find a seat. Worship happens over me: blasted music, dark space, spotlights, noise. I realize that my worship experience has changed the last few months. I am quiet when I worship alone at home, pouring my heart out before God. I'm not sure how to engage this. I don't know what this is.

From across the room, I see a few familiar faces. I hope not to be seen. I have no response for their inevitable questions. *How are you? How is Ruby?* People are praying and waiting for a good report. I don't have a good report, so I avoid them.

I sit in the dark with strangers and endure a message about faith: believe more, trust more, and surrender more. "Then…you will get your miracle." I stop listening. I must. This message is feeding my sense of guilt for Ruby's suffering. I fear these words are irrelevant to those who suffer. Constructed from an understanding of pain, they would have found a different delivery. Surely.

Holding back tears, I decide to slip out before the service ends. I've come to church and learned that I need to believe harder, do more. *Thank you?* On my way out, an old friend hands me a note and some cash. "For a haircut," it reads. I'm not sure how to take it. I don't care that my hair is a mess. I dart to my car and five minutes later am back home.

"How was church?"

Tears.

Mitch and I grieve that my much-needed outing added to my sorrow. Or maybe it just highlighted the sorrow I already had. On the back pew of rosy Christianity, I am a sorrowful mess. I don't want to reappear on that scene in this state again. I'm in a state of mourning. Jesus said that those who mourn would be "blessed." *Where is that message from the pulpit?* I find myself alienated in this community. Left out. When the church builds a room to sit and cry before Jesus, I will be happy to go. Until then, it is not a safe place for me. There's no room to grieve.

I look at the $40. I look at the note. "For a haircut." *What do I do with this?*

It feels wrong to spend time getting pampered while Ruby suffers. She has to wear medical tape on her face every day because of the feeding tube. I would rather get medical tape on my face than a makeover.

I want to remain with her.

I have not worn make-up since before Ruby was born. I have not had a haircut since before Ruby was born. I have not been consistent about anything that takes time for my appearance since before Ruby was born. I cannot remember the last time I used lotion. Soap and water are just fine. Ruby suffers; I suffer with her. It's not intentional; its just action out of reaction, reaction out of care.

Okay, I need a haircut. Okay, it would feel good to get some new clothes. Okay, I can understand how it would be refreshing for Mitch if I took care of myself. Okay, I can see that this is not entirely healthy. But personal upkeep feels out of reach. Too far out of reach.

My apologies, world, but I cannot figure out how to get this sackcloth off.

The $40 goes toward groceries.

～

Uptown Manhattan. Forget the stroller. I throw Ruby up over my shoulder. We make a beeline through street vendors, honking cabs and flocks of people to get to the riverside. Candied almonds have never smelled so good. Other smells float out of the gutters, smells that are not so kind. We land at the riverside.

"This is the city, Ruby. Do you like it?"

She looks back at me with a panicked gaze. I smile and hold her close.

"It's called New – York – City. It's a crazy place. Crazy, crazy, crazy…some people think that this place is the top of the world. Some people love this place so much that they spend their whole lives in this populated mess—can you imagine?" Ruby nestles into me. I lean into her and whisper, "There is beauty here if you choose to see."

Among the people who choose to live here is my sister Audrey. She is in grad school and has a tiny apartment on the West Side. My family piled into her home yesterday to celebrate her birthday—and listen to cars play musical horns.

Ruby and I find a bench by the river. Everywhere I look there are people, and where there are not people there are cars, and where there are not cars there are buildings. The buildings behind us are so close together you would think they crashed into each other and then got stuck. The people walk in droves, shoulder to shoulder, and rarely greet each other.

It's a mass existence in a small space.

Sunk into this space for a day, I realize something powerful: we are not the center of the universe. We are not. There are a lot of people in this world, a lot of people in this city, a lot of people in existence. These people are living their lives, navigating challenges, and dealing with losses, just like us.

Here in New York City, with Ruby over my shoulder and crowds of people walking around us, I come to a liberating conclusion: we are not sole rangers on this planet, and our crisis is not enormous. In fact, it is small.

My internal horizon stretches with this noisy skyline, view lifts.

I feel small here, and that feels right.

No longer the center of the universe, I gain perspective.

Thanks, NYC.

Chapter 15

This is Ruby's first visit to Orthopedics. An X-ray is done of her spine and she is diagnosed with severe scoliosis. The doctor is called in to consult with us about treatment. She shoots the diagnosis and treatment options to us like an archer aiming at a dartboard. We feel the hits.

"You need to have her body casted," she says without emotion.

"What does that mean?" I ask.

The doctor goes on to describe that they would put Ruby under general anesthesia and into a full body cast to force her spine straight. Every few weeks the cast would need to be replaced, and every time she would have to go under general anesthesia. "It's uncomfortable for quality of life, but it will straighten her spine."

Uncomfortable? I suspect that is a terrible understatement of this process.

Mitch and I throw each other a despairing look. Ruby has not been under general anesthesia since she nearly lost her life during it for the eye surgery. This treatment would require her to be under anesthesia regularly. In addition, Ruby aspirates, vomits and has trouble breathing on a regular basis. There's no way we can put her in a full body cast without further restricting her breathing, which will have severe consequences.

"What other options do we have?" My question hurls out with clear desperation.

"Your other option is to do nothing, in which case she will likely soon reach respiratory distress from her spine closing in on her major organs. It is unlikely that she would survive that."

I look at the lady in total shock. *Is she seriously talking to us as if Ruby were a piece of plastic?*

The doctor looks at me as if she's waiting for something. "Any questions?"

I can't think of anything, darn muddled brain. But I'm unwilling to let the doctor go; she's supposed to help us. I ask her to tell us our options again. Bad idea. Her darts come again, just as piercing as the first time.

"Body cast your daughter, or let her die" is what I'm hearing.

This is the most unemotional doctor I have ever encountered. Bone specialist, go figure.

She asks us to make a decision right there, as she is clearly pressed for time. Mitch, in his wisdom, refuses to make the decision on the spot. We are reluctantly dismissed to consider the cast and call back with an answer.

We arrive home in complete distress.

Later that day, I sit on a bench in the woods, my heart heavy with concern over pending medical decisions. *I cannot bring myself to body cast Ruby. That would be such a severe treatment, a terrible restriction to her life. There has to be another way.* In front of me, there is a broad tree. I let my eyes follow the trunk up and am somehow comforted by it's stability. This tree is settled, secure, rooted.

I hear God's voice, soft, internal, clear: "Climb up into My stability. Take My hand." The words of an old hymn come to mind and I willingly fall into them. Line by line, its lyrics give voice to my heart's cry.

Precious Lord, take my hand,

Lead me on, let me stand.

I'm tired, I'm weak, I'm lone.
Through the storm, through the night,
Lead me on to the light.
Take my hand, precious Lord, lead me home.

～

Sitting on the floor across from Ruby's physical therapist, Elizabeth, I relay the report we received from the orthopedic doctor. "There's got to be another option," I think out loud. "I cannot bring myself to body cast Ruby."

Elizabeth looks up at me and nods her head in agreement. "Have you thought about getting a second opinion?"

Second opinion? "No, I haven't. The doctor we saw is the head of the department." We have not pursued any care outside of the network of our local Children's Hospital.

"You know, there are other spine specialists within driving distance whom you could go see."

"There are?"

"Sure!" She names off a few.

"Who would you recommend?" I ask.

"Call Children's Hospital of Philadelphia. Tell them you want a second opinion."

"Are we allowed to do that?"

"Of course. It's a drive, but it may prove worth it."

I thank her sincerely. This could be an alternative way forward, and we need one badly.

I dare to hope.

A week later, I step into Children's Hospital of Philadelphia. The words "Hope Lives Here" is plastered on the walls. The environment feels different than what we are used to, in the best way possible. Perhaps their slogan is more than a slogan; perhaps hope really does live here.

We sit down in the waiting room with an expectation to wait, as we always do in D.C. Instead, we are called into the patient room within fifteen minutes. I realize that driving to Philadelphia to see a specialist here takes less time than driving a few miles into D.C. where we sit in the waiting room for hours.

In the patient room, the doctor pulls up Ruby's X-ray, which was sent ahead to him. He knows that we are here for a second opinion. I relay the report that was given to us and the options to either body cast her or let the spine curve. I explain why I do not feel safe putting Ruby in a body cast.

"Are there any other options?" My heart pounds with hope for something.

"Did they talk to you about the potential of a brace?"

"No…what's a brace?"

The doctor describes the possibility of a removable brace that would be designed specifically and carefully for Ruby's body to gently push her spine back into a straight position. It would also serve to hold her body upright, which would slow the scoliosis.

A brace. This sounds much more doable.

"The brace does not have as high a correction rate as body casting, but it still can help. In my opinion, a brace is a much better option for Ruby."

The conversation continues and it doesn't take long for Mitch and me to realize we are on board with this idea. It's a gentler approach to spinal correction, and that's exactly what Ruby needs given her other challenges. I am astounded that bracing was not even mentioned to us by the other doctor who is a renowned specialist in this field.

Second opinion. Life saver.

We find an orthotist group that will make Ruby's brace. The only problem is they are out-of-network. I sink back into my chair after the phone call. Now what? It's going to cost over $2,000, which we don't have. I pick up the phone and call them back.

"Is there any way that people who are out-of-network have successfully gotten braces paid for by insurance? Any advice of something I could at least try?"

"You'll have to talk to your insurance company."

Next phone call. I weed myself through a torrential downpour of computerized voices and finally get on the line with a person.

"Is there any way that we can get insurance to pay for something that is out-of-network?"

"You will have to file for an out-of-network appeal."

"What does that mean?"

"It means that if you can prove that no one in-network can provide the service you need, you can potentially get it covered by someone out-of-network."

"And how would I prove that?"

"Call every single provider in network and ask them if they can make the brace you need. If they can't, write a letter stating your case to insurance."

I sigh. Sounds like a long process and most definitely a tedious one.

"Okay." I hang up.

I begin my research. On the site of the orthotist that we want to use, I notice that he uses a special technique called "Rigo Chêneau." Perhaps this is something that would distinguish him. I call Ruby's doctor. "Would you be willing to indicate on Ruby's prescription that she needs a Rigo Chêneau brace?" I explain the situation and that this orthotist comes highly recommended for cases like hers.

The doctor is willing. The revised prescription is sent to me.

I then sit down at the living room table and pull up a long list of phone numbers that are all listed as in-network providers for orthotics in our region. I am going to call them, one by one, and ask if they can make a Rigo Chêneau brace. If they can't, this will prove our need for an out-of-network provider.

"Do you all make a Rigo Chêneau brace?"

"No, but we do make…"

I let them talk, thank them and then hang up. Next.

"Do you all make a Rigo Chêneau brace?"

"No, why would you need that?"

I say something that means nothing and hang up. Next call.

This continues. About ten calls into it, I start to feel hope. I think this might work. Over the next hour, I call every single orthotics option in our in-network directory. During the last call, I wait for the last no, and when it comes I hang up the phone with a wide grin. *Success.*

I write a letter to the insurance company stating our case for coverage from the out-of-network provider. Two weeks later, we receive a response that coverage has been approved. Ruby's brace will be fully paid for by insurance.

Thank You, God!

~

We drive up to a small office building in the center of an industrial zone. I wonder if we are in the right place. I look around and then see the office name on a sign above a small space. I have come to appreciate small medical offices. I find them less intimidating than the expansive hospital outpatient clinics.

Inside, I sign in and sit down. Ruby and I take a seat in the waiting room together. There is something peaceful about this place.

A mom and little girl enter the room. They check in. The mom is wearing worry. She sits down across from me. I ask questions. She unloads. Her daughter is three years old and was just diagnosed with scoliosis. She starts asking me a ton of questions about scoliosis. I answer her strategically, working to diminish her fear. Quietly, I wonder what it would be like if Ruby only had one diagnosis. This little girl runs around the room otherwise perfectly healthy.

Ruby and I are called back. The orthotist joins us. He introduces himself and takes a few minutes to hear from us. He is a kind man with a holistic approach to medicine. He asks me questions to make sure that his work will not interfere negatively with other things Ruby has going on. I appreciate that he sees his specific role as one part of her complex care. That is the reality, but few specialists recognize it. He then tells me about the brace he will create and how it will work. I see artistry in his eyes as he talks about the process.

Before long, we move to another room where a clay mold is formed around Ruby's body. The orthotist works fast. I watch his hands pressing the clay in certain spots. *He is an artist. A medical artist.* He continues with focus to form something that will support Ruby's body and fit her just right. I am moved internally to see someone applying their skill so intently to support Ruby's needs. Some call him an orthotist; I would call him a craftsman.

The craftsman allows me to choose a pattern for the hard shell of the brace. I choose purple butterflies to signify the freedom that I believe is coming for Ruby.

Ruby and I check out. Later, I tell Mitch about the office and how it seemed wrapped in kindness. We are grateful for this seemingly miraculous solution, this escape from body casting.

Two weeks later, Ruby's brace is ready and we are called back to Orthotic Solutions. The craftsman shows us his work. The outside shell of the brace is patterned with the purple butterflies that I picked out. The inside is made of foam pieces that are placed strategically to put pressure on her positioning. There is a hole in the front and on the side to give space for breathing and stomach changes due to digestion. There is a Velcro strap to tighten or loosen the brace.

The craftsman puts the brace on Ruby, and it looks like a perfect fit. Shirt on top, you hardly notice it, spare the bulging belly foam. He then begins to evaluate closely and redesigns some of the interior foam to press specifically on certain spots. The goal is to slowly push her spine back to straight by applying steady pressure, but not too quickly.

He instructs me to keep my eye on her skin and rib cage to make sure she is not bruising from the pressure and adjust accordingly.

Back at home, the brace is on. It is slowly pushing Ruby's spine. I don't know why, but she is vomiting much more with the brace on. Day two and we are catching vomit every other hour. I call the orthotist's office. They say something about an "adjustment period."

I hope this is just an adjustment period.

A few days later, Ruby seems to adjust to the brace. I don't understand how this gentle pressure on the spine can cause her body to go into an uproar, but I'm learning that the spine is much more central to the body than I knew.

The bracing treatment becomes an art of its own: it needs to be on long enough each day for effective pressure, but not too long that her muscles atrophy altogether.

We work hard to reach the correct balance with cycles of trial and error, all systems of the body seemingly affected.

In time, we find a rhythm.

The craftsman remains in our life for some time. I learn that he loves Jesus, and it doesn't surprise me. I find him to be a carpenter of his own kind. His merged artistry and medical brilliance prove invaluable. Undoubtedly, this man is an unsung hero to many, the movement of his hands forcing necessary solutions.

For certain, he is a hero in our story, but he is not unsung.

We sing his praises, often.

Chapter 16

I am walking in the forest today. The trees have dropped their leaves and the ground is covered in layers of things past. The sound of crackling leaves beneath my feet is noisy, music of its own kind. I don't realize I am the one making all the noise until I stop to evaluate what's beneath me. When I stop, the noise stops, and I see.

A pile of leaves.

In it, I catch a glimpse of my own process.

There are a lot of things that have died in my life in the last year and a half. Many things have fallen to the ground despite my expectations that they could not die. I have watched unfulfilled promises, deferred hopes and dangling injustices come to a sad end instead of moving into the powerful resurrection I expected. Things have gone missing, been stolen, run out of steam, and died.

Leaves have dropped all over my life, lifeless, to the ground.

The scene feels familiar. I feel like I have been standing in a pile of dead leaves now for some time; staring, waiting, watching, aching, and hoping that some violent and supernatural wind will blow and revive them all. I'm expecting these leaves to come back to life and somehow be replaced on the branch from which they fell.

The process of nature confronts my expectations.

These dead leaves are dead.

They will not live again in their former state. Instead, they will become the nutrients in the ground that enable a brand-new life to emerge in the surrounding trees. In time, a new bud will form at the top of even the highest tree. It will be, in every way, connected to what died and yet emerge as its own new thing.

I kick some of the leaves beneath my feet and realize that as long as I am focused on the rubble of what was, I will entirely miss the new life that will bud in the branches above. I am looking in the wrong place for resurrection. I need to look up. But that feels hard. It involves letting go of my job as watchman over my own losses. It involves a willingness first to look away from what feels validated only by my unadulterated gaze.

I pause at this internal crossroads, still standing on a pile of dry leaves. If I don't keep my eye on the vindication I deserve, who will? If I don't demand justice, will it ever come? If I don't wait for these things to live again, will anyone else care to contend for their voice?

A cold breeze blows and I realize that winter is coming. I am going into the ground, eyes focused either downward or upward, and I cannot blame anyone apart from myself for what I choose.

I choose to let go.

In this release, my job description in life simplifies beautifully and I wish I had found that pile of leaves sooner. Carrying around the responsibility for my own justice and miracle is exhausting. There is a God who is better at justice, vindication and resurrection than I am. I choose to give Him these roles in my life.

I feel the weight lift.

My vindication is with my God.

~

Last night, Mitch and I rediscovered intimacy with each other for the first time in a while. Neither of us realized how long it had been. Survival mode is picky. It picks up a handful of things and presses the rest to the sideline in wait of better days. The problem is that better days do not always come quickly. In our case, the better days have not yet come. An extended experience of survival mode can kill precious things without any announcement, without any warning.

It's a scary reality, the silent losses of a life under pressure.

I note the revelation and construct some advice to myself: *When better days don't come for months, it's important to reconstruct the survival mode you're living with to include what is important to you. Go rummaging through those sidelines of life to find out what is there that you are not willing to abdicate to crisis. Pull it out, and make room for it. Don't delay.*

For us, physical intimacy is one of those things. It was one of the first things to go when we hit a crisis, and reasonably so. Physical exhaustion and emotional depletion provide ample excuse to not go there. I wonder, however, if the real hesitance is about unprocessed emotional pain. Laid bare, we both have to face each other, and be faced by each other.

Intimacy uncovered.

We arise from the time renewed.

Physical intimacy strengthens our connection.

A strengthened relational bond simplifies everything.

It's high time to take a sledgehammer to our priority list and place this item closer to the top. It's worth uncovering.

$\sim$

The biggest day-to-day challenge with Ruby's health is reflux and vomiting. We are working hard to help her get nutrition and keep it down. Despite exhaustive efforts, she is not gaining weight or feeding successfully. As a mother who feels responsible for feeding, this feels like a personal failure to me.

I am transitioning her from breast milk, but the process has been a bit of a nightmare. I cannot pump any longer. Fourteen months of pumping is enough. I have nothing left to give. Nothing. I have spent so much time behind this machine, I cannot do it any longer. Cannot.

We are introducing formula slowly. It smells very bad. The ingredients make my head spin. *Yuck.* We are mixing it carefully for a slow introduction. Not slowly enough, apparently. The vomiting has gotten worse.

The GI team prescribes one reflux medication after another. Sometimes the medication they give her makes the vomiting worse. Sometimes she is allergic to it. Sometimes it helps, but not much. Their other tactic is to keep increasing her calorie intake with hope for growth. They prescribe increasing quantities of formula or more density per ounces of water. She does not tolerate this well at all.

You cannot force-feed a child, even through a tube.

Mitch and I know from being with Ruby day in and day out that none of the medical prescriptions are working. She is losing weight quickly. She is dangerously thin, and we need a solution.

My conviction is that dead ends are not dead ends until God says so. There has got to be a way forward for Ruby's feeding. I venture out and decide to do my own research.

In my research, I find something that ignites hope. I find something called "A Blended Food Diet." A Blended Food Diet puts real food into powerful blenders to support people who have a feeding tube. I research it and find that this real-food approach has improved the health of tube-fed children and adults. The data does not surprise me. After all, it's real food!

These days, I cringe when putting baby formula, with 54 percent corn syrup, down Ruby's tube. What if another formula is not going to fix this? What if my little girl really could eat real food? What if tube-fed children can eat real food? Is there a way?

Over the next few months, I spend myself studying nutrition, blended-food diets, and growth patterns in children with disease. I study homemade baby formula and how it compares to what older children need nutritionally. I study Ruby's condition and physical deficits and how good nutrition could improve them. In time, I develop a complex, detailed, homemade blended-food approach for Ruby. A recipe for improved health.

I need to find someone who can check my recipe plan. A professional.

I find a dietician online who specializes in blended-food diets for tube-fed kids. She practices in Arizona. She is willing to consult from a distance. I send her Ruby's diagnosis, weight, medical history, photo, and the recipes I have developed for her.

She reviews my regime for $350, sends me a detailed analysis of its nutritional value alongside Ruby's needs, and simply adds, "You are doing an amazing job feeding her good nutrition. I am very impressed." Her only recommendation is to add 2 ounces of pear juice.

Pear juice?

The stack of spreadsheet data produced by months of research lies untouched by the nutritionist who simply approves them. *We did it!*

I will start transitioning Ruby from formula to real food, one simple food at a time. Tracking nutritional values like a hawk, we begin.

I mention to a few of Ruby's specialists that I plan to transition her to real food. They are concerned, "alarmed," and generally unsupportive. I question myself in the face of their expertise. Pressed back into research, I ask more questions.

I find a forum of moms who are feeding their children real food through tubes. I express the pushback that I am receiving from medical doctors.

"Well, what's your conviction?" one of them asks me.

"Ruby is losing weight fast; she is terribly sick on formula. I believe real food can help her."

"You do not need a medical prescription to feed your daughter," she responds.

I pause and look at the screen. She is right. I agree with her. *I do not need a medical prescription to feed my child.*

This statement from a sympathizing mother becomes a lighthouse for me as I pursue this out-of-the-box feeding regimen for Ruby.

I start Ruby on trials of chicken broth and blended vegetables. From the blender, into the syringe, and down the tube it goes, her first-ever real food.

I wait for her to vomit, as she always does.

Hours later, I find…she digested it.

Over the next two weeks, I introduce one new ingredient at a time. It seems to be working. Ruby has gone five days without vomiting, which is an all-time record in her life up until now. Feeding times feel different, normalized, with real food. I am cooking for Ruby. I spend hours steaming and blending things for her, including boiling up to five chickens at a time in a monstrous pan to produce the best-gelled chicken broth to support her digestion. At night, I give her a special recipe of coconut yogurt, organic rice cereal, and pear-raspberry puree.

I carefully press it down the tube. No more corn syrup solids.

Then, something unexpected happens. We watch Ruby begin to wake up emotionally. On the real-food diet, her alertness, health and ability to interact grow rapidly. The nutrition is impacting her brain function and emotional well-being.

It turns out, the real food met another, deeper need in her too.

Here comes personality!

The only problem is, she is still not gaining weight. And therefore, her doctors want her off of this diet pronto. I am battling medical personnel on multiple fronts to keep her on it. That darn growth chart has become my nemesis.

The GI team continues to show me the chart, saying that she is diagnosed with "failure to thrive" since she is not gaining weight. Their prescription is increased volumes of calorie dense formula. I, on the other hand, am watching Ruby come to life on real food and somehow cannot ignore that for the sake of "weight gain" that has yet to be solved by formula.

I do not feel the confidence to trust myself in this process. I know my convictions, but I need to find a doctor who understands and can affirm it.

More research.

Finally, I find a homeopathic family care doctor who is willing to help. She gets it. For a little girl who suffers almost every side effect from any medication she takes, this gentle herbal care seems much more appropriate. There is space in this care for the reality that Ruby's systems are fragile.

We give it a try. We find that it works.

I work with the homeopathic doctor; the blended-food diet continues.

~

I find a parking spot across the street from a small office. Today we are going to physical therapy with Elizabeth. She is a gem in the bracelet of therapists we see. Ruby's range of motion, posture, and gross motor skills are improving through her care. The therapy is also serving to protect her from other medical interventions. Elizabeth is committed to keeping Ruby from unnecessary surgery, and I couldn't be more grateful.

That said, the appointments are not always fun. Ruby would be happy without this involuntary stretch class I am sure. I take her out of the car and pause. I look her in the eye to explain why I have brought her here again: "It's a painful process that is actually protecting you from a much greater pain. If you can embrace the process, you will see how the process itself is actually care for you."

Blank stare.

"I know. It's hard to understand. Most people don't understand this concept until they are in their last decade of life, if then. It's okay."

I carry Ruby into the office building and we make our way to the waiting room. We sit down across from a woman reading a magazine. I pull Ruby out of her car seat. The woman watches me lift Ruby up and I can see a soft spot in her eyes for us. She speaks up, "I'm Heather. My daughter Lucy is in therapy with Elizabeth."

I smile. "I'm Katie. This is Ruby."

Heather addresses Ruby directly, "Good morning, precious!" She then looks at me with compassion in her eyes and continues, "Ruby looks a lot like Lucy when she was that age."

"How old is Lucy now?

"Four."

I try to imagine what a child like Ruby at four would even be like.

Heather and I continue conversing. I hear about Lucy. Heather hears about Ruby. We share our stories. There are a lot of similarities. I feel my emotional guard coming down with her. Someone else has walked this road and come through it? I didn't know this person existed. A friendship sprouts.

I note mid-way in the conversation that Heather has not asked me for Ruby's diagnosis. Her questions are about expanding Ruby's capabilities, not about the need to define her limitations. *No education needed here; she gets it.*

"How long has she been on the NG tube?" she asks.

"Since birth."

"Whoa!"

"I pumped breast milk for over a year; and now I am trying to do a blended-food diet."

Her face lights up. "That's what we do with Lucy! Blended food!"

"Are you serious?" I respond with joy. "I have been searching the country to find someone who has successfully done this!" My mind begins to race with questions for her: *How did you develop your recipe? Were you able to find a doctor to support it?*

Just then, Elizabeth's door opens and she emerges with Lucy. My conversation with Heather dissipates. Lucy waddles out of the room, blond curls bouncing, and we all praise her. Elizabeth is helping Lucy learn how to walk, and, with a strong grip on her hand, she is doing remarkably well.

"Ruby! You're up!" Elizabeth says as she transitions Lucy's hand to Heather.

"Will you be here next week?" Heather asks me.

"Two weeks," I respond.

"Okay, here's my e-mail. Feel free to be in touch. I am happy to share more with you about blended food."

I watch Heather and Lucy leave the room and feel some sadness to see them go. *New friends.* I hope we get to see them again.

∿

It's Thanksgiving. I don't want Ruby to eat formula for dinner. I want her to have some real food, holiday food, just like the rest of us.

I put my thinking cap on and begin to strategize. What can I do for her?

The thought comes to me: *I will bake pumpkin pie from a real pumpkin. I will extract some of the cooked pumpkin, blend it with coconut milk, and serve it to Ruby through the tube for Thanksgiving.*

The kitchen becomes a love zone, and I get excited. Thanksgiving dinner is prepared. It's just the three of us this year. After I cook, I set the table for the holiday and call Mitch and Ruby to eat.

I then present…Mitch's plate, my plate, Ruby's plate.

Ruby doesn't usually have a plate, so this in itself is a moment to treasure. On it sit two little jars of blended pumpkin prepared perfectly to the consistency needed for her NG tube. On top of the blended pumpkin, I've placed mini marshmallows, just for fun.

Ruby stares at it. Mitch and I smile wide.

It's a dream come true for me to feed my little girl real food.

After all, who wants formula for Thanksgiving dinner?

Not Ruby.

Pumpkin pie through the tube it is.

Daring to live.

Part IV
Letting Go

Chapter 17

I stare at my computer screen. My friend and mentor is saying, "Come." She will buy my ticket. The thought of leaving Mitch and Ruby is unnerving. It's been almost two years. I've never left them.

But the next thing I know I'm on the plane, ascending into the clouds. It's risky. It's scary. It's happening. Three days away. The plane lands and I wonder if I've made a mistake. I miss Ruby. We've been together physically since the day she was born. I feel like an amputee, walking around with ghost pains. Part of me is missing; it's a weird feeling.

I walk out of the airport and sit down at the bus stop. The sun is shining. I wait. A van pulls up. I am off to a small town in upstate New York. I watch the airport disappear in the distance. Liberating.

My friend gives me space to be. Three days to walk, explore, and sleep through the night for the first time in almost two years. Mitch is with Ruby. I begin to feel myself emerging, much of which has felt buried due to the ongoing strikes of disease. We travel to a castle, peruse a nearby park, sit for hours in her living room, and land in a local café.

The café is called "Bombay Duck Pickle."

There my friend leans over the café table, her eyes piercing mine, and says, "Katie, you are fighting so hard." She pulls her two fists up and violently clenches them. Her face contorts as all her energy presses into her two clenched fists. It's a disturbing image. One that inevitably cannot last for long for the sheer exertion of strength it takes to maintain it.

"But who are you fighting?" she continues. "What if you let go?"

Her fists pop open; her long fingers stretch into the space. "What would happen?"

I sit silently. I think I know where she's going, and I'm not sure I like it. Doesn't she know our conviction about healing? I look at the open palms of her hands and try to think honestly. *What would happen if I let go?*

I answer honestly, "I think that if I let go, Ruby will die."

We sit in that statement. It's a true confession of a mindset I live with. My fight is keeping Ruby alive. The harder I fight, the better chance she has to live. I can't let go.

Thick compassion rolls over her face. She is well aware that she is gently challenging an exhausted soul. She dares to continue, "And whose decision is that? Who is the Author of life?"

I choose not to answer.

She sits back into her chair and waits.

"Katie, look at me. I am not saying Ruby is going to die. I pray for her healing constantly. I am just asking, do you think you can trust God with her whether in life or death?"

I am uncomfortable, and yet I know that these questions are somehow divine for this moment of my journey.

She shoots straight. "The weight of Ruby's healing will kill you if you continue to carry it as your responsibility. No matter what happens, your soul will not survive this journey with clenched fists."

"What if you let go? Dared to find out what God Himself will do when you fully entrust her to Him?" Her clenched fists rise above the table again and I see myself in them. I see that the fight that I call "holy" is, at times, just a fight.

The owner of the café approaches our table. "More?" Her quirky disposition extends an invitation to the best butternut squash soup you will ever have.

"No, thank you." I decline more and retreat out of any further conversation.

I need time with this. Space. We depart.

The next day, I travel alone to Lake Ontario. I sit on the edge of its rough waters and process the questions that confronted me yesterday with God. It doesn't take long for me to know that these questions are coming from Him. He is asking me to let go, to trust Him.

In time, I lift up my own two hands over the waters edge and clench my fists. I shut my eyes. My heart aches with longing for Ruby's healing; my body trembles with fear of what will be if I entrust her to God, if I let go. I shut my eyes and wait as the breeze blows over my face.

As I wait, I feel strength come into my heart. I sit with these clenched fists until I cannot hold the tension any longer, and then I make a decision: *I will let go.* I open my eyes and speak out loud over the vastness of the water, "God, I release Ruby to You, whether in life or death."

My fists pop open and I feel a sudden exasperated release of internal pressure. It's as if I were an overblown balloon that at last has permission to deflate.

The sense of relief is overwhelming.

I have been carrying the weight of her healing.

Deflating, deflating, deflating…I sit by the water's edge and let the tension drain. My effort to uphold this cause, my belief that the outcome is on me, and my fight to keep her alive are released to God.

I am free.

~

"Wake up, Ruby. Please, wake up."

It's been days since Ruby was fully alert, and I'm so afraid—afraid of taking her to the hospital, afraid of staying home…afraid she isn't coming back. I would do anything right now for her eyes to open again and her face to respond to mine. She is here, but it's like not here at all. My heart hurts, the pain threatening not to stop until she wakes up. I wish I could be with her where she is, wherever that is.

Long rocks, deep prayers, every effort is made—she's doesn't improve. Her body lies limp on mine. Initially, I thought she was tired, growing, just sleeping. But that's not the case.

The ER is crowded. When they see Ruby, they rush us to the back. They call her "lethargic" and people race around her like thieves in the night, no time to explain anything to me. Attaching her to monitors, they find that her oxygen is low. She is lethargic due to low oxygen.

I resist the blatant reality, consumed by internal resistance: *But Ruby has never had a problem breathing, not even since her early 4 pound days! She has always breathed on her own. She has strong healthy lungs.* Something is not right.

We are admitted into the hospital. I realize as we are led down the hallway that despite all of our outpatient appointments, we have managed to care for Ruby for two years without a single inpatient hospitalization, apart from eye surgery. This is no small feat with a child like Ruby.

Today, that streak comes to a sudden halt.

I look at Ruby lying on the hospital bed and realize she is very sick. At home, it was not as obvious to me. I'm embarrassed that I didn't bring her here sooner. Her condition has been steadily digressing over the last ten days, when Ruby's attentiveness first started to fade. Each day, I grieved fewer waking hours with her. Living even a single day without her fully awake and alert is terrifying.

I walk over to her beside and touch her shoulder. Leaning in toward her face, I beg, "Ruby, please wake up." I shut my eyes tight. Deep in my heart I know, I just know, that this thing that is on her, whatever it is, is threatening her life. I can feel the dark sense of death around even more than at her birth, despite the world announcing it. My spirit is in knots. The thought of losing Ruby makes me vomit, literally. I cannot…cannot handle this…

"Ruby, please…wake up. I miss you so much. Come back…please."

I take hold of her small hand and stand for a long time. "Ruby, please, please, wake up. It's Mom. I miss you. Please wake up."

I feel a rush of emotion: regret for not spending every waking moment with my attention on her; guilt for considering her care a burden; sick over the thought of being without her; frantic over the realization of how much I need her. My complaints about her care feel so foolish in light of this moment. It is no sacrifice, not in light of all she brings to me.

The image of the unclenched fists comes back. Was that moment preparation for this one?

In the wake of this moment, I have an unfiltered view of how much I love this little girl and how much she means to me. I don't think I could live without her. Ruby is my best friend. She gets me up in the morning. She fills my days with adventure, gives me a deep sense of purpose: a life worth living. She can't go.

"God, if You take her, take me too. Please don't leave me here without Ruby. I never want to find out what life is without her. Ever. Take me too."

I feel a hand on my shoulder. It's Mitch. I didn't know he was there; my desperate words to Ruby are ringing in the air. Mitch and I pull away from Ruby's bedside and sit together under the window in her hospital room. Things are spiraling, and we need a moment to get grounded.

"What are you sensing?" he asks me.

I hesitate, and then decide to shoot straight. "I feel like a spirit of death is looming in the air and for the first time in Ruby's life do not feel compelled to fight for her healing. I don't understand it. I wish I felt otherwise; I am trying to drown out the sense of it…" My words trail off into tears.

"Katie, I feel like God is asking us to release Ruby to Him whether in life or death, to give her back to Him. And I think we need to do it now."

For two straight years, we have repeatedly sought God for what to do for Ruby and how to position ourselves in prayer. Every single time, He has told us to believe Him for Ruby's complete healing, not in heaven but here, on this side of eternity. All of a sudden, we both feel like He is asking us to take a different position and there is no making sense of it, at least not right now.

In this paradox, the words of the disciples come to mind when they did not understand Him: *"To whom else would we go? You alone have the words of Life."*

In time, we rise and choose obedience. Bedside, we hold Ruby's hands and somehow do what we know we need to do: we release Ruby to Jesus whether in life or death.

We give Ruby back to God.

Suddenly, a sense of freedom crashes into the room, and we are drenched. It moves like rushing water around the space and into the deepest caverns of our being. It's as if Freedom is a person and He was just given full access, making all the difference in how He can reside in us. He's fully alive.

We stand in awe.

Somehow, in this awful, grief-filled moment, we discover an experience of freedom that is deeper than any we have had in our lives to date. It's the freedom of absolute surrender to Jesus, the freedom of holding nothing back from Him. I didn't know this degree of freedom was possible on this side of eternity. I feel as though nothing is holding me. Nothing.

I look up at Mitch. "Freedom. Can you feel that?"

He nods, eyes wide in affirmation.

The air is now thick and silent.

We have no idea what the next moments hold, but at least we now know who holds them.

∿

Over the next few hours, Ruby's breathing becomes increasingly stressed. Her lifeless state turns into a terrible sight of fighting to live. Her chest is convulsing up and down as her heart pounds to get oxygen through her body. Her eyes are now wide open, but she is unable to fixate. She suffers greatly. Ruby begins to vomit. She then vomits blood. I grab her hand and look away. *I must stay present, which means I must look away so I do not faint.*

As Ruby fights to breathe, her heart rate solicits alarms. Medical staff run in and out of the room clothed in fear. The attending physician pulls Mitch and me aside from Ruby's bed. "We don't feel that we can take care of Ruby on the main floor any longer. She needs to go to intensive care."

I can feel all the color drain from my face. I press my feet into the ground to maintain my balance. I look up and see pure pity looking back at me from everyone in the room. They know what his words mean; they know that she may not make it.

Ruby's bed is quickly detached and pulled out of the room. The oxygen and monitors remain attached to it. She is raced down the hallway. We run after her. Running down the hallway I feel like I am running into a black hole. But what other choice do I have? *It's forward or forward.*

At a certain point, Ruby is taken to the left, and we are stopped at the corner. We are told that we will have to take the elevator and meet her in the Pediatric Intensive Care Unit. Never has an elevator moved so slowly.

Mitch and I come running down the hallway into the PICU. We stop suddenly when we see Ruby. She is already hooked up to machines and is surrounded by medical professionals in masks. The attending physician comes over to greet us and asks whether or not we want them to intubate Ruby if it means she may die without it.

I stare at her. *Is this real? This decision being put on parents?*

Mitch asks her how much time we have. "We need to talk about it," he says.

She hesitates. "Not much time, but okay...I'll be back for your decision."

The doctor pulls the mask over her face and returns bedside with the other medical professionals who are working hard to help Ruby breathe. I watch them reposition her oxygen mask over and over again as their eyes stare down the monitors for an inclination of improvement.

Mitch and I cannot get to the bed because of the number of people surrounding it. We stand at a distance and watch, in shock. Then, I begin to see in the spirit realm, and what I see shakes me so deeply that I lose my ability to speak.

Above Ruby, I see eternity. It looks like a rip in the atmosphere and on the other side of it is the brightest light I have ever seen. The natural scene becomes dim and this bright light consumes my vision. I watch it opening above Ruby's bed. The thing that shocks me the most about this light, this space, this place beyond the torn veil, is that there is no fear there. None. On the contrary, I know that in that place, in that light, there is unending, everlasting peace and joy.

The rip in the atmosphere personifies two arms: the safest, strongest arms that I have ever seen. They reach out as if an invitation is being made into the most complete and loving embrace that could exist.

As I see eternity before Ruby, I realize that she is close to death. I realize what death means for her. The fear of death is violently ripped out of me, and I lose my ability to fear it ever again.

I then realize that she may be going there now.

I grab Mitch's arm and, unable to say much, tell him, "I can see eternity, Mitch; it's drawing close to her."

Mitch then walks over to Ruby's bedside, presses through the medical personnel, and bends over so that his head is right next to hers. He whispers into her ear, "Ruby, if you want to go home to Jesus now, we release you to go, but if you want to stay here with us and fight, we will fight with you."

He then stands up with his hand still holding hers and looks up at the monitor and waits…

And then…her vital signs start to improve.

Within minutes, Ruby takes a dramatic turn for the better. The medical staff are startled by her improvement. They stare at Mitch with perplexed looks. Relief blows over the whole room. There is cheering; there are tears. People retreat their frantic selves and let out sighs. I am still standing on the sideline. I watch the tension unravel, and I fight my way into the inner space by her bed.

"What is going on?" I ask Mitch.

Not knowing the words he had just spoken to Ruby, Mitch leans over to me and responds into my ear with confidence, "She's choosing to stay here with us."

I look up and the vision of eternity, that rip in the atmosphere, is closing. It's going away. I cannot believe it. She is staying. I shut my eyes tightly. "Jesus, thank You." It is the most sincere thank-you of my life.

We stand around Ruby's bedside and watch her vital signs recover. She is still on oxygen, unresponsive, and critically ill…but she is no longer dying.

We never had to make the decision about intubation. Ruby made a decision to fight, and, true to his word, Mitch and I determine to fight with her. And we learn something about our daughter, Ruby Joy. She is, by nature and by identity, a fighter.

Who does this?

In light of eternity, she chose to fight for life.

In light of release, she chose to stay.

In light of Home, she fought to finish her race.

I feel humbled by her strength. Inspired by her, I make an internal commitment.

> *In Ruby's honor, who chose to run her race with perseverance and live, I commit to doing the same with my life. Like her, I do not want to cut out early, but I choose now that I will live, fight the fight of life, for as long as God determines my race on Earth will be.*

And fight we do. Over the next three days, Mitch and I tag-team in the Pediatric ICU, fighting alongside Ruby for her recovery. Our space is small. It consists of Ruby's bed, her monitors, and a single metal chair with an upright back. The chair is hard, cold, with stiff arms. Brushing up on our backs is the curtain of her neighbor, another child with disease.

This PICU is nearly full of children, the sickest children in our region. It feels like a war zone. The atmosphere is intense. The lights remain on. There is no rest, no distinction between day and night, just a persistent fight for life. Disease has a sound, and that sound is here. It is heard through the children it seeks to destroy.

Parents are in and out. It seems to me that about half of the children's parents stay with them through the night. My heart breaks for the other half. I wonder if anyone would care if I crawl under some of these curtains to sit with these kids in their pain. From our small space, Ruby's space, we release intercession for them all.

As we pray, I am aware of the people around us. Here, we share the same space. The norms of life unraveling, tragedies occurring, heroic fights for life, separated by flimsy curtains. Behold our curtain community.

In honor of Ruby's decision to fight for life, Mitch and I take a stand in the room for life and healing. We turn our hearts to praise, worship, choose to love God in the face of pain. We spend hours throughout the day and night in worship, in prayer, lifting Jesus up in this space.

As we worship, the Presence of God manifests in the PICU. The sounds of disease begin to die down under the weight of the sounds of praise. We get word from behind our curtain that children around us are recovering and getting discharged. These good reports peak after twelve hours of unbroken worship in the room, bedside with Ruby.

I run into a grandmother in the waiting room who tells me her grandson has just taken a turn for the better. Others are reporting the same. Mitch and I continue to pray. We pray for Ruby and every one of her neighbors. Another mom gives me a children's book: "This is for Ruby, when she gets better." We both know this is a faith statement for a child in the PICU. Not *if* she gets better, *when* she gets better.

Mitch and I continue, day and night, night and day. We rotate, sing, and love God in that room. And as we do, we witness…

The PICU is beginning to empty out.

The PICU is now emptying out.

The PICU is nearly empty.

Three days later, we are approached by the attending physician and told that Ruby is doing really well. They are going to graduate her from the PICU to the main floor. We are overjoyed. Over, over, over JOYED.

We are escorted out of the PICU and I notice that about 80 percent of the other patients are already gone. This intensive care unit is nearly empty. It was full when we arrived.

I turn around to catch a glimpse of the pulled curtains on empty patient beds.

This is what I call Immanuel, God with us.

∼

Back on the main floor of the hospital, we search for a space to collapse from the intensity of the last few days, but we do not find it. The fight continues. Ruby is still on oxygen and has yet to regain consciousness. I begin to wonder if she will ever return to normal. It has been two full weeks since I have seen her awake and alert.

Then…one morning, it happens. From the other side of the room, I see her looking in my direction with a smile spread across her face.

"RUBY!" I scream and run to her bed. "I missed you so much!"

Up into my arms she goes, wires and all.

I throw her back into the bed and take pictures, snapping them as fast as I can. I send a picture to Mitch. "Ruby is awake!"

Later that day Mitch comes racing in from work.

Reunion.

We missed Ruby so much.

We are drunk in *happy*.

She's awake!

Over the next few days, attempts are made to wean Ruby from oxygen. The attempts are largely failing. Noisy alarms arrest us over and over again. Her medical staff run in and out of the room to adjust her levels. I watch this chaotic activity and realize that someone is going to have to watch Ruby's oxygen like a hawk and decrease it ever so slowly. Otherwise, this could take forever.

I become determined that Ruby will breathe again on her own and start my own investment to that end. It takes a lot of work, with repeated exhaustive disappointments along the way, but, in time, she gets there. She breathes; she breathes for longer. She breathes for a night; she breathes on her own that next full day.

I hold my breath, while she lets hers out.

She's off the oxygen.

Off of the oxygen for a full twenty-four hours, we are at last discharged from the hospital and sent home with Ruby.

Home.

Home *with* Ruby.

~

Walking through the shadow of death changes life. Life is different. I saw eternity. I saw it with my eyes. The sight of it ripped the fear of death right out of me. And only as fear left did I realize how constant its rumbling noise has been in me. Perhaps ever constant since the day Ruby was born. Since the day I was born?

We are home. Everything feels like a gift. Our gratitude level is so high it's intoxicating. Things that felt like a curse now display as a gift. It's weird, disorienting, but everything feels different. *We* are different.

I move Ruby from one room to another. *What a gift.*

I walk into the kitchen to get a drink. *What a gift.*

I hug Mitch without a nurse in the room. *What a gift.*

No doctors to deliberate with today. *A gift.*

Ruby is with us. *Unspeakable gift.*

I walk around our small apartment in a daze. I feel like I lost everything and am trying to figure out how it could all still be here. I feel like I don't own anything anymore. Perhaps, it no longer owns me.

I prop Ruby up on my shoulder and sit with her in the rocking chair for a long time. *Privacy with Ruby is a gift.*

I count gifts.

Pressing Ruby's body against mine the thought comes: *I think I would've died if she had not come home with us.* Tears of gratitude fall from my eyes like sprinkles onto her shoulders. We're meant to be together. It's good we are still together.

Tucked in, sweet Ruby dozes off, safe, at home.

Back in the living room Mitch and I sit down and begin to process the last week. We are exhausted from the hospitalization and yet relieved to be home. Home is a sign of recovery but not an end in itself. The work of full-time nursing staff now falls to us: medications, evaluations, feedings. Ruby is still sick.

And yet, even her illness does not feel burdensome, not right now. She's alive. And we are in awe of what we just experienced spiritually. We released Ruby to God, and He gave her back. This is hard to understand. Why would we be led through the pain of release if He knew all along she would fight it out?

Bedside, in those recent moments, we both felt her slipping away. She was near death. She was dying. I pose the question to Mitch, "Why do you think God had us release Ruby if she wasn't going to die?"

"I don't know," Mitch responds.

The verse that had emerged in the moment comes back to my mind: *"To whom else would we go? You alone have the words of Life."*

I grab my Bible and search the concordance for the reference. Maybe this passage has more understanding in it for us.

John 6.

Jesus has just said strange things.

Eat my body.

Drink my flesh.

People did not understand Him; the caption over the story reads, *Many turn away.*

I pause.

I wonder if many continue to turn away from Jesus when they don't understand Him. I wonder if there is a moment in all of our lives when He calls us beyond understanding to follow Him.

The twelve remained.

I can hear Jesus' sincerity to be loved in the midst of the falling out: *"Are you going to leave me also?"* He knows they don't understand Him.

And that's where Peter's heart is unveiled: *"Who else would we turn to? You alone have the words of Life."*

I look back up at Mitch with my finger on the page of John 6.

"It's this. This is the moment we just lived through. And somehow, by the grace of God, we did not fall away." I feel a shudder go up my spine. It's the realization that we have come to the narrow path that few choose.

We continue to process, the atmosphere feels charged as we understand more. Mitch gets a mental picture. "I see a door, and a pile of towels outside of it...many have thrown in the towel at this point in their faith journey. Many."

This door.

This John 6 door.

Towel on shoulder, bypassing the pile, we continue on.

Chapter 18

Over the next few days, I sit long in the Gospels and realize how many people fell away from Jesus when they did not understand Him. Handfuls of people stopped following Him when He stopped making sense to them. And in that falling away, they rejected their own Messiah.

Is this still happening? Is crisis the only thing that tests whether we are more committed to ourselves than Him? Could we teach people about this so that they don't have to go through crisis to learn it?

Many have bashed the Pharisees for rejecting Jesus. They are portrayed as though their inability to recognize Him was a matter of sheer stupidity. In light of this time of my life, I cannot disagree more. I understand them. It is not easy to follow Jesus when He shows up in a way that contradicts what you believe and nullifies your ability to understand.

Flipping through the pages of the Gospels, my heart grieves for the many religious leaders who could not bring themselves to follow what they could not fully understand. I get it. I was just there, at that moment of decision. Pure grace pulled me through it.

The Pharisees' firm grip of their principles, formulas, and traditions hindered their ability to fully embrace the Person of God who was their Messiah. In the face of a Man from heaven who contradicted their expectations, they were unable to let go. In so doing, they rejected their own Savior.

Unable to let go.

They had rehearsed, likely memorized, prophesies about John the Baptist. They had done the same for prophecies about Jesus. But they did not recognize either. Why? Because God's provision, His fulfilled promise, came in a way they did not expect and did not like. It came in a way that offended their minds.

Could it be that they did not understand how Person-able God is? What if this "Christianity" is not a religion at all? What's if it is flesh and blood? What if He sent a Person on purpose because this expression immediately filters those who do not personally love Him?

The whole experience shakes me to the core.

I search and search more. I question hard and long.

How many of us really know Jesus? Not just *about* Him, but know Him personally? How many of us are following traditions without a clue to the personal relationship He wants with us? And how many of us will find out where we stand on this before we die?

He is not a formula.

He's never been that.

He'll never become that.

He is the Living God, and He wants to be known.

Followed.

Loved.

Ruby came home.

He did not ask us for Ruby so that He could kill her.

He asked us for Ruby because it is only in fully trusting that we are fully free.

A lifetime of religion crumbles.

And my life, ashes on the ground, simplifies.

Jesus.

That's it.

Just lose your life—entirely—for Jesus and you will find it.

Not easy, but true.

Truth always liberates.

Three days until Ruby's second birthday.

We have much to celebrate.

Her life.

Our freedom.

~

July 10, 2011. Ruby turns two today. This birthday presents just a few days after discharge from the hospital. Our capacity is low and we do not have much to give to the day—except for gratitude, which perhaps is the best celebration tool there is; it always presents from the inside out, deeply from the inside out.

There is a tender gratitude in our hearts today for the gift of Ruby's life.

Mitch and I take Ruby to the department store. We want to buy her a birthday outfit. I put Mitch on the task and take delight in watching his process. He's a novice at shopping for clothing, but he takes this assignment very seriously. He finds a tie-dye summer dress, bright orange with in-roads of yellow, purple, and red.

I pause. And then smile and nod. *His assignment, his choice.*

I find little pink sandals with sparkly rhinestones to go with the dress. Yes, pink sandals with an orange, red and yellow sundress. Perhaps we should not have "shared" the shopping task, but, alas, this is what we want to buy. And so, we buy it.

After our time in the store, we go to a local bakery and pick out a cake. We pick out a big, expensive, ornate cake. Ruby's name is written with a sugar pen on top. This decadent piece of editable art is over the top, and we find that quite appropriate for Ruby's birthday.

We head home.

Home sweet home, sweetened by birthday merriment.

That evening, we drive out to Mitch's parent's house where his cousin has decorated the house in honor of Ruby's second birthday. It is a special time. We are there for an hour or two and then head home. Ruby is still weak from the recent hospitalization, and so are we.

That night we tuck Ruby into bed and take time to each give thanks. Mitch is thankful for Ruby's new dress. I am thankful for Ruby's curls.

"Ruby?"

We pause as we sometimes do for her to respond however she will.

A clear thought pops into my head: *I'm thankful that I'm not a baby anymore.*

I laugh out loud.

"What?" Mitch asks.

"I think Ruby is thankful today that she is not a baby anymore."

He laughs.

We stand her up on her feet. She is unable to stand on her own, as she has no weight-bearing capacity in her arms or legs. But when we hold her in a standing position, it's evident that she is actually quite long, quite like a little girl.

We lay her back down and tuck her in.

"Goodnight, Ruby."

"Grown-up you." I roll her over and give her a firm squeeze.

"Happy second birthday."

Kiss on the forehead.

Lights out.

~

I sit at the edge of the community pool. There is a mom here with twin boys, probably close to two years old. They have so many floaties strapped to them it would be hard for anyone to drown them purposefully, let alone for them to drown accidentally. The mom keeps holding them above the water and then releasing them into the pool, saying, "Look, you can do it! You can swim!"

And the boys...*panic.*

As she lets go, they start screaming, "Mom, no! No! No! Don't let go!" Frantically, they shake their little heads and hold their breath as if they are drowning, even though their heads are clearly above water and held up mightily by an army of floaties.

Over and over, I watch this occur.

She lets go.

They think they are drowning, even though they are floating.

They just don't know that they can swim! I shake my head in pity. Holy Spirit taps my shoulder. I look up. I watch the scene repeat again, but this time I see myself.

Since I came home from the hospital, I have felt like God let go. Panicked, I don't understand why we cannot seem to recover. Ruby is still sick. I can't seem to settle down on the inside.

I watch the two boys again, arms flailing. I wish they would just get it—they're floating. I get this sense from God: "I have given you what you need, Katie, to keep your head above deep waters: trouble and trial. You can do this. You can swim."

I watch.

I see the boys' panic, but I also see the mother's security. She would not let go if they were not safe. Their floatie armor is strapped on. I get the sense that God wants to teach me how to be in deep waters without panicking, not just for my own sake, but for others as well.

Okay. Stop panicking. Just float. Trust.

∽

I have been asked to come to church and teach a class on hearing God's voice. I have a history of teaching, training, and mentoring in subjects related to friendship with God. And yet, I have not done any of this for some time. I decide to say yes. This is the first public ministry that I'll do since Ruby's birth. I feel disheveled, rusty, scattered.

In a small group of thirty or so individuals, I take the microphone and share my heart. Then, I offer prayer. People come forward to receive from God.

I lay hands on the first woman before me.

Suddenly, as if she were hit by an unseen wind, she falls to the floor.

Thump.

I look around. The other leaders are busy praying for people. I crouch down on the ground next to her. "Do you feel fear or peace?" I want to uncover whether or not what just happened to her was evidence of God's Presence.

Eyes shut, body limp, she responds to me, "I feel so much peace."

I back up, still on my knees. I remember a woman who once described being slain in the spirit as "giddy peace." I think that's what just happened to the person in front of me. I don't think our church has ever seen this manifestation before. I've never seen it happen as a response to my prayer.

Wait. I didn't even pray. What just happened?

Driving home that night, I reflect. That first woman I ministered to was set free from anxiety by the time she got off the floor. I talked with her. She looked, and felt, like a new person: fear gone. The power of God had flown through her body with liberating grace after I laid my hands on her.

I'm perplexed. I wasn't looking for it; no one in our community even has a grid for this. It just happened. It was power. It was God.

That night, I reflect more. Perhaps *that* is what can happen when someone has spent fifteen months in private prayer as I have with Ruby, and then steps out and lays their hands on someone.

The power of God.

Released.

Back to my private world of prayer.

Weeks later, I'm asked to write a curriculum for a discipleship class at church. The subject is freedom and the purpose is to facilitate an experience of inner healing and deliverance for people. I agree to do it.

I devote an evening to pray about content for the class and, in that time, feel clarity on six main issues in our community where I believe God wants to bring freedom. One at a time, the topics come like clear paint strokes across my brain.

Little do I know that these six issues are areas in which I need freedom as well. As I begin my research, I find myself confronted with my own internal process. I end up being the very first student to experience this class.

One student, one Teacher, Freedom 101.

Sitting in front of my computer, with Ruby at my side, I meet with God. One issue at a time, I wrestle, and He teaches me how to wrestle free. Through repentance, forgiveness, healthy grief, gut-wrenching honesty, renouncing lies, and sitting in the love of God, I find routes out of that which binds. My personal process unpacks practically and hits the page in one lesson after another.

In my writing, I am forced to face my own chains. I wrestle until I know how to show someone else how to untie an emotional knot.

Two months later, Mitch and I stand before twelve thirsty souls and begin the process with them. The class is on Tuesdays. Grandma comes to watch Ruby. We step outside our disease-stricken world for two hours, and in that time pour our hearts out for others. Week after week, we share our stories, work through the material, and then press in together for an encounter with the Person named Freedom.

Astounding things happen.

Chains are broken.

Hearts are healed.

It's supernatural.

Beautiful.

Those twelve become our twelve, and we fall in love with them like family. We journey together into the heart of God. Together, in the midst of our pain, we learn that Jesus is what we most need.

Mitch and I find ourselves in ministry, pastoring. What we have to offer is simple; it is our lives. We are hurting and daring to live in the midst of our pain. We are not afraid to be honest about the process. We are in love with God despite what we do not understand. People respect this. And, in their respect, they find safety for their own process.

In the middle of our own combat with disease, we find a place to serve.

And in the middle of our serving, we learn that we are not alone.

The world is grieving.

Together is better.

Pain doesn't like to be pushed. It needs to be validated and then healed.

We validate.

He heals.

At the end of the semester, the fourteen of us sit around a table and one by one share testimonies of how we have experienced transformation through the class. Testimonies abound. Anxiety is gone. Cycles of depression are broken. Dignity and value have been restored. The lonely are now in a family. The insecure have found their voice. The performance-driven are free to no longer perform. Jealousy traps are gone. Sexual sin is confessed and released. Self-hatred is destroyed.

I can feel the Presence of God in the room, seemingly growing heavier as each story is shared. There is an anointing here, a charged feeling, a grace for hearts to be wide open without fear. It's striking, like naked, spiritual exposure before God. These hearts are free: free to be at home in the love of God and free to lay bare in the context of community. The anointing I feel in this room is unique, a grace for the heart.

The testimonies roll on, and the stories blow my mind. I don't know how all of this just happened. But sitting in that room together, we all know that something has begun.

The class ends, but this is the start of something.

Back home, Mitch and I are still in the crux of crisis, in a fight with disease, and under the pressure of intense medical care for Ruby.

Healing at the church, disease at home.

The paradox is strange, but we learn to embrace it. If things always have to make sense, then we will surely miss out on a whole lot of good.

Making sense of things is a task for eternity.

Chapter 19

Dressed down to a diaper, Ruby's curls tickle the changing pad. Nose to nose, I tell her how cute she is, and we giggle in the face of one another. Stretching her tiny limbs, the fun continues. I then let out a sigh. The fun stops.

"Time for a weight check."

Ruby's face dampens with mine, perhaps more in response to mine than any true understanding of the heartache we live with in the area of her growth.

Weight check.

Ruby has not gained weight for months, and her skeleton is increasingly visible through her skin. At times, when I undress her for a bath, I feel embarrassed. Her body reminds me of photos of starving children. Surely, it's my fault. I'm her mom.

I stand on the scale and hold Ruby close. My eyes peer down at the digital number between my feet. I realize there are myriads of people who stand like this on scales with a sick longing for the number to be less instead of more. I wish I could shake those people today. They have no idea the gift it is to be able to maintain and gain weight. Ruby is fighting to maintain the smallest amount of fat on her body. If only this number would be more than the last time. *If only.*

135.5

Maybe I'm the one who has lost weight.

I lay her down to double-check my number without her: 125.

135.5 − 125 = 10.5

My face grimaces. This is the lowest it's been since her first year of life. If she were to get sick there would be no room for weight loss, none at all, and we would go straight to intensive care. I have a 2-year-old little girl who weighs 10.5 pounds.

I carry Ruby back into the bedroom. She is now shivering from being undressed. The room is warm, but she has no body fat. I bundle her well. I lay Ruby down under some hanging toys and find myself slumped up against the wall behind her.

Think, Katie. Don't freak out. Use your head. There's got to be a way forward.

I talk straight to myself to keep my emotions steady. I am aware that an ounce or two more off that scale and we are hospitalized. There's got to be something I can do.

In a moment of stillness, I recognize that there is one thing that I can and need to do and I need to do it now, but I don't want to. Back against the wall, I make the hard decision I confess to myself: *The blended food is not working for Ruby.* She is healthy, but she is not growing.

Mitch's word of wisdom comes back to mind: "Sometimes the best decision is the one that you never thought you would make."

I look down at my two clenched fists. "Let it go, Katie."

Letting go feels like a death of its own kind. I have poured my heart into this project for Ruby: heart, soul, and finances. But what other option do I have? If I don't let go, I may be left gripping blended food while losing Ruby. What is that worth?

I tip over my knees and kneel next to Ruby to stroke her forehead. We are nose to nose again. "Mama's food is not helping you grow, Ruby. I'm sorry. I've tried hard. We are going to have to try something else."

I swallow my tears and can feel the burn of disappointment go all the way down to my gut, where it leaves its mark. This is devastating, but for love I will swallow my pride and move on.

"Move on to where?" I speak out loud.

Ruby's current GI specialists are as much at a loss as I am. They keep telling me to increase the volume or caloric density of her formula. Both make her vomit. They suggest we try another formula, but they all make her vomit. They recommend we hook her up to continuous feeds, which makes me want to vomit.

They're out of options.

I'm out of options.

What about CHOP? Children's Hospital of Philadelphia?

The thought dances forward on the stage of my mind. It's an idea. When we thought we were at a dead end with her scoliosis, their second opinion was a beacon of hope, and in time a viable solution. It's an idea. One idea is more than I had a few minutes ago. Perhaps it's a divine idea, a solution. I wonder how many divine solutions are hanging over my head waiting for me to let go of the man-made answers I grip tightly.

I pick up the phone and call a relative from Pennsylvania who works with children like Ruby. "Can you help me find a GI doctor at CHOP?"

A few hours later: "Dr. Gibbons."

I call his office and make an appointment. We will drive two and a half hours to see a specialist from CHOP.

Maybe, just maybe, this national specialist will know how to help Ruby grow.

~

We drive two and a half hours to an outpatient appointment in Exton, Pennsylvania. We arrive early and find a nearby park to visit. Mitch, Ruby and I stroll along a Pennsylvania trail, ground littered with colored leaves and signs of autumn. I try to enjoy it, but my heart is tense over the pending appointment.

Entering the outpatient center, we sign in and sit down. It is a small office. It feels safer to me than the hospital. Less than five minutes after arrival, we are called back. I look at my watch. The doctor is going to see us on time for our appointment. *Impressive.*

Inside the patient room, Ruby is weighed and checked in by a nurse. Enter Dr. Gibbons. He is a big, unemotional man. I tell him about Ruby, trying not to visibly tremble or cry. He interrupts me many times with flat questions.

I'm not impressed that he seems to have no emotion to share with us, but I am glad to see that he doesn't seem shocked by Ruby's case. She's an exception to so many people. Too often, I see fear in the professionals' eyes as they look at what they have never before seen. Dr. Gibbons is different; he's asking questions as if this is the hundredth child he has treated. That kind of apathy is strangely comforting to me. Maybe he'll know what to do.

The appointment concludes and he makes his recommendation. "I would like to treat Ruby inpatient. Put her in the hospital for a few days and try a few things under observation."

My heart sinks. "What other option do we have?"

"You can always stick with your doctors in D.C., but if I'm going to treat her then that's what we need to do. Her weight is low. I don't think it is safe for the trials to happen at home."

I look at Mitch. He's good at not being forced into decisions. He answers for us. "We'll think about it and let you know."

Exiting the room I catch the CHOP slogan plastered on the wall: "Hope Lives Here."

Days later, Ruby and I are in the car driving back to Children's Hospital of Philadelphia where she will be admitted. Thirty minutes away, I have been clenching this steering wheel for the last two hours, resisting the urge to take the car elsewhere. Anywhere else.

Ruby has been quiet. I am sure that she can feel my tension. It doesn't feel right to be driving toward hospitalization by choice. I must be mad.

Face the facts. Mitch and I decided to do this: admit Ruby to the hospital so that Dr. Gibbons can treat her inpatient. Ruby is vomiting and

dropping weight at an alarming rate. We do not know of any other option;
we are choosing this one as a means to choose hope.

I wish I were taking my daughter to the beach today. Or to the
zoo, to visit family, or to play on a playground. I grieve that we are
headed to the hospital. She will hurt there: stuck with needles, poked
throughout the nights, strung up to monitors with annoying noises.
She will suffer through anesthesia and medical interventions. I hate it.

Ruby, if I could take any of it away for you, I would.

If there was anything I could do to spare you more pain, I would.

If I had any power over this, I would use it.

Why is the Powerful One not intervening?

~

"I wanna build you a garden,

In a dry and weary land.

In a dry and weary land,

I'm going to find a river there."

I've found an anthem in this hospitalization. It's a phrase I heard
belted from the heart of a worshiper a few weeks ago. It's now being
released from my own heart into this lonely hospital life, over and
over and over again.

Ruby and I are here. The days and nights extend into weeks. It's
a difficult, lonely time. If I can find a purpose beyond myself, I think
it will help carry me through. I believe that being in a personal relationship with the God of purpose means that I can create purpose
anywhere I go. It doesn't hurt to try.

On my knees in worship, I invite God's Presence. I close my eyes
and press into the reality of His nearness to make this dark, cold,
wire-filled, windowless room a home for God.

And then, I dream.

God, what would happen if You moved into this hospital room?

What would happen to Ruby? To Me? To the nurses?

God, what if You moved unto this floor?

God, what if there is meaning to being a temple of the Holy Spirit, a moving tabernacle for God?

God, what if You visited CHOP this week? Made the news?

What would that look like? What could happen?

Take my life and use it, Lord.

Scenarios from another realm, where all things are possible, fill my mind, and I unashamedly ask for them all. I am a firm believer that we cannot out-dream God. In the midst of the intercession, I feel a change happening inside, an identity shift from being a victim to being a victor. *Who am I here? Am I the world's victim or the King's victor?* The hospital begins to feel less like a sentence and more like an assignment; it changes from a prison to a mission field. I begin to see opportunity all around me. Today, I have access to people to which no pastor I know has access. And I will pastor them.

Antenna up.

I find people in need, people who are ready to receive. The people I find are hungry for God. Most people are open. Contrary to popular belief about sharing faith, people are ripe for an experience with love. They are ripe. The pain in people's eyes is deep, but I watch it lessen for the simple experience of having a safe place to share it. And my hospital ministry begins.

I find children who are too sick to go to church, who are quarantined by disease. I feel honored to be this close to them, a thin wall away from their precious breaths. As we minister, I realize that Ruby gives me access to people who are in special need.

Let Your kingdom come here; let Your will be done in Children's Hospital, just as it is in heaven.

Ruby and I share days of outreach without traveling anywhere, except up and down the halls and floors of this building. Between medical consultations, we are up and around, meeting people, hearing their stories, and offering prayer. Back in Ruby's room, I notice that a thick peace is steadily increasing in her space. I sense that while we are about His business, He is in here, about ours. *Thank You.*

My heart is inspired by the sense of purpose we find as we reach beyond ourselves. If I can find a river here, I can find a river anywhere. The anthem carries me through the proceeding days.

"I wanna build you a garden,

In a dry and weary land.

In a dry and weary land,

I'm going to find a river there."

A week later, we are still in the hospital, but my inpatient experience has changed. A sense of purpose does that; it changes things that remain the same. I have become aware of the people around me, which has blown up my victim mentality. In the times that Ruby is permitted to leave her room, I put her up on my shoulder and we prayer walk the halls together, hoping to meet people along the way. The faces of the kids are becoming familiar. I am seeing the staff as people, people alive with life stories.

This morning, I connected heart to heart with the technician downstairs. Later, I noticed a nurse lingering in our presence, and I began to ask her questions. Her life spilled out like a cup begging to tip and I got to encourage her. Ruby and I have found a space, a voice, and a purpose here. At the end of the day, we sit together on the hospital room floor together and thank God for the divine encounters we got to have together.

"God, I'm not asking to stay one day longer than we have to here. But I am thankful that I've found a river here, and that river is You."

Where can I go from Your Presence?

Where can I flee from You?

If I go to Children's Hospital...You are there.

~

It's Saturday afternoon and Mitch has arrived from Virginia to visit us. This hospitalization is longer than we anticipated, a stretch from the "few days" initially quoted. Ruby's inpatient care is growing instead of diminishing. Discharge seems to be distancing.

Mitch arrives with a caravan for Ruby. He has a big bag full of things from home. He enters proudly and dumps it on the floor. Stuffed animals and toys dispense in the room. He pulls out a sign he made for her room and tapes it to the door: "Ruby's Room." The sign is regal and I smile, considering that this piece of Daddy's art is a filter for the voices permitted to discuss her life and value.

As I watch Mitch build a home for Ruby in the space, I feel my own meltdown coming on. As he steps into caregiving, I realize that it has been a lot to carry alone. The strength I have felt seems more like a pretense as the opportunity to be weak is met with a wave of acceptance.

I can hardly say hello to him without crying.

Mitch sends me outside, and I leave the hospital for the first time in over a week. Chasing nature, I find a trail near a river in the city. Crouched at the rivers edge, I quiet my heart and wait to hear God. I know I will be okay if I can just hear from God.

I let my eyes stare at the ground for a while. I stare at the dirt. I feel release in looking down. In time, I look back up. To my left, there is a bridge that crosses the river. On the other side of the river, there is a populated trail. People are walking, running, biking, playing, and strolling up and down the river's edge. On this side of the river, the trail is unpopulated. It is an empty, concrete trail with a few trees hanging over its edge. I find myself on the quiet side. The lonely side.

I think about hospitalization. I have been meeting people, but they are all new people, and I feel very lonely. Ruby and I sit together in a quiet hospital room for hours every day without a familiar face in the world. Meanwhile, Mitch is working in D.C, and I am walking this hospitalization out with Ruby alone.

In this moment of reflection, Holy Spirit speaks to me: *"I want you to learn how to live on either side of this bridge, Katie: public or private. There is great glory being opened to you in the coming days, but I want you to know how to live with or without it so that it doesn't harm you. Embrace this time."*

I sit still and contemplate the word. In light of a defined purpose, I feel gratitude for this time. I am at peace on this side of the river and can recognize the opportunity to learn contentment in hiddenness. This hospitalization is tough, and yet I am at peace with God. Our love is deepening through it.

The deepening of our love is a secret, not a soul in the world knows about it. It is precious to me in this moment. When a soul can be at rest, alone in God, fulfilled in private, thriving in the unseen, there is something of value. Inevitably, a healthy soul will grow beyond the unseen size—in time.

I pick up a dry leaf on the ground and turn it over. One side is crinkled brown; the other side is bright red. I look back at the bridge, over to the populated side of the water. *I am content here with You, God, in the cleft of the rock. I am content here with You.*

> *"My dove in the clefts of the rock, in the hiding places on the mountainside, show me your face, let me hear your voice, for your face is sweet and your voice is lovely."*

Mitch has decided to stay another night with us in the hospital, and I am so thankful! It was time for him to leave this afternoon, and none of us could bare it. He turned his curly head around and said, "I'm staying."

"What about work?"

"I'll leave early in the morning."

I dare not ask how early that will be for fear we'll both be talked out of it. Instead, I throw my arms around his neck and squeeze. "Thank you!" My heart overflows with gratitude, and I choose to conceal the extent of it. If he knew how hard this has been for me alone, he may never leave and then he would lose his job.

Mitch's presence the last day and a half has felt like a kiss from heaven. Having a partner makes such a difference. With Mitch here, I can go to the cafeteria for food without abandoning Ruby. I can step outside the hospital doors and catch a glimpse of sun. I can process medical decisions with someone who is fully invested. I have a hand to hold in the surgical waiting room, someone to share in the role of policing her treatments. This whole experience is so much easier together. Two is better than one.

I feel for the single moms whom I have met here. My last week is their everyday experience. These women are heroes in their own right. If I had a pile of priceless gold medals, I would walk around this hospital and give them to the single moms.

Evening approaches and I go down to the cafeteria to get us some food for dinner. My heart is happy: dinner with Mitch. I bring the food back upstairs and we create a picnic on the floor of Ruby's hospital room. Mitch removes Ruby from her bed and lays her on a blanket between us. The wires of her monitors barely reach, but they reach nonetheless. I set out our dinner creatively, and we celebrate family time with silly chatter and fried food. Being together is so sweet.

After we eat, Mitch and I play with Ruby. She gets rolled, tickled, talked to, played with, held and hugged. Evening turns to night and I can feel the clock ticking as if I were Cinderella and the dream is destined to dissipate all too soon. Mitch will have to leave soon. Ruby and I will have to stay. I turn to Mitch. "You should probably get some sleep. What time do you have to leave?"

I watch his head and shoulders sink toward the ground as he considers leaving. His eyes shoot up to the clock in the corner of the room. "Three-thirty AM," he answers me.

I imagine him driving from Philadelphia to D.C. in the middle of the night and then working a full day in the office; I wonder how he will do it. I find a blanket and pillow and toss them to the narrow couch in Ruby's room. The couch is plastic and smells like the hospital, but it is full length, and, to us, that is the best. We have had one too many hospital rooms with only one chair that doesn't recline, and we don't leave Ruby alone at night.

Mitch asks if he can get Ruby ready for bed. I watch him change her diaper, lotion her skin, dress her for bed through the wires and then kiss her forehead. He then lies down on the couch in her room and motions for me to join him. The couch cannot be more than two feet wide. It's narrow, but I shrug my shoulders and decide to try. I squeeze up next to him and step into stillness for the first time in my day.

Lying against Mitch, I can hear his breathing pattern and know he is slipping into rest. I lie in front of him unable to sleep. *This week I will be here alone with Ruby. I don't know if can do it. I fear the doctors, the interventions, the decisions, and most of all her health, which no one seems to fully understand. I don't want Mitch to leave.*

I stop the internal ranting and force myself into the present moment. *Mitch is here. He's sacrificed to stay another night. I need to embrace this moment; perhaps it contains the strength I need to live in the next.*

I shut my eyes and nestle my head into his chest. I can hear his heart beating and I rest in the sound of it until my own heart beats in rhythm with his. Connection. Two lovers squeezed onto a single hospital couch with our critically ill daughter in the bed in front of us. Two souls clinging to each other in the midst of shared suffering.

All too soon, an alarm will ring to separate us.

I don't care.

I grab the moment like a thirsty child, unafraid to drink. I know that a nurse will barge in soon, but I don't care to prepare for it. I can be thrust out of this moment later, but I refuse to lose it prematurely. We connect.

Eyes shut tight, I sink into Mitch's heartbeat and find safety there.

Hidden in his embrace, the world feels right again.

For just a moment, we are all three home again.

The next thing I know there is brush of a kiss on my forehead and I catch him walking out the door in his suit.

~

A team of geneticists walks into the room and I am caught unarmed, unprepared for what they bring with them: two students with curiosity about Ruby's disease. They talk as if disease were a mask and the person beneath it a mannequin. It's bothering me. I find their comments ignorant to what it is like to go through this, ignorant to how much dignity Mitch and I assign to Ruby's life. Didn't they see the sign on her door?

They are here to "evaluate" Ruby. I realize part way through that they are evaluating her anomalies. They ask me questions about her history and, as I answer, I begin to understand that these are not physicians. These are medical researchers.

I suddenly want to vomit. Why? Because Ruby is a person, not a disease, and anyone who cannot see her personhood in the midst of her ailments does not have the right to her medical information. Anyone who wants to be involved in a person's life without caring for the individual is not safe for the person. Protective instincts engage; my walls go up.

The researchers ask if they can take pictures of Ruby's anomalies, her extra finger, her merged toes. They want to take pictures so that they can display them in class to other students who have studied this disease but have never seen it. I've had enough.

I speak up. "I understand that Ruby is of some value to you because she is a living version of something you have studied but never seen."

The researchers respond with affirmative nods.

"I understand that you are here because you want to improve the education of your students so that you can help more kids."

More nods.

"However, as long as I am the mom of the kid you are interested in, you will not have access to her. If you cannot first celebrate the *person* of Ruby and give her dignity, then you have no right to assume access to information about her health, her history and this disease our family is suffering from."

I continue. "Would I want you to take pictures of *my* anomalies and put them on a screen for students to evaluate? Would that honor me as a person—at all?

Silence.

"And what if my mom said you could, but I didn't want you to and was embarrassed by it? Would you still do it?"

Blank stares.

"Ruby gets the same respect that you would give to me, because she is a person just like I am. My answer is no."

One of the ladies begins a quiet rant about the benefits of research in helping find cures for disease like this. If they have more information to study, they can make more progress. Makes sense. Perhaps I should care more.

But I don't.

Not my baby.

Not on this mama's watch.

Ruby is a person, and she will not be objectified. No matter how good the cause. I'm defending her dignity, even if it does totter on the morality line for others.

If I were the one with the disease, I could decide for myself. Perhaps, in benevolence toward the future of medical research, I would yield. However, this is not about me. It's Ruby they are interested in. I will not expose her anomalies for the sake of "research." She will not be objectified. Period.

"No."

The people leave.

I'm left frazzled and upset.

Bad day in the hospital.

I just want to get out of here.

The difficulty of this hospitalization is proving hard to bear and I cling to Scripture. I think of Mary outside the tomb of Jesus.

> *"Mary stood outside the tomb crying.*
> *As she wept, she bent over to look into the*
> *tomb and saw two angels in white."*

What if Mary had not taken the time to cry? What if she had pretended that she had no reason to weep, or gone right back to life, trying to gloss over her loss instead of expressing how she felt? Could it be that her tears positioned her, with her body bent over from weeping, to encounter heaven?

I don't know, but I do know that I want to be positioned to encounter heaven. I lean into this suffering and weep.

Chapter 20

Days turn to weeks and holidays approach. It's Thanksgiving day. We are still in the hospital. Ruby was unable to have the G-tube surgery this past week because they found that her vitamin K levels were too low for surgery. I am so thankful someone knew to check it. Low vitamin K means that her blood cannot clot normally. A hematologist is treating her, and we are waiting for the levels to come up.

In the meantime, Thanksgiving has come, and in the hospital we stay.

This morning, my sister came with her three kids. They brought us cinnamon buns, and it was a real treat. Her kids went running around the hospital room like it was a playground, and that made us happy. Children sliding under the hospital bed, throwing things across the room, and squeezing Ruby despite all her tubes brightened our day.

I am now standing in line at the hospital cafeteria. There is a mom in front of me and a mom behind me. I am sandwiched between two mamas whose children are hospitalized on Thanksgiving day, and mine is as well.

I begin talking with the lady in front of me. She has been here for three months and doesn't see an end in sight. "We will probably be here on Christmas too," she says with flat emotion. My eyes broaden. I can't imagine the dread of a hospitalization that stretches on indefinitely. This lady is a champion. I wonder if she has anyone who takes care of her. I bring the lady behind us into the conversation. Her son has been inpatient for three weeks. They are in the hospital on Thanksgiving unexpectedly, and she seems devastated by it. I share some of our story and we all three connect. The conversation dies down and I am left sandwiched again in line. Here we are. Three sad mothers, all waiting in line for microwaved turkey and gravy on Thanksgiving day.

I connect with as many people as I can in the cafeteria. This is my community today. Life has put us in the same room on Thanksgiving, which in my book makes us family, even if only for a few hours. I manage a few bright conversations and a few sad rejections. It's okay. I don't always want to talk either.

It's strange to see this side of a holiday, where the families of sick children gather behind barred windows to buy a piece of pumpkin pie. It's an eclectic group of people, and yet we share something today. What binds us together? We all want mashed potatoes. Why? Because somehow this powdered fluff makes us all feel a bit at home in this alien environment. And in that, we are part of something that is bigger than this facility.

I believe in comfort food. I believe in sharing it with strangers as a way to connect. I believe in adopting whoever you're with on Thanksgiving. I believe this holiday will prove a special one for me in hindsight.

I return to the hospital room.

Mitch wants a Philly Chicken Cheesesteak instead.

Seriously?

I question, contemplate and then…wholeheartedly agree.

Rubber turkey is tossed. Cheesesteaks happen, in Ruby's hospital room, for Thanksgiving dinner. We enjoy it.

Best Thanksgiving dinner ever.

⌒

The NG feeding tube is out.

The tape is off her face.

At two years old, Ruby has a "button" surgically implanted in her stomach for a feeding tube to attach. G-tube surgery happens. She does well in it. I am shocked to see Ruby's face without medical tape. I am sad that a more permanent feeding tube is now with us. I still believe she can, she will, eat. I *think* I believe.

But for now here we are, G-tube surgery. Thank God that is over. My expert NG tube skills are tossed, willfully and thankfully. I wonder how hard it is going to be to learn this new tube. It is wider; blended food would be easier. Perhaps she'll get to go back on it.

G tube is in.

We are still in the hospital.

Time to recover from surgery.

∿

Ruby is being discharged.

They say we can go home.

I am shocked giddy.

They unplug her monitors.

I put her in the car seat.

We walk out of the hospital.

We drive away from Philadelphia.

Hands clenching the wheel, I recall the drive to this hospital a few weeks ago. I had no idea we would be there for so long. I look back at Ruby. *Champion.* This moment calls for the discipline of celebration that we have learned throughout her life. I ponder how we can celebrate this hospital discharge. A party is designed on the screen of my imagination, and it's just a matter of time until it presses into reality and hangs balloons in the sky of our home.

I don't know if we will get to celebrate standard graduations of our daughter in the same way other parents do, but I do know that our little girl has surpassed in greatness what some accomplish in a lifetime. This day calls for a graduation party. Ruby has fought, persevered, held on, come through…again.

The moment we arrive home, Mitch welcomes us with a firm embrace. I can see from his face that the distance has worn on his soul. He looks drained. He worked in D.C. while we were in Philadelphia. The medical care at CHOP was worth it, the distance a hardship for us. We collide back into the same space. It's not all roses, but we do have balloons. Mitch and I have some work to do to reestablish our sense of partnership.

Overnight, Ruby does okay. I am so happy to be in my own bed. Lying flat is a gift. Lying down without the fear of medical personnel, a grace.

In the morning, I find that Ruby's G tube has leaked considerably. Her bed is soaked, and so is she. I doubt an ounce of the feed was absorbed and this is very concerning. I get online and do my research. I check the G-tube button, re-gauze the site, and try feeding her again. Again it fails.

This begins my downward emotional spiral.

We are finally home from the hospital, but the challenges persist; and I fear I do not have the strength for them. I am here without nursing support and Ruby's health is still declining. I feel worn out, disappointed, and I begin to feel sorry for myself. That self-pity thing should be an alarm to anyone, no matter how grim the circumstance. It's not a safe leader, and yet I fall for it.

Lying in bed at night, I start to feel the urge to run away. It's not for lack of love; my heart breaks at the thought. But something inside has let go, and I feel carelessly in need. My level of stress has gotten so high, and without reprieve, I fear it is overtaking my will. My emotions are freezing, and there's this harrowing voice inside my head that keeps telling me to break free from it all by cutting loose. I heard the word "leave."

This mental fight continues for days.

On its silent backdrop, my world begins to support the thought of running away. Mitch and I fight: I think about leaving. Ruby starts vomiting: I think about leaving. I survive another sleepless night: I think about leaving. I wake up to another hard day: I think about leaving. G tube is leaking: I think about leaving. Dishes pile up in the sink: I think about leaving.

The rationale behind the thought disappears as a sense of entitlement overtakes my process. It's like I can hear the song of entitlement in my mind, dancing on the stage of self-pity. "Your needs are not getting met here. You have the right to go somewhere else!" It's the voice of temptation, wrapped in a pretty package and offered to me like a gift. It feels good to be validated, and I listen to the voice, receiving its handout willingly. But when I open the gift, I find that its wrapping was merely deception, its contents ugly.

In a moment of grace, the voice of truth interrupts, causing me to recognize that a selfish dart into the unknown would leave a wake of destruction behind me. I would lose the gift I live with, the gift I live *in*.

The internal fight continues. I become afraid. What if I can't resist this? What if I run?

I wish I could say this struggle dissolves overnight, but it does not. On the contrary, it continues until it is obliterated in the face of a moment that stripped bare my love to shine again. I pen my experience in my journal.

> *Today, Ruby had a terrible episode—aspiration—and time passed with no breaths. No matter how many times I walk this life-and-death line, it never dims in trauma.*
>
> *"Breathe, Ruby! Breathe!" I shook her and yelled. More time passed with no sign of breath. I flung her over my knee to lengthen her diaphragm. She suddenly gasped and screamed and I felt an overwhelming sense of relief.*
>
> *She recovered. She breathed. She settled down. She is okay.*
>
> *Somehow in those seconds, I was totally delivered from my internal darting game, delivered from wanting to leave as, in my heart I knew, she nearly left us. I have now searched thoroughly, inwardly and outwardly, and found the urge to cut loose completely gone. It is dead. It died in those two breaths she did not take.*
>
> *I'm all here now. Shaken back into my rightful place by an awful moment that deserves thanks. Mitch, Ruby and I—in life together—together will stay.*

This is all too short for me to cut out early.

~

Doorbell rings. It's a package. "For Ruby."

Inside are homemade Christmas pajamas. They are long, just for her, with a zipper and bright red trim. I lay them on the floor and take a hard look. As I do, I catch my lips pressing into a smile. *Christmas.*

Things have been hard. Ruby has been sick. The G tube is leaking. Ruby is still vomiting. Her alertness draining. If I'm honest, I don't know what is happening with her, but I feel too burned out from the last hospitalization to take her back to find out.

My heart's cry for Christmas is, "God, please don't let us be in the hospital on Christmas."

A faint attempt at festivity.

A few lights go up in the house.

Some sparkling juice.

We're off to the in-laws.

Relatives ask why Ruby is yellow. I hadn't noticed. Gifts are given to Ruby. She responds with a blank stare to the blinking noisy toys. She's sick. We drive a few hours to the next set of parents. It's Christmas Eve. All night long Ruby vomits on the hour. She cries and cries hard. I barely sleep. Away from home, I try to keep our night noise to a minimum. Suffering is not easy to hide.

Christmas sunshine hits the room and I am so thankful the night is over. Ruby falls asleep. I am left to face family. I have little to say. Sweets taste bitter. I just want my daughter to feel better. Later that day, I have a hard time waking Ruby up. Something is not right. Her skin is turning increasingly yellow, the whites of her eyes a strange pale orange.

We sleep at that house Christmas night and drive to the ER at Children's Hospital first thing the next morning. I beg God in the waiting room that they will find nothing wrong, that we will not need to be admitted and that we can go home.

Ruby is evaluated and quickly admitted into the hospital.

We are inpatient again.

She is diagnosed with liver disease.

Merry Christmas.

In her room, I pull Ruby's Christmas pajamas out of her diaper bag and manage to get them on around the wires and monitors. We'll do what we do. Make the most of it.

Alone on a hospital chair, I shut my eyes and pray: *For Christmas, I give You shattered emotions. What do You give me in exchange?* This clear statement from Scripture hits my mind: *"Treasures in darkness, riches stored in secret places."*

～

We are a few days into another hospitalization. Mitch is back at work in Virginia; Ruby and I are inpatient again at Children's Hospital of Philadelphia. Doctors have confirmed that Ruby's LFTs, which indicate her liver health, are dangerously high and rising. They have been unable to identify why her liver has become sick.

I am angry. *What has Ruby done to deserve this? She's not an alcoholic; she's not even three years old. It's not right. She doesn't deserve to have a sick liver. It's not fair.* Thinking like this drains my needed strength, so I force my brain to stop.

Stop. Just love her; be with her.

I fight to keep Ruby from vomiting throughout the day and realize how severe it has become under the watchful eye of others. In the evenings we have sleepless nights, which are all too familiar.

A team of doctors visits us each morning and I watch them prescribe by trial and error medication we worked hard to wean over the last few months. I wonder if it isn't medication that has caused Ruby's liver to grow sick. I dare not blame doctors.

I feel helpless and out of control.

Then, I begin to fight. I interrogate the people. "What exactly is keeping us here?" "When can we go home?" I do my research and learn that this liver issue will likely be a process, a process longer than I want to be in the hospital. It seems that much of what is happening could be happening as outpatients.

"Can we please go home?" I pull out the "out of town" card, telling them that we were in Philadelphia for Christmas and got stuck here. I want to go home.

The attending physician looks at me on December 31ˢᵗ. "You can go home if you promise to continue to get blood draws on Ruby's liver locally and see a doctor there for ongoing care. We have not solved the problem yet. Do you understand?"

"Yes. Bye."

〜

That night, I am sitting on the floor of a friend's house surrounded by people worshiping God. We were supposed to host this meeting for New Year's Eve but were uncertain if we would get out of the hospital in time, so it was moved to another location. We barely made it. Ruby is upstairs in their spare bedroom, sleeping. I am sitting on the floor wondering what possessed me to come.

I pull out my journal. I need to connect with God. This is one of those times when I might run far from Him if I don't run into Him right away. I write: *What would make sense for what I am feeling tonight? Screaming, giving up, pounding my fists, running away. Finding a way to express this jumbled, frantic, detached, broken space inside.*

I pause and then take a courageous leap into the arms of God.

"God, I am hurting. There is noise inside of me that resists You. I don't want it. I give You anger, resentment, hardness of heart, vengeance, my demand for justice, hurt, pain, offense, discontentment, a racing heart, misunderstanding, and all the hardness that has stuck itself to me this year through all the hard things that have happened." I don't want to carry any unclean thing with me into this New Year. Only that which You have filled with purpose for my future.

I open my Bible. In it, I find promises that I never recall seeing before and they are bright, weighted with hope. I feel capacity to receive them, to believe them, to see them as the frame of a doorway between this year and the next. These words carry the incline of sun after rain, satisfaction after hunger, and release after tension. They carry a resolve that there will be an end to this suffering. Suffering will end.

I read passages from Isaiah over and over, soft whispers to my weary soul. Each time I read them I feel a little stronger and, through this doorway, I enter the New Year.

> *"Those the Lord has rescued will return. They will enter Zion with singing; everlasting joy will crown their heads. Gladness and joy will overtake them, and sorrow and sighing will flee away. I, even I, am He who comforts you."*

> *"Your sun will never set again, and your moon will wane no more; the Lord will be your everlasting light, and your days of sorrow will end."*

The clock strikes 12:00 AM. I crawl through the transition, managing to shed a load of burdens on my way in and catching a bright glimpse of hope for what is to come.

It's a new year.

Part V

Mining for Gems

Chapter 21

We are going to the beach. It's January. It's cold. The beach is out of season. We're exhausted. Ruby is sick. It's a weird time to go, but we're going. We need to see the ocean. I need to see the ocean.

I book a "snow-bird" special online and we get in the car. The three of us drive for six hours and arrive at night. We pull up to a tall sparkly hotel; lights dance up and down its architectural lines. It is bright but deserted. The parking lot is empty. It's winter. We enter the lobby alone. Check in.

The elevator carries us up to our room and we discover that it is beachfront. I walk straight over to the sliding doors of the deck and press them open like it's my destiny. Two feet outside, I cling to the rail and hang my head over the edge to catch the beach breeze. Deep inhale. *The ocean.*

I stand outside until the feeling of frigid presses me back. Reluctantly, I return to the indoors only to pin back the curtains so that the water remains in full view. Mitch smiles. Ruby is in a daze. I feel hope. Hope to heal.

The pressure of disease has been heavy on all of us. Perhaps we can escape it here, even if for a day. Perhaps we will be permitted a chance to breathe, breathe and remember that there is more to life than hospitals and doctors.

There is always more. We're out to find it.

Mitch and I create a bed for Ruby near us. We unpack her medications, set up the feeding machine, and prepare for a night away from home. Ruby has been crying a lot. She's not feeling well. Her eyes are yellow with jaundice and she's vomiting regularly. I wonder if this trip is safe for her, and yet my deeper conviction is that the ocean breeze is very safe for her. So very safe.

Mitch and I have a long night of relaying medical care for Ruby. This is our normal, although it still does not feel normal at all. Sleep deprivation never becomes normal.

I rise early in the morning to capture the time we have on the beach. Mitch and Ruby are asleep. I sneak downstairs and out to the shoreline. I walk until I cannot walk anymore. I wrestle, argue, and then settle things in my heart with God. There is something healing about the ocean.

A few hours later, I return to Mitch and Ruby who are content indoors. I press them for some adventure, and they agree to come with me to the nearby lazy river. Mitch hangs close to Ruby while I swim—in January. It is a need, this feeling I have, to get out of the box before it kills me. And so, I break out. I swim. I shiver. I smile.

The weather warms up in the afternoon and we are able to take Ruby out for a walk in the stroller. The three of us explore the shoreline and it dances with art. The wind sketches wild designs in the sand and we marvel. Shells sparkle. The waves tumble. We get a taste of beauty. *The ocean.*

In the midst of all this, there is a looming sense that we are acting out of our reality, and it could get popped at any moment. I fear that Crisis will become unhappy with me for not coinciding with it for a day. I fight the urge to live the day in fear, and beg God to make this day the longest we have ever had. I don't want it to end.

Being winter, the sun sets early, and we are back indoors all too soon. Mitch gets food for us and brings it back to the hotel room. We eat together by the window with the curtains pinned back. I sit back in my seat. *Fun. Hi, it's been awhile. Sure hope you can stay.*

A good evening together, a night at the shore, a taste of another reality, and then we're back in the car. But I feel different, somehow restored. There is something profound about the spray of the shore. I don't think this could've happened anywhere else in the world.

The ocean is, at times, a most necessary drink.

∿

Home again. Ruby dozes off at the table. Her head collapses to the side of her highchair. The great undertaking begins. Mitch gently lifts her finger, hand, wrist, arm, and then ever so slowly lifts her small body up out of the seat. Slower than a snail, he moves her from the kitchen, through the living room, and gently releases one limb at a time into her bed.

The goal is to not wake her.

He succeeds.

And then…a great sigh tumbles out of us both, almost simultaneously. Rest for Ruby is not taken for granted. Congestion, strained breathing, relentless reflux overpower these quiet moments most of the time, but not tonight.

I watch her sleep. *God, when will this suffering end for her?* Soft curls laid out on her pillow, she continues to face life courageously. *But she shouldn't have to; she's a child. Why is it so hard?* I sit next to her bed and realize that I am exhausted. I would like to go to bed too, but the medical routine knocks hard for more work.

I complete the 9:00 PM feed. I start it and crawl into bed and set my alarm for 12:00 AM, 3:00 AM, 6:00 AM, and 9:00 AM. Mitch and I will rotate feeds. In between those feeding times, vomiting, coughing fits, repositioning, breathing, changing, comforting, and recovering from these episodes will all take place. As the world around us sleeps, we lift our lead heads up off the pillow again and again to care for this one we love.

The schedule of a newborn for two and a half years.

Our nightly routine.

Before the night begins, I step outside into the snow, the first of the season. The first grace we've seen in a long time. I had an evening

call from Ruby's doctor. Her liver levels have started to trend down—
at last.

Grace. A blanket covering of white.

It hushes the scene and gives me a moment to be.

I walk in the quiet of a snow globe night, keenly aware that the
weight of this liver disease has been heavy on me. The weight of Ruby's inability to eat, the mental chaos, the emotional tipping points
are beginning to manifest through illness in my own body.

Will you extend this blanket of white to me, God?

Is there grace for me too, God?

~

"Oh, Mighty breath of God,

How things change when You come into the room.

Oh, Mighty breath of God,

How things might change if I would make more room for You."

I sit on the chair in our bedroom as this ballad plays over and over
from our computer. It's been a long hard day of medical trauma. I'm
exhausted, and yet I know that if I do not take a moment to think, the
internal pressure could pound me overnight.

I sit and let the music wash over me. I can feel His Presence. I can
feel His breath, I can feel His wind, and…I don't understand if He
is here why things are not changing. I peer over the edge of Ruby's
bed. Her face is pale, energy drained, breath heavy. She is suffering
from disease. I stroke her head as my heart breaks even more. "I wish
I could take your place, Ruby. I wish it were me and not you."

It seems like the doctors are shooting their arrows into thin air.
Despite the appearance of confidence, I can tell that no one really
knows what to do. Efforts are proposed, debated, at last executed…
and prove ineffective.

I am beyond sad.

I want Ruby to get to live her life without disease. I want for us to share in her eating, playing, growing and developing like other children. My heart aches to acquaint her further with life outside the hospital, to share experiences as mother and daughter, to get to choose how we spend our days, to explore who we are as a family.

I kneel down on the floor of our bedroom and flip my heart inside out toward heaven. "God, You are our only hope." My hope becomes a song and I sing.

"Oh, mighty breath of God, how things change when You come into the room." My song is choked out with tears.

Please, Jesus, heal Ruby.

Heal my daughter.

My pounding whisper.

~

Dr. Gibbons calls. Ruby's liver numbers are dangerously high. He wants her back in the hospital. He wants her to have a liver biopsy to see if he can determine why her liver is sick.

I don't feel ready to give up on treating her at home. I feel like I should be able to fix this, find a solution, pull one down from heaven— something. This call to me feels like, "You're not enough as a mom; bring her to the professionals."

The liver biopsy is an inpatient operation requiring general anesthesia. He wants Ruby in this week. I sigh. Medical intervention to me means that Ruby suffers even more now in the hopes that it will produce something that can help her. I hate seeing Ruby suffer.

I hang up the phone without a commitment. I sit uneasily with the call for the day and wait to talk with Mitch until after his workday. When Mitch gets home, I relay the call.

We sit in silence.

The silence breaks.

"It's for Ruby, Katie. She needs help. Are there any other options?"

"I tried, Mitch. I asked questions, tried to pull on any alternative options. He said this is the only option he sees right now."

"Well then, let's move forward with it."

I know he's right, and I agree, but it doesn't help my stomach from suddenly turning into ugly knots. Ugly, ugly knots.

Ruby and I pack up our things *again* to go back to the hospital.

I feel really sad.

One hour on the road and Ruby and I have both been silent. I feel that she can discern my heavy heart. Her eyes stare straight out the car window as our home city, the one we waited for weeks to come back to, disappears into the distance.

We are driving back to Children's Hospital of Philadelphia.

My eyes look straight ahead. I begin to pray. Rather suddenly, I get a mental picture of myself standing at the doorway of a house that has a top floor and a bottom floor. There is a staircase in front of me and the steps contain letters that read an ascending "optimism." The lower level is clearly pessimism.

I let out a sigh. It's my choice. I can climb into optimism, or I can stay downstairs in pessimism. It's not an easy decision, because the upper room requires me to release disappointments that are heavy on my heart right now. If I choose optimism in this hospitalization, does that mean that my disappointments don't matter?

I don't know the answer to the question, but as I sit with my options I realize that I am the one who has to live with what I choose. Part of me wants to stay in pessimism to prove something, to prove my crushed hopes. But prove to whom? No one else is watching me right now. Ruby and I travel alone. She and I are the ones who have to live in this house with whatever floor I choose.

Love for Ruby compels me to release my disappointments to God and climb the steep steps into optimism. It's a strenuous internal hike up into a new perspective. En route, I wrestle into release. *God, I give You permission to give me a new perspective. I ask that You would make me grateful; help me to see Your gifts in this day. I choose optimism. Holy Spirit, help me to see.*

I pull into the hospital garage and sit still for a few minutes inside the car. Head bowed, I commit this time to God and feel a renewed sense of internal peace. I am going to expect the best. Perhaps there is someone here we need to meet, or another child we will get to pray for. Maybe these doctors will find a solution for Ruby's liver disease. Maybe we will be happily home before we know it.

I get out of the car and open Ruby's door. She is asleep. I kiss her forehead and then gather up her things before clicking her car seat into the stroller base. I kneel down in front of her stroller and squeeze her feet. Her eyes slowly peel open.

"We're here, Ruby. You and I were chosen for another adventure with God. I don't know what is going to happen, but I do know that this is a special time for us to spend together. We are going to look for every opportunity to share God's love, like a scavenger hunt for Jesus. While we are here on mission from Him, Dr. Gibbons wants to do a liver biopsy to see if he can make you feel better. I am going to help take care of you and will stick with you. You are an amazing, brave little girl, and I am so happy to have this time with you."

I stand up and put my nose against hers, "And...I've decided that you and I are going to have fun this week!"

She looks at me with dreary eyes, seemingly uncertain about the fun part. I take hold of her hand and as I do, I can feel her spirit standing up with mine upon the invitation to hope for the best. We are going to do this hospitalization together, in the upper room, where hope and optimism live.

I hold Ruby's hand until I feel that we are connected emotionally. We have learned to bond through touch, as that remains our primary form of communication. I wait to feel that emotional bond, and then I stand up behind her stroller and begin to push.

Onward.

Top floor optimism begins to spill out of me as I remark, "Good morning, Children's Hospital of Philadelphia. Queen Ruby is on your deck again!"

I push her stroller with a sense of pride.

I believe Ruby is one of the most important people in the world.

~

A kind lady in a blue vest leads Ruby and me to our room on the GI floor. Room 16. The number catches my eye and I have a sense that it contains a gift.

When the bustling of check-in dies down, I dive into the psalms to find out if Psalm 16 is the gift bannered over our door. I read it, and then read it again. I'm uncertain of what it means, but I feel that it contains something for me.

Business ensues, doctors visit and I relay Ruby's medical history as I have a thousand times. Monitors are hooked up, pajamas are strung through wires, food is refrigerated, egg yolk blender is connected, and the room is anointed with oil. The night shift begins.

We have one tall window. It looks out to a corridor between two buildings. The view out of the window is of another building, but if I look sharp left I can see some of the sky and the street below. With that narrow view of the sky, I open up my Bible and decide to sit with Psalm 16. I sit with it, meditate on it, and then rewrite it in my own words:

You assign my portion.

You secure my lot.

You set the boundaries.

I have a delightful inheritance, because You are mine.

You give me counsel.

You help me know what to do.

You provide ideas that enlighten my life.

You stand at the place of authority over me.

Because You are with me,

I am not shaken.

As a result, I experience joy out of season.
Gratitude tumbles out of my mouth at unexpected times.
Peace arrests my body in high-anxiety circumstances.
I enjoy my life, because You are tangibly in it.

You are with me. You are here. You are good.

You set the boundaries for what happens to me.
I am not outside Your care.

You will not let us die, God.
You will not watch idly as we decay.
You oversee my lot.
It's Your job to keep it safe.
You cannot be robbed, and therefore I cannot be robbed.
I will not come out with less.
It's impossible.
Through You, I gain in all things.

You have taught me what life is made of.
It's all about knowing You.
Loving and being loved.
In the midst of whatever.

When everything else ends,
This joy,
This pleasure of knowing You,
Will last forever.

The pen takes on a life of its own, and I receive a response:

I am your portion.

I am your cup.
I am your lot.
I am secure.

I am your inheritance.
I am not second best.
I am the best inheritance you could have.

I never leave.
In bright times and dark times,
I am always near.

I oversee your process.
I am your counselor.
I instruct you carefully.
I provide for you in the night.

You have given Me authority in your life.
I take My job seriously.
I am holding you so tight that
You are unable to shake.

I will not abandon you.
You will not decay.
Life will always increase for you,
Because I am life.
I am here.
I don't wear out.

I show you the path of life.
I am the path.

I am the life.
I am joy.
I am pleasure.
I am significance.
I am eternal.

I give you Myself.
I am yours to enjoy.
To have and to hold.
No matter what.

Do you know that I am yours?
I am your great reward.
Your inheritance.
Your prize.

All of Me is given to you in Christ.
Take hold of your inheritance.

I AM.
Yours.

I record it in my journal: *"An unexpected love exchange in Room 16 of Children's Hospital. Psalm 16."*

Chapter 22

We have been here for two days and something unexpected has happened: I've found myself relieved to have help with Ruby's care. The stress of her medical schedule is falling to the nurses, and they are on top of it. I can actually take a step back! I am so used to watching Ruby's breathing like a hawk for any signs of distress, but here I don't have to do that, confident that her monitors will beep and let me know if something is not okay.

In the release from constant medical responsibilities, I recall that inside of Ruby's diaper bag there is a children's book that I have been carrying around for months. It's called "Ruby, In Her Own Time." It's a story about a duck named Ruby who learned how to swim later than all her duckling siblings. My friend sent it to us months ago. I have not had time to read it to Ruby. I fear my role as a mom has been consumed by the role of a home-based nurse.

I feel a pinch of regret realizing that we could have had more help before now, help that in essence could free me up to do mom things, like read stories. I didn't realize how much work the medical care has become until I am watching three nurses juggle what I generally do by myself at home.

I ponder this. *I wonder if we should've had a home-based nurse before now.* I consider it, but I am honestly not sure. I value being Ruby's closest caregiver and getting to take care of her medical needs through the love of a mom. I think it would make me sad if there were things she needed that I didn't know how to do. I feel bonded to her through the intimate connection in caregiving.

No, I don't regret it.

And yet, perhaps this time is a gift to us. I should accept the help.

I find it hard to let go, to stop micro-managing the doctors and nurses as a mom who has held the advocate role with strength for a long time. And yet, here lies a children's book five months in the waiting. *I've got to let go.*

I purse my lips and then let out a sigh. I pull the children's book out of Ruby's bag. I am going to let the nurses do their job, and I am going to try to rediscover my job as a mom, unconsumed by syringes.

And at last, Ruby and I meet a special yellow duck named Ruby.

Ruby, In Her Own Time.

∼

The following days prove precious. Ruby and I play together like we have not for a long time. I let the nurses do their job while I read stories, sing songs, and make stuffed animals talk. I show Ruby the world as far as it can extend from her monitor. We peek out the door, out the window, under the bed, over the sink, and any other facet of her room that could prove interesting to her.

I manage to set up a play mat on the floor. We sit there for hours: playing, stretching, and tumbling with her little monkey, Swinger, until all three of us are fit for a nap. Every few days, we are joined by a physical therapist who sits on the mat with us. I like her. She is hopeful about what Ruby can and will do.

We are actually having fun, making joy the chief goal each day. It's just Ruby and me here in these quiet days in the hospital, waiting for her name to rise to the top of the wait list for the OR. I don't mind waiting longer. I dread her having to undergo another medical intervention.

Evening of our third day, and I write:

"Sometimes this place feels like a gift; the care, the facility, the service, the help. And then there's a moment, like this morning, when someone barges into the room to do a blood draw, can't find a vein, and Ruby starts vomiting from the pain and stress. My screaming child is overlooked to find a vein, as if that were honestly more important. The whole thing eventually wraps up and a moment later I hear it repeated in the room next store. I'm reminded…this is not a hotel, it's a hospital."

~

The liver biopsy is scheduled for today. I just read through all the risks involved and had to sign the bottom of the page on Ruby's behalf. It did not feel good. I feel flushed. I'm trying to be courageous. *Trying*.

I didn't realize that the liver biopsy requires an incision, like surgery. Ruby will be undergoing general anesthesia, which remains scary to me as she nearly lost her life the first time she was put under. She has been so sick. I hate for her body to have to undergo additional stress.

The morning hours crawl by, and my need to get the operation over with rises like water in my soul. I fear if they don't call us soon I may back out.

In time, the nurse comes to bring Ruby and me down to the operating room. Ruby is rolled on a bed, and I follow close behind. We go down the hallway to the main elevator and take it downstairs. The nurse tries to make small talk. I end up sharing with her, and there is a connection. A God moment happens in the elevator; the nurse is touched by God.

Outside the elevator, we continue down another corridor. And then…those glass doors, those barriers that I am not allowed to cross. I hate this part…

They take Ruby through the glass doors, and I am left standing outside them, holding back tears. She is so precious to me, the most precious thing in the world. I hate not being able to remain at her side in times like this.

They take her away.

Behind me is the surgical waiting room, where parents of all kinds sit anxiously, waiting for their children to come out of surgery. I am not ready to go in there. I want to remain unmoved in the middle of this hallway until those glass doors reopen and they give Ruby back to me.

Hospital life bustles around me and I stare at the glass doors.

At last, I decide to turn around and sit in the waiting room. The waiting room is busy today, full of families in crisis. I am among them. I am one of them. I am them.

The lady at the door asks me to check in. She tells me that they will provide updates on my child.

I find a chair. Time crawls. Crawls. Crawls. Crawls.

Ten minutes.

Twelve.

Fifteen.

I stop checking.

At last a man in a hospital gown comes in and calls her name, "Ruby Luse." I identify myself as if for the lottery. He tells me that the operation has gone well and I can see her now. He then shares that they are having trouble calming Ruby down. She is in a lot of pain waking up from the surgery. Someone in the room recommended they go get her mom to help. *Whoever made that call is a genius.* I stand up fast.

I am escorted quickly into the post-operating unit. I push past a few people to get to Ruby. Her face is so pale it is hard, even for me, to recognize her. She's crying out in anguish, and I can see the eyes in the room shooting worried looks at her blood pressure. I get my hands around her face and notice that she is bleeding from the mouth. At closer glance, I see that her front tooth is knocked out of place. I begin to speak to her, "Here I am, Ruby. Mommy is here." I feel a sting of guilt that I have not been in the room until now but manage to continue, "It's okay, Mommy is here."

Ruby immediately starts to calm down, and the medical professionals watch in amazement. I manage to thank whoever had the wisdom to bring me in. *Should it be any wonder that her own mother can comfort her better than strangers?*

I continue engaging Ruby with my focus zeroed in on her. Her blood pressure comes down; her yells for help turn into whimpers of suffering. These do not cause the monitors to beep, but they do break my heart, like a plate being stepped on by a boot heel.

The room empties out until I am left with Ruby and one nurse. This is a good sign. It means she doesn't need all those eyes on her anymore. I ask the nurse what happened during the liver biopsy. I want to know why her tooth was knocked out of place. "What happened? Did she feel that happening?"

The nurse says that she doesn't know, and that no one noticed. I get upset. "I notice, and I would like to know what happened to her tooth."

The anesthesiologist comes in and is patient with me. He says that he has no idea what happened, but its possible that she bit down on the breathing tube while they were trying to intubate her. The scenario is not comforting. He then leaves his name with me for any liability. He is willing to take responsibility.

I stay with Ruby in the post-op. Eventually, the doctor approves her to be transferred back to the main floor.

Back on the main floor, Ruby continues to wake up from the anesthesia, and it's as if she is waking up into a pool of pain and suffering. Her suffering seems to increase with the passing of time. I am at a loss of how to help her. She has an incision in her abdomen from the biopsy, and the only medication they can give her for the pain is Tylenol. This is in part due to allergies and in part due to her liver disease. The Tylenol is not helping, the screams rising.

I stand at her bed as her face grimaces in pain and find myself collapsed over the rail. Exhaustion from months of fighting this fight is upon me. I am worn out to the core. I've got nothing left. Nothing.

Ruby is suffering, and there is nothing I can do about it. My heart is shattering into a thousand pieces. I feel at the end of myself.

Standing there, I am faced with a choice. Right now, in this moment, I know that I can either throw in the towel and curse God, or choose to love Him in the midst of my suffering. It feels like I have two seconds to decide.

I shut my eyes and center myself in Him. I then begin to worship God, and I do it out loud. "You are good. You are beautiful. You are right. You are true." I continue with heartfelt conviction. *I refuse to attribute this disease to God. I refuse to blame Him for what I do not understand. I choose to worship.*

I begin to cry. I don't know if what I am doing is crazy. I wonder if I've lost my mind. No one is here to tell me to stop, so I continue. I manage to sing through tears, declarations of love encircled by throbs of pain.

This is worship.

Suddenly, I have a vivid vision. I see demons all over the room and they are weeping violently in anguish of defeat. I'm startled. I see ugly, evil, contorted beings crying out in despair around me. I don't know what to make of it. I wonder why God is showing me this. I wonder why they are crying. I wonder if this means Ruby is healed?

Then I realize…they are weeping because I am worshiping God.

I had no idea that a decision behind closed doors to worship could wreak such havoc on the enemy. You would think he just lost the war. Perhaps he did.

In time the air clears, the vision dissipates, and my worn-out heart lies still in the hand of my Maker.

⌒

Ruby continues to suffer throughout the night. The Tylenol is not working, the site of her incision swelling. My heart is in shambles from watching her endure this pain. I end up collapsed over her bed feeling that we both might die before morning.

One thing I know, live or die: I will be found worshiping Jesus.

My thoughts are interrupted: *"You will not die tonight."* I respond from a weary soul: "God, I've run my race. What good is a broken heart anyway? What in the world could You do with a heart that is as shattered as mine?" I wait, expecting God to realize I have a good point. Instead I hear clearly, *"I will give you the compassion of My Son, Jesus."*

I am left with this picture of liquid compassion being poured into the crevices of my broken heart. I feel that it will profoundly affect my life from this moment on, but I have no idea how, where, with whom, or for what. Still, I'm feeling a sense of purpose, even significance. Miracle.

Even in this, my night of terror, I have found that He is good.

"He is near to the brokenhearted,
and saves those who are crushed in spirit."

Chapter 23

It looks like we may get to go home tomorrow! I feel like Ruby and I just climbed Mount Everest, again, and I am near tears considering that we may actually get to go home soon. I can't wait to be with Mitch again. I am so proud of Ruby. She is about to graduate, again.

The hard part about discharge this time is that the liver biopsy report came back with no new information. They searched the sample of her liver and were unable to identify anything that is causing her to be sick. This means that they know nothing more about how to treat her illness than they did a week ago before we came here. The thought that this whole time was a waste of time is so discouraging I force my eyes off of it. I search for my pen, chronicle gratitude.

> One of the things I have inherited in this hospitalization is the understanding of how precious Ruby is and how much I love taking care of her. We have bonded so much through the first few days of playtime, into the trauma of the biopsy, and right up into this time of intense recovery. I know inside that it is my honor to care for this little girl.
>
> People here have also loved her well and helped me to remember just how lovable she is. We had a nurse in the PACU who just adored her. She kept saying, "Ruby, I could just look at you all day. You are so adorable!" This nurse told me that when she heard Ruby's name, she thought it was the most precious thing,

like a unique, irreplaceable gem. I felt proud, and agreed. Yes, that is true about our Ruby. She is precious, unique and irreplaceable.

This time in the hospital has silenced a lot of the external noise of my life and I have gotten to focus solely on caring for Ruby. This is a good thing.

I stop short when that "good thing" rolls off of my pen. Psalm 16 comes back to mind. Could it be?

Delightful?

Inheritance?

I squint my eyes as my brain fights to consider what this could be. Psalm 16, a pathway through this time. Can I see its fulfillment in the midst of this chaos? Is that stupid optimism, or is it present hope? The facts hit my journal with a splash of confident ink.

I've fallen into a whole new level of love for Ruby this week: acceptance that her life is a gift, and it is my gift to be with her. We found each other in a new way, and it was bright.

Yes, this is a delightful inheritance.

∿

Ruby and I arrive home later that afternoon. Mitch has meticulously cleaned the house and is trembling with anticipation for our arrival. Our car pulls up, and he runs down the steps and out onto the porch. We embrace in the street. I have so missed him. He sweeps Ruby up and carries her indoors. Mitch takes a few trips and brings in all our stuff.

I carry myself, and only myself, for the first time in days.

Smiles cover our faces as we cross the threshold back into shared space. The clean house means the world to me. I suddenly feel so exhausted I might be sick. I was doing just fine while I maintained full responsibility for Ruby, but the moment it is shared I find that I can barely uphold my part.

Mitch sends me outside. He knows me. He knows that a bit of

sunshine, wind and the voice of God can repair just about anything for me.

That evening, we celebrate together. Ruby has graduated once again. We honor her, love on her, and then tuck her into bed. She is still very sick. We are home, and yet we are left with the stress of undefined care.

Over the next few days, Mitch works full-time and cares for Ruby with every spare moment. He wants to be the one to change her, care for her, bathe her, and spend time with her. They reconnect through his tender care, and Ruby begins to find her smile again, which is somehow very connected to her daddy's voice.

I am not able to do much besides write cross words in my journal and cry out for help from God. I am drained. I've begun to tremble physically, lose stuff, drop things. I keep breaking glasses accidentally. It's weird. I'll be standing in the kitchen holding a glass and, suddenly, will drop it. It shatters on the kitchen floor into a sharp and scattered mess. Mitch keeps moving in behind me and sweeping up every last piece of glass. He doesn't ask questions. He just tells me that it is okay, and he cleans up the mess.

I feel afraid that it is all a sign that I simply cannot hold on any longer, not even to a glass. I begin leaning hard on Mitch as I feel myself collapsing. Perhaps between the two of us, we will yet have strength to stand.

Mitch takes on Ruby's care and mine, both of which become intense. He is pouring out every spare minute of the day, and often throughout the night. I try not to bother him at work, but my panicked text messages seem to slip past my good intentions and litter his day with grief. When he gets home from work, he drops his briefcase at the door and enters into another workday with us, which often lasts through the night until his business day begins again.

There are moments when I catch Mitch's eye and can see the ache of his enormous heart. Deep in those brown eyes, I see fierce love that will not die. His love for us is tenacious: it is wild, it is whole, and it is practically tangible. I don't see Mitch counting the personal cost of being a husband and dad, both of which are costing him everything right now. No. I see him freely giving away everything he has—for love. I feel confident that he would give his life for us.

He is giving his life for us.

I live with a hero.

I wonder how long he can extend this kind of support.

Who is charged to take care of Dad?

~

Ruby and I are standing in a room full of whole-hearted worshipers. The sound of love songs dance in the atmosphere around us. The music transcends this realm and merges with the one to come. Hundreds of people are packed into this room to meet with God. Ruby and I are among them.

I decided that I was going to take Ruby to a conference in Pennsylvania. It is hosted at a church that is very precious to me, an altar of encounter. I am here for me. The Presence of God is the one thing I know can refresh a weary soul. I am also here for her. This place is full of faith for miracles, and miracle workers are among us.

The sessions of the conference come and go with the outpouring of revelation about God. I am reminded of who I am, and who He is. Something inside seems to stand up in response to the King who is in the room. I am being strengthened.

I take Ruby to one of my favorite places in the world, the Prayer Room. I lay her down on the floor, and I lie down next to her. I cry out as only a mother can. *"Please, God. End this trouble. Heal Ruby."* I then cease striving and lie still. Together, we rest in God's Presence.

That evening, I press through the crowd with my little girl. She is clearly ill, her face yellow with jaundice, her alertness fading. I get her into the hands of a miracle worker. This sought-after minister holds her and prays for her. I wait for Ruby to revive. Instead, she hands her back to me and says, "You are an amazing mama. Do you know this?" I begin to cry hard.

God sees Ruby, but He sees me too.

I linger in the front and press in for more prayer for Ruby. We manage to make it to the pastor. He turns to me and asks about Ruby. I peer into his eyes to check if he really has time to hear. He does. He listens and then prays for her. His prayer of faith is like healing balm to my heart. His faith is strong. For a moment, I am not a lone fighter.

The pastor spends time with us. He then calls people to come surround us, and many begin to pray for Ruby. I sit in the middle of a concert of prayer, holding her close. I feel that it is impossible for her to not be healed right now. Jesus is among us. A little boy stands in front of us and says, "Wake up, Ruby, wake up!" My heart echoes the same. We all cry out. In this moment, Ruby and I have a family, a faith-filled family.

I close my eyes and the strength of this family washes over me. Their faith for Ruby is alive. I think of the recent report of the doctors. Doctors are at a loss of what to do. I bow my head: *"God, it has to be You."*

Weeks later, I notice that Ruby has stopped using her eyes. She stares blankly and has ceased to track. I miss her. I miss her ability to interact. I echo the prayer of the little boy we met at that church: "Ruby, wake up, wake up!" Deep plea.

With a heavy heart, I decide to take her back to the hospital. I recall the events of last summer and fear she is not getting enough oxygen. In the hospital, she is checked for pneumonia. It comes back negative. They tell me she is fine and send us home.

I wish I could believe them, but I'm her mom and I know better.

She's not fine.

I am teaching tonight for a class at church. Pulling up my boots, I wonder what this will be like, stepping out of my house for more than the hospital, more than Ruby, doing something for others. It's been months.

I stand in front of a room of aching hearts. They want to be free. They signed up for this "Freedom" class on purpose. It's the class Mitch and I wrote, now multiplied at the church and taught by others. I have not touched its material for months. Tonight, I return as a guest teacher.

These students have high expectations. They want to meet Jesus.

I stand before them with crisis screaming in my personal life and a hard-pressed decision to see beyond myself into their broken lives to release His love.

I preach.

I talk about crisis.

I talk about process.

I talk about the only thing I really know right now—His Presence.

God's Presence falls and falls hard in the room.

The people cry.

The place is shaken.

Hearts crack open.

Healing happens.

I finish the class and no one wants to leave, no one except for me. I need to get back home to my sick girl. I question if I should've even left. The love-soaked faces of the people before me speak that it was the right thing to come. I still question it.

Home again, I lie next to Ruby and put my head against her chest. I track her breathing and feel better knowing she's breathing. I close my eyes and can see the faces of the people who got touched tonight by the love of God.

I'm living in a mystery.

From one friend to another, God, I am thankful for what You did tonight, but I really don't understand it. Why did You just heal all those people with ease while Ruby is still here sick?

Chapter 24

Ruby and I return to the genetics clinic; her geneticist is not happy. He is not happy that we went to Children's Hospital of Philadelphia for a second opinion, and he is not happy that he was not consulted prior to her liver biopsy.

"Honestly," he tells me, "that doctor made a bad choice."

"Okay," I respond, emotionless.

I am well aware that Ruby is worse off after this intervention and has yet to recover from the trauma of it, but none of us knew it would turn out this way. We believed that the biopsy would yield information on how to treat her liver. I am also aware that this geneticist was not in the room when Ruby's liver was failing and the biopsy was our only known strand of hope. *I can't look back in regret; his comments are not helping me.* I choose not to defend myself, but rather sit quietly before this disgruntled man and wait.

The geneticist then turns his chair around and says, "There's something I need to tell you, and there's no good time to tell it to you."

I stiffen. I prepare myself, and then the pistol fires.

"Ruby's case of Smith-Lemli-Opitz syndrome is the severest I have ever seen, and it is fatal. She may have come through the respiratory virus last summer, she may have come through the worst of the liver disease, and she may come through whatever she is battling now.

But at some point, something will take her out. This disease will take her life…"

I lose him right there. That last phrase threw me up against an internal wall; I'm pinned there, spear in hand, wanting to kill him. In my shock, I fail to stop him, and, although I miss most of what he says, I hear the bullet hit with "She will die."

Ruby is sitting on my lap looking straight at him. She has two neat French braids in her hair and a bright pink sweater on. Her innocent eyes stare at him as he breathes death over both of us. He may not believe she understands him, but she does. I know she does. I turn her around in an effort to protect her; French braids now turn against the doctor; her face is now toward me.

Gathering myself I fire back, "Do you have any idea what Ruby has come through? The odds she has already beaten? They told me she would only live for seven days! Ruby has been defying medical prognosis her entire life!"

I'm angry.

I get a flat response. "We can keep hoping for that, but it is also my responsibility to tell you what I know based on research."

Research. I hate that word. It's like the medical bible. A bible with no faith, hope or love. Imagine prophesying from something like that.

"I don't want to talk about it," I shoot back.

He looks back at me with pity on his face. I am not hearing him and it is making his job hard. I am throwing his words back into his face with no shame.

Awkward silence fills the room.

In an effort to end the conversation, I relent. "I am aware of her prognosis." As the words come out of my mouth, my heart sinks. I feel sick for needing to satisfy his need to make me see. "I appreciate you wanting to help, but I don't want to talk about it." I add, "Especially not with Ruby sitting right here."

I guess that is enough for him, because his face changes and he wraps up the appointment in a professional manner.

Driving home, I'm shaking. Ruby is silent. For all the awful times we have endured together, this is one of the worst. Words can kill. We're going to have to detox this poison and fast.

Try as I might over the next few days, I am unable to shake his words. They torment me. The phrase "something will take her out" rolls over and over in my tired brain. I don't understand why this is holding weight when it never has before.

~

It's mid-March and my sister is coming to visit. I'm excited. Fresh air. She is in graduate school and on spring break. She's choosing to spend her break visiting us, visiting Ruby.

Ruby is sick. My hope is that this visit will help distract me from that. Audrey loves Ruby. She is good with her, relates to her, talks right through the disease to her, and loves her. I anticipate that a third party present will help alleviate some of the recent medical stress.

Audrey arrives, and we are excited to be together.

First night of her visit comes and goes. In the morning, we decide to go to the park. While feeding Ruby in the morning, I notice that she is less responsive, again. I brush it aside in hopes that she will improve during the day.

The sun is bright in the sky. Audrey, Ruby and I get on the trail at the park and enjoy the outdoors. Spring seems to be coming early this year. It's March but there are already little green buds on the trees. The air is warm and Ruby is in her slip-on shoes with no socks. Her pink Mary Janes catch the warmth of the sun starting at the two white bows atop each shoe; it soaks right into her happy sock-less feet.

We return home after our walk. Within an hour of being home, I realize that Ruby's lack of responsiveness is quickly getting worse. I hold her close and try to get a sense as to whether she is okay. In doing this, a fierce uneasiness unearths in me.

She is not okay.

I call Mitch. "Ruby's not doing well. I think I need to bring her to the ER." Mitch and I have a shared understanding that it takes a whole lot for us to bring Ruby to the ER. We would live in the hospital full-time if we brought Ruby to the ER as much as we "should."

Considering this, he is taken off guard. "Okay. If you feel you need to, then you probably do." He continues, "I don't think I'll come right now because of work, but let me know how it goes."

I bite the bullet and tell Audrey, "I think we need to take Ruby to the ER."

She's fine with it. I feel disappointed. This is not what I was hoping for this week. Audrey cooks us up some hot dogs to pack for lunch while I prepare Ruby's things. As I pack up Ruby's things, I feel a pit in my stomach growing. *Something is not right. We need to get to the ER.*

Inside the ER, Ruby's intake is completed and finds that her oxygen is low. She is cultured and found to have pneumonia, which is affecting her breathing. None of this feels out of the ordinary. I fight hard for a few hours to not have her admitted.

Unable to stabilize her oxygen levels, I am informed that it is not safe for Ruby to go home; we will be admitted. Heart sinks.

The geneticist who we saw outpatient just a few days prior comes in to visit. Ruby was sick then too, but not like she is right now. We hoped that it would pass without the need for inpatient care.

He smiles as he evaluates Ruby. "Looks like she's been outside." He points out tan lines on her feet.

"Yes, we went for a walk this morning," I respond.

He looks pleased. He had kindly urged me the other day in clinic to seize the day with Ruby. I think he sees evidence of that on her sun-kissed feet.

In the ER, I watch Ruby closely. She is starting to work harder to breathe. I'm studying her numbers and realizing that her oxygen level is decreasing steadily despite being on support. The nurses keep coming in and slightly increasing her oxygen. *She's getting worse. This is not like her.*

I text Mitch. "I think you need to come here now." He takes off of work and arrives in the ER. I am already starting to tremble. He's trying to understand what is going on.

"Mitch, I don't know if anyone else has even picked up on it, but Ruby's oxygen is dropping steadily, and this is not like her. Something is off; she's not okay."

Mitch convinces me to go get some food with Audrey. He will stay with Ruby. Reluctantly, I leave the room. Too many times I have been unwilling to take care of myself in the midst of these events and end up crashing. I reject my own discernment to try to do what is best and step away.

In the elevator headed toward the cafeteria, I start to get texts from Mitch.

"She's not doing well."

"You should come back now."

"Come quick."

My stomach flips and I try to reverse the elevator to get back downstairs. It is the slowest moving machine in the world. When the door finally opens on the floor of the ER, I go running; Audrey is behind me. The guard stops me at the door of the ER. I tell him that my daughter is back there and is not okay. He starts asking me questions and I burst into tears.

"I need to get to her now!"

With little compassion, he holds out his arm to stop me.

"Only one of you can go back there."

"Go ahead!" Audrey pushes me from behind.

Frustrated by an unkind man at the worst moment of my life, I race into the ER and find that Ruby has been rushed into another space where she is convulsing and surrounded by medical staff. The air is thick with fear and panic.

I find Mitch. "What is going on?"

"Her oxygen dropped to critically low. It was close, Katie. She's not doing well."

I kick myself for leaving. *Did Ruby just nearly die while I was out of the room?* The first of many coming regrets washes over me like a sick blanket, and I can't shake the feeling. I knew she was getting worse. I sensed it. *Why did I leave?*

Mitch looks in shock. For the state of crisis we live with daily, I think there was an expectation that this too would pass. The degree of her illness at the moment, however, is unprecedented.

We are approached by an attending physician. "Are you Mom?"

My eyes tear up. "Yes, proud mother of Ruby Joy." I feel so guilty for not having been here when whatever happened took place.

"Ruby may need to be intubated, but it is your choice whether you want us to do that." The scene from last summer flashes before my eyes. They want us to decide again whether or not to keep Ruby alive. *I hate this.*

"I understand that the geneticist had a talk with you recently?"

"Yes."

"We understand that you will factor that conversation into your decision."

I nod.

I now get it. The geneticist needed to tell me his honest opinion of Ruby's condition to inform decisions coming down the pipe, like this one. That "something will take her out" lingers.

Mitch walks over to Ruby's bedside and leans into her. I know what he is doing. He is talking to her and listening for her response, spirit to spirit. Stepping away, he returns to me.

"Katie, Ruby is really suffering and she doesn't want to be intubated. 'Please, Dad, no!' is what I heard. I think that intervention would make her suffering extreme right now."

We don't relay this to the doctor, but instead ask if we have any other options besides the intubation.

"We can do a Bipap," she responds. "It may or may not help her, but that is the only other thing I know to try." She explains further, "Basically, it is a stronger oxygen mask that we can give her externally. I cannot guarantee that it will help, but it will at least provide more support than what she is on right now."

We choose the Bipap for the time being and relay how Ruby has recovered without intubation before.

The doctor makes it clear that we understand Ruby could die without intubation. Our heads nod in a response no parent should ever have to make. She then says they will start with the Bipap and see how she does.

Mitch and I press through the medical cloud of people to get to Ruby's bedside and explain to her what is happening. She is not responsive, but her body is working really hard to breathe. The high blood pressure from this work is causing everything to be tense, including open eyes that see nothing.

Mitch leans over to her, and I place my hands on her body. "Ruby, we are not going to have them do intubation. They are going to do a Bipap instead." There is a peace that comes over her when we tell her this. Mitch and I feel strongly that her suffering would peak to unbearable if she were intubated right now.

I then step away, shaking. I can't handle seeing her in this condition.

Things are moving too fast to process further. Trembling, we leave that room and follow Ruby's trail into intensive care. Before we do, however, we have to sign a paper saying we know she could die on the way there. I don't have time to process this, but I can feel my body tensing and my heart racing.

Must keep moving.

We have been on this life-and-death line before, but something is different. I can feel it inside. *Something is not right.*

I text my sister: "Ruby's not doing well. We are headed to intensive care." I can't imagine my sister alone right now in the same building while all this is transpiring. But I also can't think of a single thing I can do for her. *Moving on.*

In the ICU, we are put into a private room and greeted by staff. Ruby is put on the Bipap to increase her oxygen support. Mitch and I stand at the head of her bed while medical staff work tirelessly to help her breathe. I hold Mitch's hand tight.

"She might go home, Mitch."

"Ruby's a fighter, Katie. She'll get through this."

The attending physician approaches us within a few minutes.

"I'm really sorry, but the Bipap is not working. Ruby's heart is wearing out."

I stand silent. She is fighting to the very end. Her heart is wearing out. I can't imagine anything more sorrowful than that statement or this experience. I begin to cry.

"I'm so sorry." The doctor tries to comfort me and then continues, "She will probably die soon. We can still intubate her or shock her heart if you want. That said, those interventions will definitely be very difficult for her to endure right now, and even if we do them she may not make it. And if she does, she may not ever be able to come off the breathing support."

"Or wake up?"

"She may not ever be fully alert again."

I know what this means. It means she would lie like a vegetable on a breathing machine "alive," but the furthest thing from life.

We can't do this to her.

We ask the doctor for a minute.

Mitch and I deliberate on what no parent should ever have to decide. *Do we have them shock her heart in the hopes that she will live? Do we have them intubate even though we sense strongly Ruby doesn't want it?*

It doesn't take long to know what we need to do. We need to release Ruby to God. Clear as it is, I cannot bring myself to say the words. Cannot. I look Mitch in the eye. "You have to tell the doctor. I cannot bring myself to say those words."

Somehow he does. Mitch tells the doctor that we are choosing not to have them intervene any further.

When he does, I start weeping.

I just know. She is going home.

I tell Mitch to text family. "This is serious, Mitch." He sends the text: "Ruby is very ill; she may not make it through the night."

The next thing I know, the doctor is grabbing me and telling me to get on the bed and hold Ruby. All wires are detached from her. The room empties out like lightning, and we are left alone. I am holding Ruby. I am holding Ruby as her heart wears out.

I hold Ruby tightly and weep.

Mitch begins to weep too.

Mitch sits behind me. "No, Ruby, please don't go."

"No! No! No!" I bury my head into her chest and cry out.

I never believed she would die.
I always believed she would be healed.

Shock hits me violently, and I start shaking uncontrollably.

Ruby is dying.

This moment of realization brings excruciating internal pain, and I feel my own breathing become hard work. I could die with her.

Keep breathing, Katie.

It's as if my heart is physically being ripped out of me. I do not expect to survive this pain. "God, please, take all three of us."

A peace comes over Ruby.

She lies still.

Her heart is still beating, ever so slowly.

She is not suffering.

I feel grateful her heart was not shocked.

She is dying in peace.

I look at the peace on her and wish I could feel it. But I cannot. All I feel is anxiety and pain packaged in panic. I cannot feel peace. I don't know where God is. I feel abandoned. *This can't be happening.*

Holding Ruby, I suddenly feel her explode out of her body. Like a little girl who has waited for years to run, she runs Home. The sense of running wildly is so strong, I feel like she might not stop for a decade, as if all her desire to move was pent up and just let loose.

The Father catches her. I see it.

She is completely, *completely*, free.

For the very first time.

And…she is gone.

I hold Ruby's lifeless body, "No! Don't leave us! Jesus! Bring her back! Please!" I place my hand on her body, "LIVE! LIVE! LIVE!"

Mitch releases his cries, "Jesus, please, heal Ruby. Please, heal Ruby."

Mitch's cries pause my screams. He is praying a phrase that I have heard him pray a hundred thousands times in the last few years. Flashes of Mitch's faith journey come before my eyes as I recall his conviction that God called him to believe for Ruby's complete healing. Mitch never gave up, never. In the face of it all collapsing, he is still asking, still believing God for the best thing. "Raise her from the dead, Jesus. It's not hard for you." I hear him continuing.

This is not denial. This is true faith. I can feel it.

Eternity then opens up to me again through the eyes of my heart, but this time it is over Mitch. I see Mitch running past his finish line and the great stands of heaven giving him a standing ovation of applause. He has believed God, and I believe it will be credited to him as righteousness.

The doctor comes in and gently puts her stethoscope up to Ruby's chest.

There's no heartbeat. She looks up at me, "She's gone."

I weep heavily.

Mitch weeps too.

"You can take your time." The doctor departs.

Four PM we checked into the ER.

Nine PM we sit alone in a pile of blood and tears.

Holding our dead daughter.

Who, now, is somehow the most alive of any of us.

For is it not so, that we, the ones who are in this side of eternity, are the ones who are dying?

～

Mitch and I are told by the attending physician that we can linger as long as we want. The thought of leaving Ruby's body is incomprehensible to me. I could never leave her. They will have to drag me out of here. *I will not leave.*

Family shows up at the hospital, as well as pastors and close friends. It means a lot that they are here, although I have nothing to give in interaction with any of them.

Time passes, and Ruby's body is changing. It becomes increasingly cold and dark with splotches of blood gathered beneath the surface of her skin. Blood drips from her dry mouth. Mitch and I lie next to her, and I take hold of her hand. It is cold.

She is cold, lifeless, gone.

Our lead pastor comes into the room, and Mitch steps aside to make room for him. Condolences are made. I look up and see that Mitch's face is white. "I don't feel well," I hear him mutter under his breath. He then catches himself as if blacking out. I'm holding Ruby's dead body and cannot let it go to help him. Pastor asks Mitch what he needs. Mitch looks up at him with a blank stare. "I don't know."

The word "release" is given to us by the pastor.

I tuck it away. No room for words at the moment. No room.

Family comes in to see Ruby and say good-bye with long breaks between them. I cry for a few straight hours until I run out of tears, at which point I stare at people with no feeling at all. Part of me has just died with her. I feel the shock of an amputation, uncertain as to what part of me is gone and what part is still here.

In exhaustion, Mitch and I eventually fall asleep on the hospital bed with Ruby's body between us. We rest together physically for the last time.

$$\sim$$

The light hits my eyes, and I open them suddenly. For a moment, I think that I have had a bad dream, and then I turn over and see Ruby's body covered in the face of death. This is no dream; it is a waking nightmare. She has gone.

At the sight of Ruby's deteriorating body, I am suddenly done. Ready to leave. Ready to do what last night I never thought I could do. Release her body and get out of this room. Morning light shines into the room. Somehow it speaks to me that Ruby is no longer here. I feel compelled to chase that light and find out where she has gone.

Nurses come in.

I dress Ruby for burial.

I clip one of her braids to keep.

A hand mold is made.

Family comes in to say good-bye.

I'm in a daze.

And then, I watch my life end.

They wrap Ruby in a white sheet like a mummy,

And take her away.

Mitch and I step into a terror walk out of the hospital. I wonder if Jesus' walk to Calvary felt like this. We walk with our empty stroller, across the PICU to the elevator. Down the elevator and onto the main floor, across the main floor and into a buzzing lobby. Passing families with full strollers, we make our way through Children's Hospital with an empty stroller.

I make it halfway through the lobby when I feel my heart shatter, and I break down. I cry uncontrollably and then fight like a wild woman to find the exit of the hospital. Parking garage nonsense catches me. Our car sits.

The empty stroller is put into the empty car. Empty car seat snapped in. And we exit Children's Hospital. Without Ruby. We drive home.

Without Rubes.

"Empty" screams at me from the back seat of the car. That "empty" beast gets on my tail and stays there for a long time. It is a deafening, chilling, silent scream that will shake me and chase me for a long time.

As we drive, Mitch notes that the trees have exploded with blooms. He is right. The day Ruby died, spring erupted on the outdoor scene. Bloom, bloom, bloom. Color arrived today. It is bright outside, but dark inside of us.

We pull into our driveway.

We go inside.

We shut the door.

And sit, in disbelief.

Ruby's things are scattered around the house from use just yesterday. I had no idea she would not come home. I look around our house and nothing looks familiar. Everything sits untouched, and yet it all wears the impact of loss. Everything has changed. Nothing has escaped this destructive blow of Ruby's absence.

I cannot recognize a single thing in my house.

I do not know what this place is.

I do not know where I am.

I cannot grasp what is happening.

I look around, I look for Ruby, and then I scream back at "empty."

"WHERE IS RUBY??"

I tremble, physically shake, for days.

Chapter 25

In a split second, Ruby shoots through the cosmos and is in the arms of God.

Light.
Light.
Light.
Embrace.

Before she can even think, Ruby is swallowed in an embrace with Love. Her head buried in His chest, she can feel the very heartbeat of God, the sound, the source—of Love. With every beat of His heart, life and light are released into her being and she is fully revived.

Locked in this embrace, she is Home.
Held—she is made whole.

Inside of this embrace, all effects of disease disappear.
All weariness from suffering is dispelled.
All regret for half living—gone.

Ruby is washed by Love in a hug.

And every trace of darkness leaves.

She is made whole. And the moment she is made whole, she makes a decision—to run. Her legs tremble with desire as muscle tone forms—and Ruby runs.

Somehow still wrapped in that same embrace, she finds her feet and takes off. Running, running, running, she allows herself to explode out of the confines that held her body in disease. She is now running, wild and free.

He lets her run.

The Father has waited long to see her run.

She was made to run.

The release He feels for her is even greater than the release she feels herself.

At last…Ruby Joy…is free.

As she was always meant to be.

The Father lets her run for as far and as long as she wants to.

And it is far, and it is long.

Embrace.

Run.

Stand.

Ruby stops running and stands.

She stands tall.

She stands healed.

The arms that held her loosen as He touches her shoulders. The Great Embrace transforms into a Being. Her eyes straighten, and she sees clearly—the face of Jesus.

The light in His eyes dance with joy, and she finds that her own eyes cannot help but dance in return. This is the dance of lovers who need not speak. Ruby and Jesus have found one another and will never let go.

Ruby takes a deep breath in, and on the exhale learns that she can speak. And speak she does. A mile a minute, she talks, every pent-up word, released. Talk, talk, talk, talk, talk. All the things she wanted to say but couldn't, all the things she wants to say and now can. She talks until she gets delirious from talking so much and ends in a fit of laughter.

Laughter.

Ruby's sweet laughter is heard.

Paradise unearthed.

Jesus pulls a key out of the pocket of His robe and it reads "Ruby." Ruby stands up before him, tall and proud; she wants what He has for her. He reaches into her heart and unlocks her.

Jesus unlocks Ruby, and an explosion of color is released from her being. It is living color with emotions, dreams, destiny coiled into it like strands of DNA.

Ruby is unlocked.

She becomes confident.

She becomes strong.

She becomes unfiltered beauty.

She becomes herself—fully.

On becoming herself, Ruby realizes she is hearing. Hearing the sound of cheering. Cheering for the glory of what He just unlocked. Cheering for the glory of who she is. Cheering for the masterpiece of what He has made. *Ruby Joy.*

The sound of cheering is intermixed with singing. To the singing, she dances, to the cheering, she bows. Dancing and bowing, dancing and bowing, dancing and bowing—Ruby expresses herself before heaven and is wildly received.

Jesus takes hold of her hand and motions to lead her somewhere new. They walk together. A slow walk. Endearing communion. Lingering friendship. No one here is in a rush.

Ruby looks down as they walk and sees her bare feet on a golden street. She has heard about this. "Streets of gold." It is brighter and purer than she ever dreamed.

On either side of the street there are people intermixed with angelic beings. Some are centuries old, heroes of faith, family who beat her Home. Every one of them feels somehow familiar, like family lost and now found. They are watching her, and she has a knowing that they have been watching her for a long time. The people love Ruby; adoration soaks their faces as she walks by.

She likes being liked.

At the end of this particular golden road, there is a piece of red tape hanging across it. Jesus steps aside, Ruby breaks the red tape, cheers go wild.

She has finished her race.

On the other side of that tape is a cloud of glory: a circular rainbow around the floor of the space, and inside of it is the throne of grace. Pure light is shooting out from the throne and Ruby can hear the tinkling of golden crowns being cast down.

She steps into the cloud of glory and then hears the Father running toward her. Somehow she knows that this has always been His position toward her, but here in Glory she can feel and experience what has always been true. He runs toward her and she is caught in another embrace, the same embrace that took her Home.

Father God steps back slightly and lifts His hands to silence heaven. The Creator of All gets on His knees and looks Ruby straight in the eyes. She stands boldly before Him; it's just who she is—unafraid.

Heaven goes quiet.

All eyes are on Ruby.

The Father speaks.

"Well done, good and faithful servant."

"You have finished your race."

"You have earned a great reward here."

"Ruby Joy, we welcome you Home."

Ruby jumps into Him with a confidence only a child can have and throws her hands around His neck. "THANK YOU!" Holding onto Him she realizes that she doesn't ever have to let go. This, holding onto Him, is Home.

She holds onto Him for a long time. Dangling as a small child from His broad neck. She doesn't care that all of heaven is on hold until she moves.

He doesn't rush her.

He waits.

And then, into her ear, He whispers, "Ruby, I have something for you."

At this, she jumps off of Him and, rather innately, opens her hands and shuts her eyes. Ruby hears gasps of observers circling over her head as something is being brought out. She shuts her eyes tighter, determined not to peek. And then she feels, not into her hands, but onto her head, something is being placed.

The Father takes her hands in a soft squeeze and lifts them to feel the crown that He placed on her head. "Ruby Joy, behold your crown."

Before her eyes open, a broad smile crosses her face. She already loves it. She knows she is going to love it.

She wonders if she should ever open her eyes, for what she imagines is so beautiful she is content just to know something like it is there.

This lasts for a moment, and then, in suspense, she opens her eyes. Her eyes open slowly, and she sees her reflection in the light bouncing around the room.

Pure beauty.

She is.

Ruby stands tall in the center of heaven—crowned—unveiled in eternity.

She has been embraced.
She has run free.
She has stood with Jesus.
She has finished her race.
She has become herself.
And now she is unveiled in Glory.

The beauty of who she is rests indescribable in words.
An indescribable gem.

A trumpet sounds, and an angel with a scroll appear next to the Father.
He nods at the angel and the scroll is rolled out and read.

"Ruby Joy."

Ruby looks up with a grin.

"She enters into the ranks of heaven first as a daughter, and second as a warrior."

Heaven listens intently; this is indeed a special little girl.
"She is given a place of honor in the Father's house, the house with many rooms. She is also given a place of stature in the armies of heaven, a place of historic assignment. She will love God and make history with men for eternity."

Ruby listens as these details and others are read from the scroll. Her mind, however, is distracted by the love of the Father. She stares at Him. *How can He be this good?* All of what she is being given is wonderful, but all she really wants or needs is Him.

He stares back, as if He feels the same about her.

Knowing her thoughts, He interrupts the reading for a moment.

"Do you see this little girl? She loves me well."

This makes Ruby dance.

And she does that for a long time.

When she settles back down, the scroll reader continues.

No one is in a rush.

"Her parents demonstrated great faith for Ruby's life, and this honored heaven. Their faith has materialized here as an inheritance that she now receives. Ruby has entered our world with a great inheritance through the faith that was held in her life. She is given wealth, access, and heavenly rewards allocated by the Father."

Ruby screams and cheers.

"Yeah, Mom! Yeah, Dad!"

A light giggle is heard throughout the crowd. Heaven loves children. Children are allowed to act like children here.

Ruby's love for her parents has not changed. They are her heroes. And somehow, she does not feel far from them. It seems to Ruby that they are very near, maybe even here.

She then motions for the Father to come near.

"Tell them I am happy here.

"Tell them I am free.

"Tell them I am—what they've always wanted for me—whole and healed.

"Tell them *I love it here!*"

He nods and smiles.

Only a few notice that, buried in the Father's eyes, is also a deep sorrow. For He knows that Ruby's parents are the ones who still suffer. His heart breaks for the long road of grief they have ahead. He cries with and for them. Loss of life was never intended to be.

"I love your parents, Ruby," the Father responds. "I love them so much. They love me so well. They are not finished with their lives on Earth, and neither am I finished with them there. There are more, many more people, who will come to know Me through their lives, and so they must hold on. I must help them hold on."

Ruby listens intently.

"And," He adds with a fatherly grin, "someday, they will join us here. I promise. They will."

Ruby smiles again. She suddenly feels that she will not have enough time to prepare all that she wants to for her parents before they arrive. There is so much she wants to do for them before they get here.

And right there, during her first visit into the throne room, she plops down on the floor and starts making plans for when her parents arrive. Already, she has so much to show them, many for them to meet.

The scene around her changes.

The rainbow remains.

She looks up and there is a sea of glass, a field of wildflowers, a mountain of grandeur, an arena for worship, a house with many rooms, a living rainbow, a boatload of shooting stars, and the softest grass she has ever imagined. She is standing in the center of it all. *Paradise.*

It seems to Ruby that all things beautiful are here, unveiled and on full display before the throne of God.

"I love it here!" She collapses into the ground. Lying on the ground she senses that the wild flowers around her would taste good. She picks one, and into her mouth—chews, chews, chews—swallows.

Ruby swallows food for the first time in her life.

And she really likes it.

A group of angels flies in with a tray.

"Your grandma ordered this for you for your first meal here."

Ruby laughs. "Oh, Grandma, thank you!"

Behind the angels are a group of children waiting to meet Ruby. She has not felt lonely at all, and yet is happy to see them. *Friends.* Ruby invites them to share her meal. They sit together in the field of flowers and eat Delight.

Then, when her tummy is quite full, she jumps up and tells the kids she will see them later. She wants to begin her exploration of a world we have yet to see.

And so, she does…

Tight roping the sea of glass.

Flipping against all odds of gravity in the field of flowers.

Catching shooting starts with a silver net.

Leading worship in the Great Assembly.

Resting and reading in the house with many rooms.

Setting out for heavenly warfare in her crown and purple robe.

Dancing before God with the living rainbow.

And this is just the beginning of Ruby's life—in eternity.

"Mama, can you see me?
Daddy, can you feel me?
I'm at home!
I'm made whole.
Dancing on the streets of gold.
Don't stop holding on."

The End.
The Beginning.
The End and the Beginning.

Epilogue

Five years later, I stand at the finish line and wonder how I will ever cross it. It is time to finish the memoir. Finishing this story feels like a cruel task, as it has just begun, and yet the narrative must land somewhere, or at least pause with peace. As is the case with any piece of art, it is never really done, but rather the artist arrives at a necessary surrender of it. I unclench my grip to release this story to you and consider.

If I wrap up my loss in a bow for you, I run the risk of making the entire narrative inauthentic in a single page. The loss of a loved one is a tragedy that begs for words it will never find. Even the wildest verbal expressions fail miserably to convey the depth of this experience. Loss of a loved one is a terror, a terror that is awake.

And yet, if I choose not to wrap up the story for you at all, and leave it dangling in the raw loss, I also find it inauthentic to its true shape. For there are deep beauties that I have excavated in and through it—comforts that overwhelm sorrow, gains that shout into eternity.

Therefore, I will do my best to land this plane with both tensions present. When you exit this narrative, I want you to go in the direction in which it points you. I anticipate that to be different for every reader. My goal here is simply to get the plane on the ground, boldly holding the tension of both realities: the loss and the beauty.

As I contemplate my own emergence from this narrative, I can see myself holding the thread of Ruby Joy's written story as I have countless times before. This time, I dare to follow it to its end. Surprisingly to me, I find that it is not leaving me off in a dark corner, but rather leading me out of a pit of darkness and into the light. The release of Ruby's story is a release of my process into light. The light feels scary to me, unfamiliar. And yet, I choose to step into it, even with my skeptical, squinting eyes.

A few strides in the light, and I find that my dreams are being uncovered like the excavation of artifacts I thought were long gone. I am recovering beyond what I initially thought possible. Life is still offering me breath, and I am accepting it, breathing deeply. I have noticed that I am smiling more. Laughter sometimes finds me, and, in the midst of it all, I feel a growing capacity for what is ahead.

The grief is real; the beauty is more real. The grief feeds the beauty, for those who have eyes to see it. But what is most important to me in this moment is neither the grief nor the beauty. It is the importance of celebrating this one beautiful life: Ruby Joy, my girl. I am privileged to be that girl's mom and share her story with you.

I dare to pick up my pen and finish this book.

Hello world,
I have a story to tell you.
It is called Ruby Joy.

Katie Luse

Postscript

Thoughts on Navigating Disappointment & Loss

Gems in Darkness

I want to take the final pages of this book to speak directly to readers who relate to Ruby Joy's story out of your own experience of disappointment and loss. After Ruby went Home, I entered headfirst into grief. In grief, I found that I was not alone. The world is grieving. We are all grieving something. I want to share some gems from my grief process. Gems that I hope will illuminate your path where needed.

I'll start with an image, a vision that I received during Ruby's first year of life when Mitch and I found ourselves in an unexpected pit of emotional darkness, not unlike the grief after Ruby went Home. It is a vision that sheds light on my personal process and the invitation extended to you.

In the vision, I was standing in a dark pit screaming, "Out! Out! Out!" Eyes shut tightly, I refused to look up, certain that rescue would come and I would never be forced to really see. I heard God speak to me, "You will get out of this pit the day I decide you will get out, but you have a choice. You can either come out empty-handed or come out rich."

I then opened my eyes in the vision and saw the walls of the pit lined with exquisite gems. Gems lay in piles at my feet. The sense of wealth and value around me was overwhelming. I had a knowing inside: *You already paid the price to inherit the promises to those who suffer. You may as well stop screaming, pick them up, and come out rich.*

And so is the choice to all who suffer. Will you come out empty-handed or will you come out rich? Will you find the treasures in darkness that are yours to possess?

I want to share with you some of the treasures that I have collected relating to navigating disappointment and loss. I cherish the opportunity to give these gems away, as any who take them then carry a redemption stone from my story. Take one. Take all. Partake.

Love God

Many people ask me, "Are you angry with God?" My thought is that *it is easy to judge what you are not close to*. God is the hero of my story. He is the one who was with me every day of Ruby's life, and every day since. He never even slept. He is comfort. He is peace. He is hope. He is relentlessly present, presented love.

God is the reason why I am still here, and not only here, but also living, breathing a full life, hunting beauty, and kissing my world with healing.

God.

I love God.

I still love God.

I still miss Ruby.

I am convinced that grieving and loving God are not in contradiction with one another at all. It is my conviction that God did not make Ruby sick, and neither does He celebrate that she died of disease. I do not believe that He causes suffering like this, ever. A good father would not, could not, and He is the best Father I could ever imagine.

Embracing the mystery of what took place produces far more peace in my life than needing a rational answer as to why she was not healed. God grieves with me in my loss. He is for me and not against me. I know this like I know my name, because I have known Him in darkness, and His light never dimmed.

Be careful what you are willing to lose in times of loss. Loss of love for God will open another door of death in your life that is unnecessary and subtly, but violently, destructive. I am convinced that loving God is what keeps us feeling alive.

Protect your love for God.

Face Your Grief

When it comes to loss or disappointment of any kind, you cannot jump over, under, around, or otherwise ignore it with an expectation to heal. You must go through it.

Through.

In it, there is a place of intimacy with God where your raw heart is exposed to His raw love, which you will find is more than enough for your needs. The fellowship of suffering is a real place where beauty beckons deep to swallow hard and really live.

Grief is a non-linear, aggressive friend. The sooner you respect it, the sooner you can receive its graces. In the *through*, there is grace to heal. There is.

Pain does not like to be pushed; it needs to be validated and then healed. Grief is a divinely designed gift to process pain. It cannot be rushed, it cannot be directed, and it cannot be prescribed. It must be embraced, wholly, as it comes—respected deeply, faithfully. It is both holy and terrible. This holy terrible is another story for another time.

Many tears.

Much grace.

Unexpected joys.

I grieve because I love.

You grieve because you love.

We grieve because we love.

Don't let anyone rob you of your grief. Whether in big losses or small, it is in the grief that love can breathe. Pain doesn't like to sit still. It will move you unless you move it. Either you direct it or it directs you. Choose the direction of your pain carefully. My advice is to run into God with your pain and grieve there.

Grieve.

You must.

Choose to Heal

Recovery is a choice. It is not automatic. Time in itself does not heal. Healing happens when you courageously face the pain and encounter who God is for you in it. Healing requires a thousand courageous decisions that no one sees or knows to celebrate.

There are days when I want to heal, and other days when I do not. I have found it important to know that my healing does not mean further distance from Ruby. In reality, Ruby beat me Home. She ran her race and won, fast. She is alive, along with all the others who have gone before us. *We are the ones who are still dying.*

When I realized that Ruby was not behind me but ahead of me, I gained fortitude to stand up and move forward. Every day that I live, I am one day closer to my own entrance into eternity where she now runs. Keeping eternity in view is how I live with hope, even as I live with loss.

Beauty for ashes is a real thing; letting go of ashes is a choice. Our role is to loose the ashes; His role is to create the beauty.

Will you let Him?

Will I?

Value Life

As for Ruby, I need the world to know that she lived. From the inside out, her life redefined my sense of greatness, my pursuit of purpose, my deep experience of what matters. I call her my "opportunity child," because she came holding the opportunity of a lifetime. I embraced the gift of her. I will never regret that.

Ruby came in a package that is often murdered, one of the many innocent lives that people validate discarding as garbage because of deformity and disease. I am a mom of a child who was born with a fatal genetic disease, a condition in which abortion is encouraged. I am a mom who has something to say about this. Hear me.

Anything that threatens the value of a life is a chief enemy.

Whether this enemy is found in the shadows of suicide, the wasting away of waists to bulimia, apathetic acts of violence, cuts on arms, the killing of the unborn—whatever its form, this enemy turns humankind against itself in an atrocious robbery of life. History cries out for these lives, these destinies that are meant to contribute to our time.

Ruby came attached to pain, and yet I found in her the most profound beauty, the kind that every soul thirsts to experience in any day of our brief lives. She came with an invitation to live, and live fully. She came clothed in opportunity, drenched with purpose. She lived, and many will live more fully because of her life.

Her life had value, as every life has value.

Mine for Gems

Finally, as for you and me, we are not living in paradise yet. One of the things that Jesus assured us was that hard things would happen. "In this world you will have trouble, but take heart because I have overcome the world." There is an opportunity in times of suffering to overcome in a way that we will not be able to in eternity.

I believe that what we choose to do in times of disappointment and loss are defining moments of our lives. In order to make courageous decisions, we have to know that we are not victims but survivors. Victims do not have choices, but you and I do. While we cannot choose what happened to us, we can decide what to do about it. We can answer the question "What am I going to do now?" In that choice, we discover personal courage that can break open the hard rock of circumstances for mining of gems.

The most precious moments of my life to date are those wherein I decided to worship with a broken heart, allowing the gift of worship to transform my low position into a position of eternal weight. These moments were rare opportunities that I deeply treasure.

In honor of Ruby Joy, I implore you, find your ruby and let it lead you to joy. Learn to love what is in your hands. Refuse the escapism fantasy. Mine the reality of your life for beauty. Make the world around you wealthy through the graces you carry. And remember: when you suffer, all the promises of those who suffer belong to you.

> *"And the ransomed of the Lord will return,*
> *They will enter Zion with singing;*
> *everlasting joy will crown their heads.*
> *Gladness and joy will overtake them,*
> *And sorrow and sighing shall flee away."*

Don't stop holding on,
Katie Luse

For more information and book orders visit:

www.katieluse.com

Notes

Chapter 2

"The Lord is my Shepherd. I shall not want. He makes me lie down…" Psalm 23 (New International Version)

Chapter 3

"For Zion's sake, I will not keep silent; for Jerusalem's sake, I will not remain quiet, till her vindication shines out like the dawn, her salvation like a blazing torch." Isaiah 61:1 (New International Version)

Chapter 4

"I am the Lord, is there anything that is too hard for me?" Jeremiah 32:27 (New International Version)

"To you we call, O Lord our Rock; Do not turn a deaf ear to us, If you remain silent, we will be like those who have gone down to the pit. Hear my cry as I call to you for help, As I lift up my hands towards your Most Holy Place." Psalm 28:1-2 (New International Version)

"I will not in any way fail you nor give you up nor leave you without support. I will not, I will not, I will not in any degree leave you helpless nor forsake nor let you down (relax my hold on you). Assuredly not! So we take comfort and are encouraged and confidently and boldly say, 'The Lord is my helper: I will not fear or dread or be terrified.'" Hebrews 13: 5-6 (New International Version)

"Have not I commanded you? Be strong and courageous. Do not be afraid; do not be discouraged, for the Lord your God will be with you wherever you go." Joshua 1:9 (New International Version)

Chapter 6

"...like a champion rejoicing to run his course." Psalm 19:5 (New International Version)

"Greater love has no one than this: to lay down one's life for one's friends." John 15:13 (New International Version)

Chapter 7

"The Lord...has become my salvation." Psalm 118:14 (New International Version)

Chapter 9

"From the ends of the earth I call to you, I call as my heart grows faint; lead me to the rock that is higher than I." Psalm 61:2 (New International Version)

"Abide in me." John 15:4 (New International Version)

Chapter 12

"Man looks at the outward appearance, but God looks at the heart." 1 Samuel 16:7 (New International Version)

"Fix your eyes not on what is seen, but what is unseen. For what is seen is temporary, but what is unseen is eternal." 2 Corinthians 4:18 (New International Version)

Chapter 14

The lyrics "I am the richest man in the world, because I have your Word" are credited to Justin Rizzo and his song "The Richest Man on Earth." (Justin Rizzo, *The Richest Man on Earth (The Word Is Light)*, Forerunner Worship, 2007)

Chapter 15

The lyrics "Precious Lord, take my hand, lead me on, let me stand" are from the gospel hymn "Precious Lord, Take My Hand," by Rev. Thomas A. Dorsey.

Chapter 16

"Let my vindication come from you; may your eyes see what is right." Psalm 17:2 (New International Version)

Chapter 17

"Lord, to whom shall we go? You have the words of eternal life." John 6:68 (New International Version)

Chapter 19

The lyrics "I wanna build you a garden" are taken from "The Garden Song," by Jason Upton. (Jason Upton, *Glimpse*, Key of David Ministries, 2012)

"My dove in the clefts of the rock, in the hiding places on the mountainside, show me your face, let me hear your voice, for your face is sweet and your voice is lovely." Song of Songs 2:14 (New International Version)

"Mary stood outside the tomb crying. As she wept, she bent over to look into the tomb and saw two angels in white." John 20:11-12 (New International Version)

Chapter 20

"Treasures in darkness, riches stored in secret places" references Isaiah 45:3 (New International Version).

"Those the Lord has rescued will return. They will enter Zion with singing; everlasting joy will crown their heads. Gladness and joy will overtake them, and sorrow and sighing will flee away. I, even I, am He who comforts you." Isaiah 51:11-12 (New International Version)

"Your sun will never set again, and your moon will wane no more; the Lord will be your everlasting light, and your days of sorrow will end." Isaiah 60:20 (New International Version)

Chapter 21

The lyrics "Oh, Mighty breath of God, How things change when You come into the room" are taken from the song "Hallelujah (Spontaneous)," by Anthony Skinner. (Anthony Skinner, *Forever and a Day*, DC3 Entertainment/Orphansake Records, 2003, compact disc)

"You assign my portion, You secure my lot, You set the boundaries, I have a delightful inheritance, because You are mine…" Psalm 16:5-11 (New International Version)

Chapter 22

"The Lord is close to the brokenhearted and saves those who are crushed in spirit." Psalm 34:18 (New International Version)

Chapter 25

The lyrics "Mama, can you see me? Daddy, can you feel me? I'm at home! I'm made whole, Dancing on the streets of gold, Don't stop holding on" are taken from "Amy's Song," by Jonathan and Melissa Helser. (Jonathan and Melissa Helser, *Walk Through the Walls*, Bethel Music, 2008, compact disc.)